FOUNDATIONS
Society, Challenge and Change

Second Edition

Alex Colville, *To Prince Edward Island* (1965). Acrylic emulsion on masonite, 61.9 X 92.5 cm.

FOUNDATIONS

Society, Challenge and Change

Second Edition

Brian Burnie, Editor

George Brown College of Applied Arts and Technology

The editor would like to thank Fran Dungey and other members of the George Brown College faculty for their help in the preparation of this second edition.

THOMPSON EDUCATIONAL PUBLISHING, INC.

TORONTO

Permission to reproduce copyrighted material in this book should be obtained from the
original copyright holder as indicated on the sources page at the end of the book.
Permission to reproduce unsigned material not otherwise credited should be obtained
from the publisher:
  Thompson Educational Publishing, Inc.
  www.thompsonbooks.com / email: publisher@thompsonbooks.com

Orders: Copies of this book may be ordered from:
         General Distribution Services, Inc.
         325 Humber College Boulevard
         Toronto, ON   M9W 7C3
         Tel: 416-213-1919, Ext 199
         Toll Free (Ont/Que): 1-800-387-0141
         Toll Free (Canada): 1-800-387-1083
         Fax: 1-416-213-1917

Canadian Cataloguing in Publication Data

Main entry under title:
Foundations : society, challenge and change

2nd ed.
First edition edited by James V. Rudnick.
Includes index.
ISBN 1-55077-109-4

1. College readers. I. Burnie, Brian.
PE1122.F68   1999   808'.0427   C99-931677-X

Credits for text and images are to be found at the end of the book. Every attempt was
made to obtain permission to reproduce the material contained in this book. Corrections
or omissions sent to the publisher will be included in future reprints.

Cover: Elan Designs
Printed and bound in Canada.
1 2 3 4 5   1999 00 01 02 03 04 05 06

CONTENTS

To the Student

This book is about lifelong learning. Whatever career you eventually pursue, many of the issues raised in this book will pop up again and again. The aim is to bring some issues to your attention that so that you can begin to think about them.

Three criteria guided the selection of material for this book, and we think they make it rather unique:

- The selections had to be **intrinsically interesting** (and, therefore, at least somewhat fun to read). Though there were certain pieces we had to include, we tried to avoid material that most people would find absolutely dull.

- The selections had to be **well written**, if possible by professional writers. Good writing should sell itself, or so we believe. On the other hand, we did not shy away from material that used difficult vocabulary. In other words, the selections are lively to read, but you might need a dictionary by your side.

- The selections had to raise some **"big questions."** Yet, we did not wish to imply that these questions are simple and straightforward, nor did we wish to imply that all the answers already exist.

A good approach to this book, and the course as a whole (if not life as a whole), is for you to be **pro-active.** While reading each selection, try to think of interesting questions to ask your friends or raise in class. This way you will get more out of the course and it will be more enjoyable.

You cannot learn the material in this book simply by memorizing—you will also have to think about it and work at it. However, a little memorization will help, especially if you are having difficulty. We have highlighted **key terms** in the main articles. At the end of the day, you should ensure that you know these key terms well enough to be able to explain and discuss them with your classmates and friends. You should be able to discern the meaning of the term from the context in which it arises in the text itself—if you cannot, or if you are unsure, go back to your dictionary. Looking up the word or phrase, thinking about it, and using the term is an essential part of the learning process. There is no easy way around this; it takes work.

Finally, we would like to hear from you if you have material that might be useful in future editions of this book. Please send a copy of the material to the editor (a mailing address and email address can be found on page 4).

Good luck with your studies!

Modern Ode to the Modern School

John Erskine

Just after the Board had brought the school up to date
To prepare you for your Life Work
Without teaching you one superfluous thing,
Jim Reilly presented himself to be educated.
He wanted to be a bricklayer.
They taught him to be a perfect bricklayer.
And nothing more.

He knew so much about bricklaying
That the contractor made him a foreman
But he knew nothing about being a foreman.
He spoke to the School Board about it,
And they put in a night course
On how to be a foreman
And nothing more.

He became so excellent a foreman
That the contractor made him a partner.
But he knew nothing about figuring costs
Nor about bookkeeping
Nor about real estate,
And he was too proud to go back to night school.
So he hired a tutor
Who taught him these things
And nothing more.

Prospering at last
And meeting other men as prosperous,
Whenever the conversation started, he'd say to himself
"Just wait till it comes my way—
Then I'll show them!"
But they never mentioned bricklaying
Nor the art of being a foreman
Nor the whole duty of contractors,
Nor even real estate.
So Jim never said anything.

INTRODUCTION

"So Jim never said anything," reads the last line on the page opposite. The School Board had brought his "school up to date" to prepare him for his "Life Work." Indeed, he was taught not "one superfluous thing" and, in the end, he presented himself "to be educated." His tutors showed him how to be a bricklayer, a foreman, a contractor, a bookkeeper, a real estate agent and "nothing more." But poor Jim was not prepared for the modern world.

Jim's dilemma—exaggerated by poetic licence, perhaps—captures the rationale behind this book; namely, that there is a need to expand the amount of "general education" in the colleges and universities. The reasons are simple.

First, in today's labour market, at least in the advanced industrialized countries, the demand is for people who have good communication skills, can take the initiative and can quickly adapt themselves to the needs of the workplace. This is, in effect, how to get ahead. To be sure, technical skills are needed more than ever, but an increasingly necessary complement is a broader education and transferable skills. Employers are demanding it.

Second, while one purpose of an education is to get a job, another is to gain a broader awareness and a sense of personal fulfilment, which can lead to a balanced and satisfying personal and family life. The world is very complex today, and it takes time for young people to get a personal perspective on it. Having time, and making time, to discuss broader issues in science and technology, the social and psychological sciences, and the arts and humanities can help in achieving this important second objective.

Too often, both goals are lost in the drive to produce a work force with only a narrow skill set. It is now widely accepted that the emphasis needs to shift more in the other direction—towards courses that can help foster highly skilled persons who can also move with the times, live satisfying personal lives and contribute to society.

The Road Not Taken

Robert Frost

Two roads diverged in a yellow wood,
And sorry I could not travel both
And be one traveler, long I stood
And looked down one as far as I could
To where it bent in the undergrowth.

Then took the other, as just as fair,
And having perhaps the better claim,
Because it was grassy and wanted wear;
Though as for that the passing there
Had worn them really about the same.

And both that morning equally lay
In leaves no step had trodden black.
Oh, I kept the first for another day!
Yet knowing how way leads on to way,
I doubted if I should ever come back.

I shall be telling this with a sigh
Somewhere ages and ages hence:
Two roads diverged in a wood, and I –
I took the one less traveled by,
And that has made all the difference.

PART 1

GENERAL
EDUCATION

The school system, custodian of print culture, has no place for the rugged individual. It is, indeed, the homogenizing hopper into which we toss our integral tots for processing.

Marshall McLuhan

GENERAL EDUCATION

AN INTRODUCTION

Technical skills alone are not enough in today's world; employers are demanding more. Education must also teach students how to think critically with an eye to acquiring knowledge that will help them shape the rest of their lives. That is the underlying argument for "general education."

Two **macroeconomic** developments are helping to shape the curricula of Canadian colleges and universities. One is the gradual shift of manufacturing industries to the less-developed countries of the Third World–that is, there are now simply fewer and fewer traditional manufacturing jobs. The other is the emergence in Western developed countries of sophisticated high-tech industries (computers, biotechnology, telecommunications and so on) that require a highly skilled and technically competent work force.

An important feature of many of these new high-tech jobs, in addition to high levels of expertise, is that they require high levels of flexibility and creativity, advanced communications skills, and broad-based knowledge. These are the "new" characteristics that employers now routinely look for on job résumés, in addition to high levels of technical proficiency. The problem is that, in the context of a near-insatiable **labour market demand** for employees with high-tech skills, it has been relatively easy, until recently, for educational establishments to overemphasize **skills training** and underemphasize **broad-based education** (communications, generic skills and general education).

All that is changing. There is now a movement in the colleges and universities to correct imbalances that may exist in this regard. The colleges and universities want to ensure that the education system is geared to developing young people who are technically skilled, and therefore able to get work, but who also have advanced communications abilities and a set of knowledge skills that are transferable to a variety of work contexts.

The re-thinking in this regard began in the 1980s. In 1988, the Ontario Council of Regents, the agency that oversees colleges in Ontario, was asked to develop "a vision of the college system in the year 2000." The outcome, known as *Vision 2000,* acknowledged the major changes taking place in Canadian society. It called for a greater emphasis in the colleges on

There is a shift in the developed countries away from traditional manufacturing industries and jobs.

developing skills and background knowledge with broader applicability to the current and future interests of the Canadian economy and society. For the authors of *Vision 2000*, "general education" and generic skills were not substitutes for job-specific skills but rather an increasingly necessary complement to them. Such skills were, as the report noted, also important in promoting **citizenship participation** and helping people cope with the changes taking place today in all aspects of their lives.

This book has been developed essentially to introduce students to the topics, issues and concerns outlined in the *Vision 2000* report.

BROAD-BASED EDUCATION

This first unit begins with an extract from *Vision 2000*. The extract describes some of the large-scale economic and demographic changes taking place in Western industrialized countries. These changes involve not only the macroeconomic changes noted above but also such things as the ageing of the Canadian population ("greying"), the multi-ethnic base of Canada ("multiculturalism") and the changes in workplace relations ("skills and deskilling"). All these trends will affect each and every one of us, whether we like it or not.

The next article, entitled "Who Gets the Jobs?", warrants an especially close reading. Who does get the jobs? It is now common to answer this question by saying that "it is college grads who get the jobs," and this is largely true. Indeed, a recent trend is for university students, especially those graduating with arts degrees, to go "back to college" in order to acquire technical skills that will enable them to secure a decent job.

However, there is a concern that students graduating from technical programs at both colleges and universities are not sufficiently equipped in terms of communications skills and broad-based knowledge. In university technical programs in business, science and engineering, there are now mandatory "general education" courses in place in an effort to deal with this problem. This has certainly helped. For college students, the problem is somewhat more acute. Students who go directly from high school to college often do not have the same opportunities as university students to gain a broad-based education. General education courses and programs at the colleges are aimed at dealing with this problem.

The seriousness with which **educational policymakers** in both colleges and universities are addressing this problem, and finding solutions, should not be underestimated. A concerted effort is in place to upgrade the quantity and quality of general education courses for both university and college students, and this is to be welcomed.

You will find that there is enough information in this first unit to provide a good basis for discussion and debate, both within the classroom and outside the classroom. The remaining units are devoted to exploring issues and topics under the headings "Science and Technology," "The Social Sciences" and "The Arts and Humanities."

KEY TERMS

- Macroeconomic change
- Labour market demand
- Skills training
- Broad-based education
- Citizenship participation
- Educational policymakers

Good communications skills and a general education are necessary complements to job-specific skills.

THE NEW WORLD ORDER

Vision 2000 and Beyond

THE ONTARIO COUNCIL OF REGENTS

In today's fast-changing marketplace, workers who lack appropriate language and communications skills or basic technological literacy are at a distinct disadvantage. Major social changes are taking place in Canadian society that are affecting each and every one of us, young and old, and whether we like it or not.

PREVIEW

In 1988, the Council of Regents, the body charged with overseeing community colleges in Ontario, was asked to develop "a vision of the college system in the year 2000." Their report, known as **Vision 2000**, acknowledged the major changes taking place in Canadian society. It called for a greater emphasis in the college programs on generic skills and background knowledge with broad applicability to Ontario's economy and society. Edited selections from the report are reproduced here.

When Ontario's colleges were created 25 years ago, it was a time of massive growth and change in the educational system. The **baby boom** was engulfing the system: new schools and university facilities were being built at an unprecedented rate to accommodate the demand. Not only were there more children coming into the system than ever before, but students were staying in school longer. In addition to the pressures of expansion, school curricula were being overhauled, secondary school programs were being reorganized and a host of new vocational schools were being built.

It was also the decade in which a human being first walked on the moon; scientific discovery and technological change were starting to accelerate, and a growing gap between the emerging needs of the economy and the skills available in the labour force was seen as a cause for concern. It was to the educational system that leaders turned to ensure that Ontario would have the skilled human resources it would need for the coming decades.

A NEW EDUCATIONAL ENVIRONMENT

The environment of the 1990s is very different from the one in which the colleges were created, when the economy was dominated by manufacturing and the natural resource sector; the technological base was relatively stable; and production was becoming increasingly automated. At the beginning of the 1960s, population growth rates had reached an historic peak; the population was fairly homogeneous, mainly of European origin, and the traditional household was the nuclear family supported by a male breadwinner. There was a steadily expanding, youthful labour force, and most workers could expect to have one career last a lifetime.

The trends that were just beginning to take shape—and that helped to give rise to the creation of the college system—are in the process of transforming Ontario's economy a quarter of a century later. The demographics of the province are changing significantly, and the social priorities set at that time—the emphasis on equality of opportunity and the responsibility of the colleges to meet the needs of the wider community—have found new impetus in the realities of the 1990s.

Trends such as the ageing of the work force, industrial restructuring, technological innovation, and the changing skill content of jobs highlight the need for a dynamic college system which provides high-quality, relevant career education for a broad range of learners.

Ontario's work force is undergoing some fundamental changes because of demographic trends. The population growth rate is slowing down. Coinciding with the lower population growth will be a fairly dramatic increase in the median age of Ontario's population. The median age is projected to rise from about 32 years at the close of the 1980s to 40 years in 2011.

As the supply of young entrants to the labour force declines, the province is shifting from labour surplus and a relatively young work force to increasing labour shortages in a number of sectors and a "greying" work force. Critical labour shortages in some industrial fields are already occurring, but at the same time there is unemployment in others, mainly among lower-skilled and older workers. This is occurring at a time when increased competition on a global scale and the race to keep up with the latest technological innovations are forcing industrialized economies around the world not only to "retool" their factories, plants and offices, but also to retrain their workers. The ability to adapt quickly to **new technology** and other changes in the marketplace has become a major challenge for employers and employees alike.

Many traditional **manufacturing industries** are undergoing difficult adjustments in this new environment. Success in many industries is no longer predicated on mass production of a single product, but customized production of products geared to the specific needs of the client. The assembly line is being replaced by multiskilled teams, quality circles and other new-style work environments. Many employers are emphasizing the need for workers who can think critically, communicate well, and work with others in solving problems.

The **service sector** has become the fastest growing sector of the economy. However, many service jobs continue to be dependent on the goods-producing sector. Many of the high-growth service occupations are low-skill and low-paying, with limited prospects for promotion. On the other hand, the service sector is creating a whole range of new highly skilled professional-level occupations, in finance, communications and other fields.

Most of the workers in Ontario who will be required to adapt to new technologies, economic restructuring and increased **global competition** in the year 2000 are already in the labour market. Many of these adult

The new trend is towards high-tech industries that increasingly involve high-skill occupations.

workers will need retraining not just once, but several times in the course of their working lives.

Canadian employers have tended to exhibit significantly lower rates of investment in training than many of this nation's major trading competitors. In the past, employers have been able to import skills from outside Canada to compensate for skills shortage. But the supply-demand disparity in skilled occupations is also being experienced in other industrialized countries; it is not expected, therefore, that immigration will provide the solution. Canada, and Ontario, will have to train–and retrain–their own.

Economic trends are not the only forces for change in the new environment; Ontario is changing in other ways. We have become an increasingly **multicultural society**; fewer immigrants now come from Europe, and more from the nations of Asia, Africa and Central and South America. Many new immigrants require language training before they can participate in education or work, and many come from countries which do not have highly developed educational and training opportunities. Those who do have qualifications for professional and technical jobs in Ontario find it difficult to get their credentials validated here. People from other cultures want to be assured that their customs and heritage are respected, and that they will have an equal opportunity to succeed.

The role of women has changed. Women now make up 45 percent of the provincial labour force, and their **participation rate** continues to increase; however, they continue to earn, on average, only two-thirds of what men earn. Women are also under-represented in many of the occupations that are experiencing critical labour shortage. Many women need support services, particularly child care, to enable them to take advantage of available training opportunities. Other groups, such as persons with disabilities, want better access to education and the labour force so that they, too, can realize their potential.

Demographics may also affect the colleges in future in a more indirect way, through the government's ability to pay for post-secondary education. … The ageing population means that a greater proportion of public resources will likely need to be devoted to the health sector.

Together, the economic and social changes in Ontario are putting new pressures on the colleges. While the colleges have filled a much-needed role in career education in the last 25 years, they are being challenged to update their mandate in order to remain relevant to the real needs of the province and its people.

REORIENTING THE CURRICULUM

Vision 2000 believes that the provision of general education and generic skills should be significantly increased in programs which receive a college credential.

Notes
[1] Michael Park, "Expanding the Core: General Education, Generic Skills, and the Core Curriculum in Ontario Community Colleges," in *Challenges to the Colleges and the College System—Background Papers* (Toronto: Ontario Council of Regents, 1990).

Insufficient general generic education. In the four principles for the colleges outlined in 1967, colleges were directed to "embrace total education." But from the beginning of the college system, general education (e.g., studies in sociology, world events or the environment) has received less emphasis than vocational skills training in college post-secondary programming, and its position has further declined in the last decade. When funding restraints squeezed college budgets in the late 1970s, program hours were cut back, and the major casualty was general education. General education is supposed to constitute at least 30 percent of post-secondary program content; however, most programs have considerably less.

The rapid pace of change in the workplace, particularly that caused by new technologies, has increased the need for students to acquire generic skills—such as problem solving and critical thinking, as well as basic literacy, numeracy and computer literacy—so that they can learn new skills or adapt old ones. A worker who does not have the **transferable skills** to advance to better positions in his or her field may become trapped in a particular job. An over-concentration in many college programs on narrow **occupation-specific skills**, to the detriment of generic skills and general education, is restricting career opportunities for some college graduates and affecting the ability of business and industry to adapt quickly to the demands of the marketplace.

A greater emphasis in college programs on skills and knowledge that have broad applicability to different current and future uses is needed to serve the interests of Ontario's economy and society. If the diffusion of new technology is dependent on a broadly educated and skilled population, it is important to ensure that as many people as possible have technological literacy and other skills which are transferable to other jobs and occupations. These skills are not a substitute for job-specific skills, but are complementary to them. Moreover, general education and generic skills are important tools for good citizenship and help people cope with change in all aspects of their lives.

General education and generic skills. In the context of the colleges, we define general education to be: "the broad study of subjects and issues which are central to education for life in our culture. Central in, but not restricted to, the arts, sciences, literature and humanities, general education encourages students to know and understand themselves, their society and institutions, and their roles and responsibilities as citizens."[1]

We define **generic skills** to be: "practical life skills essential for both personal and career success. They include language and communications skills, math skills, learning and thinking skills, interpersonal skills, and basic technological literacy. They are not job-specific, but are crucial to mastering changing technologies, changing environments and changing jobs.... Facility in some generic skills—reading, listening, writing, learning—is a prerequisite for success in most college level courses."

If A is a success in life, then A equals x plus y plus z. Work is x; y is play; and z is keeping your mouth shut.

Albert Einstein

A broad-based education and good communications skills are the keys to a successful high-tech career.

REVIEW

1. Economic and social changes are placing pressure on colleges to meet the needs of Ontario. What factors have necessitated this pressure?

2. How are demographic changes affecting the work force?

3. What essential skills can general education provide for today's worker?

In the current environment, a worker who lacks appropriate language and communication skills or basic technological literacy is at a distinct disadvantage. In today's fast-changing marketplace, workers require a portable and expandable skills base. Such a base gives them greater security of employment by enabling them to adapt to changing job demands by updating or upgrading skills and to shift between jobs with different skills requirements.

Increasingly, employers are asking that college graduates have ability to learn additional skills, to work with others, to solve problems and to communicate clearly. These skills are becoming more valued because both the speed and nature of economic change make adaptability a requirement. From the perspective of employers, a focus on a generic skill assists them to use both capital and human resources more flexibly in adjusting to the impact of change and competitive pressures. While specific skills training may be firm or job-specific, a focus on generic skills as a foundation of the college curriculum would benefit employers as a whole.

In addition, the communications revolution has expanded the horizons of citizenship so that people can and should feel part of local, national and international debates on issues that affect them, their families and their futures—issues such as poverty, the environment, the Canadian constitution or political change in other parts of the world. To participate actively, they should be aware of the background and context of current events and issues. Helping people to be good citizens, as well as productive workers with marketable skills, should be part of the educational experience at a college. We are advocating nothing less than major reorientation of the curriculum in the direction of general education and generic skills.

It may also require some reorientation in how students view a college education. Many current students are attracted to the college because programs are perceived as providing training which enables them to immediately perform on the job at a high level. The colleges and the secondary schools will need to demonstrate to students the necessity of embarking on a **lifelong learning** process and the importance of solid foundation skills to this process.

EDUCATION FOR WHAT?

IN THE "Technological Society"

JAMES TURK

Far from de-emphasizing a solid general education in the humanities and in the social and natural sciences, the conclusion is that, on the contrary, perhaps we should be stressing this type of education more than ever.

Let me begin with a myth which does not serve us well in our discussions of education and technology, namely, that the new microelectronic technologies will require a more highly skilled, better trained work force. Generally, the opposite is the case. The history of the development of the **microelectronic technologies**, and of their subsequent use, is a history of designing and using machines which deskill work and diminish the role of workers. Insofar as possible, decision making, which formerly was undertaken on the shop or office floor, is removed to the confines of management.

The **deskilling** is not inherent in new technologies. There is nothing natural or inevitable about deskilling. The new technologies have been consciously designed to deskill work—to allow employers to draw from a larger (and therefore less highly paid) labour pool. Technologies could be designed which enhance and make use of workers' skills, but designers and purchasers of new technologies have little interest in such approaches.[1]

The result is that the design and use of the new technologies is creating a pear-shaped distribution of skills. On the one hand, jobs are being created for a relatively small number of highly skilled people to design, program, and maintain the equipment. On the other hand, the present skills of the great majority of workers are being diminished, and many of their jobs eliminated....

The point of these comments is to argue that contrary to the widely held (and widely perpetrated) view that the new technologies are increasing the demand for a more highly skilled work force, the opposite is the case. Evidence for this claim comes not only from scholars studying the workplace, but also from organizations like the U.S. Bureau of Labor Statistics which projects job growth over the next decade or so.

Its projections, the most sophisticated in North America, are quite startling for proponents of the high-tech future. Not one technologically

PREVIEW

Microelectronics and the shift from a manufacturing to a service economy are altering the nature and organization of work today. What are the implications of these changes? In a presentation at a conference on liberal education at Ryerson Polytechnical Institute, James Turk challenges conventional views about these changes and their educational implications.

"Deskilling" may not be inevitable in high-tech microelectronics, but it is an area for serious concern.

sophisticated job appears among their top 15 occupations which are expected to experience the largest job growth. The category which will contribute the most new jobs through 1995 is janitors—alone accounting for 775,000 new jobs or 3 percent of all new jobs created in the United States. Following janitors, in order, are cashiers, secretaries, office clerks, sales clerks, nurses, waiters and waitresses, primary school teachers, truck drivers, nursing aides and orderlies. If you want to go down the list further, the eleventh occupation with the most substantial growth is salespeople, followed by accountants, auto mechanics, supervisors of blue-collar workers, kitchen helpers, guards and doorkeepers, fast food restaurant workers....

DEFINING "SKILLS"

Many who would dissent from my argument would point to the fact that workers are (and presumably therefore need to be) better educated now than 20 years or 40 years ago. Certainly workers today—from the shop floor to the manager's office—on average, have far more schooling than in the past. But that is no evidence that they are, or need be, more skilled. The lengthening of the average period of schooling has relatively little to do with changing occupational requirements for most workers. Rather the lengthening of years in school has resulted from attempts to decrease unemployment levels (beginning in the 1930s), to use the educational system to absorb some of the returning service personnel after World War II, to changing social expectations about the right to more education, and so forth.

In response to the higher level of average grade attained, employers have introduced higher minimum levels of education as requirements for hiring—whether it be a retail clerk at Eaton's, a machine operator at Canadian General Electric or an entry-level management trainee at General Motors. But there has been no study which has demonstrated that the higher levels were a result of the changing nature of the jobs rather than an increased supply of people who had spent longer in school.

Moreover, one must recognize that traditional designations of "skill" have only an inexact relation to what we would commonly mean by "skill." To put it differently, the definition of "skill" must be understood politically as well as descriptively. For example, things that are required in jobs done primarily by women tend to be defined less as skill than things required in jobs done traditionally by men.

Similarly, there are often necessary "skills" required in the most "unskilled" work—a point employers often discover when they open a new plant in a low-wage area and find that they cannot get the production they expected initially because the inexperienced work force does not have the "skills" required by the "unskilled" work.

I mention this only to highlight for you the fact that the definition of "skill" is more problematic than we conventionally take it to be. When I

Notes

[1] See David Noble, *Forces of Production: A Social History of Industrial Automation* (New York: Knopf, 1984); and Andrew Zimbalist, ed., *Case Studies on the Labor Process.* (New York: Monthly Review Press, 1979).

[2] Harry Braverman, *Labor and Monopoly Capital.* (New York: Monthly Review Press, 1974) pp.443-44.

[3] Quoted in Braverman, p.447.

have argued that work is being deskilled, I am not referring to job classifications of skill, nor to educational requirements imposed by employers, but to the mastery of craft, that is the knowledge of processes and materials; the ability to conceptualize the product of one's labour and the technical ability to produce it. As Braverman notes, most discussions of skill use the term as a "a specific dexterity, a limited and repetitive operation, 'speed as skill', etc." He goes on to say that the concept of skill has been degraded to the point that:

> ...today the worker is considered to possess a "skill" if his or her job requires a few days' or weeks' training, several months of training is regarded as unusually demanding, and the job that calls for a learning period of six months or a year—such as computer programming—inspires a paroxysm of awe. We may compare this with the traditional craft apprenticeship, which rarely lasted less than four years and which was not uncommonly seven years long.[2]

To this point I have attempted to argue that new technologies in workplaces from a manufacturing plant floor to **software** production houses to offices are designed and used to deskill the work of the vast majority of workers, and concomitantly, the definition of skill is also being degraded, giving the impression that the real degradation of skill is not as stark as it is. What has come to be defined as **skills training** is a distorted and narrow kind of job training of the sort described many years ago by the Gilbreths in the *Primer* on scientific management: "Training a worker means merely enabling him to carry out the directions of his work schedule. Once he can do this, his training is over, whatever his age."[3]

Even today, with all the mystifying hype about **job enrichment** and new forms of work organization, Frank Gilbreth's characterization of training is a perfect description of most so-called "skills training."

EDUCATIONAL IMPLICATIONS

The implications of all this are what concern us today. The most obvious and important implication is that there is little foundation to the view that rising skill levels for the labour force as a whole demand the reshaping of school, college and university curricula to provide more emphasis on mathematics, computer science, and technical training.

While some jobs will require a significant amount of this type of education, the great majority (and a growing percentage) will require little of this knowledge in order to fulfil the requirements of the work. If anything, on average, there will be a diminution of the need for this kind of technical education as essential job prerequisite.

The dangers of a misplaced emphasis on more **technical knowledge** at all levels of the educational system are several.

First, false expectations are being created. Students will be primed with the myth about the skills their future jobs will require, and then, when they get jobs (if they get jobs), they will discover the cruel joke of their skilled training for what they find to be deskilled jobs.

Training is everything. The peach was once a bitter almond; cauliflower is nothing but cabbage with a college education.

Mark Twain, author

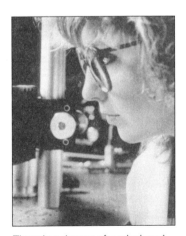

There is a danger of a misplaced emphasis on acquiring more and more technical knowledge alone.

REVIEW

1. How does author James Turk refute the view that "the employment future lies with those able to perform professional and technically sophisticated work"?

2. What is Turk's main point in his discussion of the term "skills" and how the term is defined?

3. According to Turk, what should be the ultimate goal of a solid general education? Does this goal seem reasonable in today's transition from school to work?

Second, the rush to emphasize **computer literacy** and a more technical curriculum can force a de-emphasis of more important educational priorities that today's and tomorrow's students will require, not only for their jobs but for greater fulfilment in their lives.

The deskilling of work means that people will have increasingly to find meaning outside their work. The rapidity of technological change means that people will likely shift jobs (regardless of whether they shift employers) more frequently in their working lives. The greater availability of information and the burgeoning quantity of that information will put greater pressures on people who want to be informed and active participants in their society.

All of these factors mean that the priorities for education from kindergarten through university, including technical and vocational programs, must be to provide people with the capabilities to think critically, and to develop their cognitive, expressive and **analytical skills** to the fullest. It must, as well, provide people with extensive knowledge of their social, cultural, political and economic institutions, and prepare and encourage them to participate actively in the shaping of decisions that affect their lives.

Far from de-emphasizing a solid general education in the humanities, social and natural sciences, the implications of the emerging "technological society" are that we should be stressing this type of education more than ever.

Certainly there is a necessary place for people specializing in technical matters, but that may be no greater a need in the future than it has been in the past. More likely, there will be a lesser need for such specialized education. Given the power of what can be done with the new technologies, even our scientists will need a sound, general education more than ever. It will be essential for them to have a **humanistic perspective** from which they pursue their scientific achievements. The quality of our everyday lives, even the future of humankind, is dependent on scientists realizing the broader implications of what they are doing.

Our production and office workers will need narrow job training, which should be provided by the employer. Our skilled craftspeople that survive the deskilling mania of technology designers will continue to need proper apprenticeships (which have increasingly disappeared over the past 40 years). But all will need, as well, a tough, critical, informative **general education**—beginning at the primary level through to the highest levels—if we are to achieve our fullest potential as individuals and as a society.

WHY COLLEGE GRADS GET THE JOBS

SHOW ME THE MONEY!

ROBERT SHEPPARD

Nimble as ants, Canada's colleges have become so flush with their ability to place students in real jobs—most boast a success rate in the range of 90 percent—that nothing seems to daunt them or their students.

When the Kanitz twins completed high school in 1988, they went their separate ways. Kristi, the brainer, headed to the University of Western Ontario in London—as far from their King City home, north of Toronto, as her scholarship money would take her. Her brother Justin enrolled in auto mechanics at Centennial, a college of applied arts and technology in Toronto. For Kristi Kanitz-Woolsey, the penny dropped when she completed her BA in 1992 and both she and her brother applied to teachers' college at the University of Toronto. Justin was accepted. Kristi was not. "It was a huge blow to my ego," she says, laughing about it now. "I was supposed to be the academic in the family." Indeed, first in her geography class at Western, she retreated to a two-year master's program where she became increasingly disillusioned with the prospect of getting a job in her field. Today, Kristi, 28 and the new mother of twins, is the contented manager of a small Waterloo manufacturer of U-bolts—an unusual fit for someone with an MA in international relations—and Justin teaches in the tech shop of a Toronto high school. Says Kristi: "My father used to say, 'You go to university if you want a challenge, you go to community college to prepare yourself for real life.' And after going to university for six years, I tend to agree with him."

So do an increasing number of today's young people. To a generation scarred by recession and reared on consumer choice, the exalted **university degree** is fast losing its traditional allure to the more prosaic **college diploma**. One reason is cost: the typical diploma carries a tuition of $1,500 to $2,200 a year, while the university equivalent is in the $3,300 range and rising. The second reason is the rush for jobs, for security in an insecure world, that is reshaping social attitudes and the post-secondary universe in its wake. This summer, when management consultant Ernst & Young asked pollster Angus Reid to explore how Ontarians felt about jobs and education, 35 percent of the respondents said a college diploma in a technical

PREVIEW

A tough-minded generation, scarred by recession and concerned about debt, is stampeding to colleges across the country. This article explores how the traditional barrier between education and training is rapidly falling away, and job-ready colleges are becoming "the finishing school of choice" for many university grads.

occupation was the most valuable type of education they could envision. Only half as many believed a university degree in science would do the trick; only 3 percent had faith in a BA. The mood has been changing since at least 1993, when Environics Research Group Ltd. began asking whether people would direct a high-school graduate to a trade school or university, and subsequent polls showed a widening gap in favour of the former. Parents with university degrees were still keen to see their children follow in their footsteps. But for almost everyone else, including the pollster's top category of professionals, senior administrators and business owners, the job-focused college came out on top.

But never mind what adults think. The real trend in the postsecondary ranks is that many of the larger colleges report that up to 30 per cent of their students already have a university degree—a phenomenon that has been growing right across the country for several years. That trend has colleges crowing and universities rethinking their roles as students question the value of investing six or seven years to get the right mix of the theoretical and the practical. Stephen Quinlan, president of Toronto's Seneca College, the largest in the country, runs what he calls "the grad school of choice" for nearby York University....

Universities are alert to the trend. Says York University president Lorna Marsden: "We are certainly becoming much more aware of what's really going on by virtue of students' feet." York is one of those at the forefront of those, at least in Ontario, trying to shorten the learning experience for students by negotiating program-specific arrangements with certain colleges—"without giving up our brand name," says Marsden....

After 30 years of being the **junior partners** in the country's **postsecondary system**, Canada's colleges are starting to show what Seneca's Quinlan likes to call "upstart tendencies." Seneca's most recent exploit—a 24,300 square-metre building of its own smack in the middle of the York University campus—is a case in point. The high-tech outpost, scheduled to open in the spring, will house 4,000 college students and whatever university ones come around seeking technical skills. Interest is such that work has already begun on an expansionary second phase. A modest 1,100 square metres is being set aside in case York wants to set up any high-tech labs itself.

Nimble as ants, Canada's colleges have become so flush with their ability to place students in real jobs—most boast a success rate in the range of 90 percent—that nothing seems to daunt them. Colleges are in the business of producing not only welders and machinists, but world-class chefs, a new generation of multidisciplinary health care workers—and whiz-kid animators for Nelvana and Disney. Need more computer technicians? Seneca says it can produce as many as any university can, and at half the cost. But this may be comparing apples and oranges. Colleges produce more of the well-paid workers in **information technology**, the ones who set up and monitor a company's computer networks. Universities tend to provide the more analytical programmers....

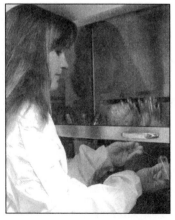

Many large colleges report that up to 30 percent of their students already have a university degree.

Many business leaders—and many universities—argue that a degree is worth more in the job market and offers better protection against an economic downturn. It may. But with the recent movement between universities and colleges, the value of a simple undergraduate degree is becoming harder to measure. What is unassailable is the penalty for stopping at high school: between 1990 and 1996, the number of jobs for those without a degree or college diploma fell by 910,000, while employment for those with a **postsecondary credential** increased by more than 1.4 million.

But scratch the surface and it is more than just the old political slogan—"Jobs, jobs, jobs"—that is driving the college option. Eighteen-year-old Tantray Walsh from Cold Lake, Alberta, had her choice of universities when she completed high school last year. But her armed forces family was moving to Calgary, and she followed her guidance counsellor's advice, enrolling in Calgary's Mount Royal College in a two-year program aimed at helping people with disabilities. Walsh believes she will "most likely" go on to university—Alberta's transfer system enables her to apply her college credits towards a university degree—but this year is opening her eyes to other options, including colleges in the United States. "We are such a close-knit group here—small classes, my teachers know me by name," says Walsh. "I know people who went to Mount Royal first and then to university and didn't like it. I'll have to see...."

"This is a tough generation," says Durham's Polonsky. "They are more like their grandparents' generation than their parents'. People in their early 20s have lived much of their life in a **recession**, and they will always be wary of economic cycles." Indeed, today's college student, with an average age of 26, is slightly older than his or her university counterparts and has spent more time in the work force, often being buffeted from job to job. At Durham, Polonsky estimates that about 1,000 of the 4,500 full-time students have children and many are single parents juggling jobs and kids....

In an age of perilous government support, even the slightest shift in student preference can disrupt the postsecondary universe. The current demand for cheaper, more relevant education is not lost on the universities. When colleges such as Humber in Toronto moved to offer a variety of one-year certificates for those with university degrees or advanced standing, several universities followed suit with similar add-ons of their own. In the past several years, a wide range of creative partnerships have taken shape, from the university buildings springing up on college campuses to joint ownership of facilities where common programs are taught....

Unlike universities, hampered by governing senates and hundreds of years of tradition, colleges are much more free to spin on a dime and offer courses on the latest computer or health services technique—whatever the market will bear. "I spend my days talking to business people, trying to find what they want," says Seneca's Quinlan. His tactic for not being bamboozled by half-baked ideas: he asks companies for a commitment to hire Seneca grads three years down the fine if he sets up a program, or to loan him that $100,000 piece of new equipment for training. College presidents say

Master and Doctor are my titles;
For ten years now, without repose,
I've held my erudite recitals
And led my pupils by the nose.

Johann Wolfgang Von Goethe, poet

Many college students are lured away by good-paying jobs before graduating.

KEY TERMS

- University degree
- College diploma
- Junior partners
- Information technology
- Postsecondary credential
- Recession
- Developing countries
- "Education" and "training"

REVIEW

1. Colleges were created in the 1960s to deal with the effect of the baby boom. How have they evolved since then?

2. What factors, other than economic ones, might motivate students to choose the college option?

3. We need "greater clarity" in the roles of colleges and universities. What traditional barriers between the two need to be addressed?

they can zap a new program in place in anywhere from six months to a year, depending on the availability of the training materials and instructors. "It's tough to do," says Michener president Renate Krakauer. "But otherwise, the world passes you by...."

When they were created in the 1960s, products of social and educational upheaval, colleges were designed in large measure to deal with the fallout from the baby boom, to cushion the entrance to the job market of a growing number of young people. Since then, they have evolved on many fronts–skills merchants, career reshapers, credentialists for everyone from journalists to funeral-services workers. Now, they are approaching the final frontier: international respectability.

Developing countries are tired of sending their best and brightest to become doctors or engineers at North American universities, only to see them stay. With Canadian colleges bringing their computer or health-care technician courses right to Chile or Trinidad, these countries are now able to envision building their own infrastructure. Toronto's Seneca earned $10 million last year, 20 percent of its revenue, on international ventures mostly in developing countries. Together, the country's colleges have been involved in at least 300 educational development projects in 70 countries. Red River College in Winnipeg and Camosun in Victoria have joined forces to develop a program on child care standards at the University of Danang in Vietnam; Grant MacEwan Community College in Edmonton recently established an office in northern Russia to maintain contact with the graduates of its health care administration program. On the Team Canada trade mission to Latin America earlier this year, colleges turned out to be the big draw at breakfast business meetings, surprising many who wondered why they were along in the first place.

The irony is that colleges can sell abroad what many of them cannot sell at home–a coherent system of flexible postsecondary education. "The advantage of the community college is its tremendous sense of place," observes Ray Ivany, head of Nova Scotia Community College, a single administered body with 13 campuses. "You cannot imperil in any way that primary connection to the communities they serve." But at the same time, he says, "that old dichotomy between **'education' and 'training'** is rapidly falling away. Students are moving back and forth between college and university. They pop in, they pop out of the workforce. What this province needs, what Canada needs, is greater clarity in the roles of colleges and universities and a seamless transition so the debt-load of students can be reduced." How easy it will be, given their years of mutual mistrust and competition, for the institutions of higher education to muster that sort of clarity is anybody's guess. But for this generation of students, with a tight grip on their education dollars, the assault on the old barriers and attitudes has already begun.

A NEO-LUDDITE REFLECTS ON THE INTERNET

NON-LINEAR THINKING

GERTRUDE HIMMELFARB

Over-exposed to "multimedia" and "hypermedia" replete with sound and images, do we risk being unable to concentrate on mere "texts" (formerly known as books), which have only words and ideas to commend them?

On the subject of our latest technological revolution, cyberspace, I am a neo-Luddite. Not a true **Luddite**; my Luddism is qualified, compromised. I revel in the word processor; I am grateful for computerized library catalogues; I appreciate the convenience of CD-ROMS; and I concede the usefulness of the Internet for retrieving information and conducting research. But I am disturbed by some aspects of the new technology–not merely by the moral problems raised by cybersex, which have occupied so much attention recently, but also by the new technology's impact on learning and scholarship.

Revolutions come fast and furious these days. No sooner do we adapt to one than we are confronted with another. For almost half a millennium, we lived with the product of the **print revolution**–the culture of the book. Then, a mere century ago, we were introduced to the motion picture; a couple of decades later, to radio and then to television. To a true Luddite, those inventions were the beginning of the rot, the decline of Western civilization as we have known it. To a true revolutionary, such as Marshall McLuhan, they were giant steps toward a brave new world liberated from the stultifying rigidities of an obsolete literacy. To the rest of us, they were frivolities, diversions, often meretricious (as some popular culture has always been), but not threatening to the life of the mind, the culture associated with books.

Not that the book culture has been immune from corruption. When the printing press democratized literature, liberating it from the control of clerics and scribes, the effects were ambiguous. As the historian Elizabeth Eisenstein pointed out in her seminal 1979 work *The Printing Press as an Agent of Change*, the advent of printing facilitated not only the production of scientific works, but also of occult and devotional tracts. It helped create a cosmopolitan **secular culture** and, at the same time, distinctive national and sectarian cultures. It stimulated scholarship and high culture, as well as

PREVIEW

The technological revolution has brought us from the culture of the book to motion pictures, radio, television and cyberspace. What is the impact of the latest technology on learning and scholarship? In this article, Gertrude Himmelfarb, a professor of history, explores the pros and cons of the Internet as an educational tool.

ephemera and popular culture. It subverted one intellectual elite, the clergy, only to elevate another, the "enlightened" class.

Yet for all of its ambiguities, printing celebrated the culture of the book—of bad books, to be sure, but also of good books and great books. Movies, radio, and television made the first inroads on the book, not only because they distracted us from reading, but also because they began to train our minds to respond to oral and visual sensations of brief duration rather than to the cadences, nuances, and lingering echoes of the written word. The movie critic Michael Medved has said that even more detrimental than the content of television is the way that it habituates children to an attention span measured in seconds rather than minutes. The combination of sound bites and striking visual effects shapes the young mind, incapacitating it for the longer, slower, less febrile tempo of the book.

And now we have the **Internet** to stimulate and quicken our senses still more. We channel-surf on television, but that is as naught compared with cyber-surfing. The obvious advantage of the new medium is that it provides access to an infinite quantity of information on an untold number and variety of subjects. How does one quarrel with such a plenitude of goods?

As an **information-retrieval device**, the Internet is unquestionably an asset, assuming that those using it understand that the information retrieved is only as sound as the original sources—an assumption that applies to all retrieval methods, but especially to one whose sources are so profuse and indiscriminate. Yet children and even older students, encouraged to rely upon the Internet for information and research, may not be sophisticated enough to question the validity of the information or the reliability of the source. A child whom I saw interviewed on television said that it was wonderful to be able to ask a question on one's home page and have "lots of people answer it for you." Before the age of the Internet, the child would have had to look up the question in a textbook or encyclopedia, a source that he would have recognized as more authoritative than, say, his older brother or sister (or even his mother or father).

As a **learning device**, the new electronic technology is even more dubious—indeed, it may be more bad than good. And it is dubious at all levels of learning.

Children who are told that they need not learn how to multiply and divide, spell, and write grammatical prose, because the computer can do that for them, are being grossly miseducated. More important, young people constantly exposed to "multimedia" and "hypermedia" replete with sound and images often become unable to concentrate on mere "texts" (known as books), which have only words and ideas to commend them. Worse yet, the constant exposure to a myriad of texts, sounds, and images that often are only tangentially related to each other is hardly conducive to the cultivation of logical, rational, systematic habits of thought.

At the more advanced level of learning and scholarship, the situation is equally ambiguous. Let me illustrate this from my own experience. I used to give (in the pre-electronic age) two sequences of courses: one on social history, the other on intellectual history. In a course on social history, a student might find electronic technology useful, for example, in inquiring about the standard of living of the working classes in the early period of industrialization, assuming that the relevant sources–statistical surveys, diaries, archival collections, newspapers, tracts, journals, books, and other relevant materials–were on line (or at least that information about their location and content was available).

This kind of **social history**, which is built by marshalling social and economic data, is not only facilitated, but actually is stimulated, by the new technology. One might find oneself making connections among sources of information that would have had no apparent link had they not been so readily called up on the computer screen (on the other hand, now one might not make the effort to discover other kinds of sources that do not appear).

But what about **intellectual history**? It may be that the whole of Rousseau's *Social Contract* and Hegel's *Philosophy of History* are now on line. Can one read such books on the screen as they should be read–slowly, carefully, patiently, dwelling upon a difficult passage, resisting the temptation to scroll down, thwarting the natural speed of the computer? What is important in the history of ideas is not retrieving and recombining material, but understanding it. And that requires a different relation to the text, a different tempo of reading and study.

One can still buy the book (or perhaps print out a "hard copy" from the computer), read it, mark it up, and take notes the old-fashioned way. The difficulty is that students habituated to surfing on the Internet, to getting their information in quick easy doses, to satisfying their curiosity with a minimum of effort (and with a maximum of sensory stimulation) often do not have the patience to think and study this old-fashioned way. They may even come to belittle the intellectual enterprise itself, the study of the kinds of books–"great books," as some say derisively–that require careful thought and study.

Perhaps I am exaggerating the effect of the **electronic revolution**, just as critics have said that Elizabeth Eisenstein has exaggerated the effect of the print one. She sometimes seems to suggest that printing was not only *an* agent of change, but *the* primary agent. Without the printing press, she has implied, the Renaissance might have petered out or the Reformation been suppressed as yet another medieval heresy. "The advent of printing" she notes, preceded "the Protestant revolt."

The electronic media cannot make that claim to priority. The intellectual revolution of our time, **postmodernism**, long antedated the Internet. Nonetheless, the Internet powerfully reinforces postmodernism: It is the postmodernist technology *par excellence*. It is as subversive of "linear," "logocentric," "essentialist" thinking, as committed to the "aporia," "indeterminacy," "fluidity," "intertextuality," and "contextuality" of discourse, as deconstruction itself. Like postmodernism, the Internet does not distinguish between the true and the false, the important and the trivial, the

I find television very educational. Every time someone switches it on I go into another room and read a good book.

Groucho Marx

KEY TERMS

- Luddite
- Print revolution
- Secular culture
- Internet
- Information-retrieval device
- Learning device
- Social history
- Intellectual history
- Electronic revolution
- Postmodernism
- GIGO

REVIEW

1. How did the advent of printing "liberate" the culture of the book?

2. As an information-retrieval and learning device, how has the Internet affected the quality of learning?

3. How does the Internet "reinforce" postmodernism?

enduring and the ephemeral. The search for a name or phrase or subject will produce a comic strip or advertising slogan as readily as a quotation from the Bible or Shakespeare. Every source appearing on the screen has the same weight and credibility as every other; no authority is "privileged" over any other.

The Internet gives new meaning to the British expression describing intellectuals, "chattering classes." On their own home pages, subscribers can communicate to the world every passing reflection, impression, sensation, obsession, or perversion.

Michael Kinsley, editor of the new cyberspace journal *Slate*, defensively insists that his magazine will retain the "linear, rational thinking" of print journalism. To have to make that claim is itself testimony to the non-linear, non-rational tendency of the new medium. Each article in *Slate* gives the date when it was "posted" and "composted" (archived). Composted! One recalls the computer-programming acronym a few years ago—"**GIGO**," for "garbage in, garbage out." (As it happens, the articles in *Slate* are not garbage, but much on the Internet is.)

One need not be a Luddite, or even a neo-Luddite, to be alarmed by this most useful, most potent, most seductive, and most equivocal invention.

HONING GENERIC SKILLS

SOME FALLACIES OF THINKING

ROBERT H. LAUER

How do we know which explanation is right? How can we distinguish fact from fiction, the logical from the not-so-logical? Are there certain "fallacies of thinking" we should watch out for before passing judgement?

PREVIEW

In this piece, Robert Lauer uses the analysis of American social problems to illustrate mistakes that are commonly made when thinking things through. He argues that familiarity with the fallacies of reasoning will help us to formulate our own analyses and to evaluate the arguments of others.

Why do people use drugs? And what can we do about the drug problem? These questions took on an urgency for Americans in the 1980s and early 1990s. The answers given are many and diverse. Here are a few that appeared in a popular column in 1989:

- It's an education problem. We need to guarantee every child as much education as that child can handle, so no one has to grow up in poverty.

- It's a religious problem. God is punishing us for deviating from His ways. We must return to the ways taught in the Bible.

- The problem is one of our willingness to get tough. We need to crack down on the dealers. They should be put to death, like they do in the People's Republic of China.…

- The problem is that we are a sick society. Our nation is full of people who abuse their children. Our kids are unhappy because they have parents who are full of anger and greed. You can't expect well-adjusted kids when the parents are so screwed up.…

To these analyses we could add others.… We could say, for example, that drug abuse results from the breakdown of rules that followed the rapid change in all **social institutions** in our era, from the labels applied to young people who experiment with drugs, or from the definitions of appropriate and inappropriate behavior that prevail in juvenile groups.

There are, in other words, myriad explanations for drug abuse, and for all other social problems as well. The question we raise in this chapter is "How do we know which explanation is correct?" All of the above may sound reasonable, but not all are necessarily true. In fact, many myths surround social problems. How do we distinguish myth from fact?…

THE SOURCE OF MYTH

Here we will look at nine different fallacies that have been used to analyze social problems. A familiarity with the fallacies will help you to logically formulate your own analyses and to evaluate the analyses and arguments of others.

• Fallacy of "Dramatic Instance"

The **fallacy of dramatic instance** refers to the tendency to *overgeneralize*, to use one, two, or three cases to support an entire argument. This is a common mistake among those who discuss social problems, and it may be difficult to counter because the limited number of cases often are a part of the *individual's personal experience*. For example, in discussing the race problem in the United States, an individual may argue that "Blacks in this country can make it just as much as whites. I know a black businessman who is making a million. In fact, he has a better house and a better car than I have." You might counter this argument by pointing out that the successful businessperson is an exception. The other person might dismiss your point: "If one guy can make it, they all can." The fallacy of the dramatic instance mistakes a few cases for a general situation.

This fallacy is difficult to deal with because the argument is based partly on fact. There are, after all, black millionaires in America. But, does this mean there is no discrimination and that any black person, like any white person, can attain success? Many Americans believe that welfare recipients are "ripping off" the rest of us, that we are subsidizing their unwillingness to work and supporting them at a higher standard of living than we ourselves enjoy. Is that true? Yes, in a few cases. Occasionally, newspapers report instances of individuals making fraudulent use of welfare. But does this mean that most welfare recipients are doing the same? Do people on welfare really live better than people who work for a living?

The point is, in studying social problems, that we must recognize that exceptions always exist. To say that Blacks are exploited in America is not to say that *all* Blacks are exploited. To say that the poor are victims of a system rather than unwilling workers is not to say that one can't find poor people who are unwilling to work. To say that those on welfare are generally living in oppressive circumstances is not to deny that some welfare recipients are cheating and living fairly well. To use such cases in support of one's argument is to fall into the trap of the fallacy of the dramatic instance, because social problems deal with general situations rather than with individual exceptions....

• Fallacy of "Retrospective Determinism"

The **fallacy of retrospective determinism** is the argument that things could not have worked out any other way than the way they did. It is a *deterministic* position, but the determinism is aimed at the past rather than the future. The fallacy asserts that what happened historically *had* to happen historically, and it had to happen just the way it did. If we accept this fallacy, we would believe that our present social problems are all inevitable. We would say that avoiding racial discrimination or poverty has always been impossible, that there were no alternatives to the wars in which we have been involved, and that the nation's health could not have been any better than it has been. However regrettable any of the problems are or have been, the fallacy of retrospective determinism makes them the unavoidable outcomes of the historical process. This fallacy is unfortunate for a number of reasons. History is more than a tale of *inevitable tragedies*. History is important in enabling us to understand social problems, but we will not benefit from history if we think of it merely as a determined process. We cannot fully understand the tensions between America's minority groups and the white majority unless we know about the decades of exploitation and humiliation preceding the emergence of the modern civil rights movement. Our understanding will remain clouded if we regard those decades as nothing more than an inevitable process. Similarly, we cannot fully understand the tension between the People's Republic of China and the West if we view it only as a battle of economic ideologies. We must realize that the tension is based in the pillage and humiliation that China was subjected to by the West. Again, our understanding will not be enhanced by the study of history if we regard the Western oppression of China in the nineteenth century as inevitable.

If we view the past in terms of determinism, we will have little reason to study it, and we will be deprived of an important source of understanding. Furthermore, the fallacy of retrospective determinism is but a small step from the stoic *acceptance of the inevitable*. That is, if things are the way they had to be, why worry about them? Assuming that the future will also be determined by forces beyond our control, we are left in a position of apathy: There is little point in trying to contest the inevitable. This fallacy is probably less common in discussions about social problems than the fallacy of the dramatic instance, but it does appear in everyday discussions....

• Fallacy of "Misplaced Concreteness"

There is a tendency to explain some social problems by resorting to *reification*—making what is abstract into something concrete. "Society," for example, is an abstraction. It is not like a person, an animal, or an object that can be touched. It is an idea, a way of thinking about a particular collectivity of people. Yet we often hear people assert that something is the fault of "society" or that "society" caused a certain problem. This is the **fallacy of misplaced concreteness**. In what sense can society "make" or "cause" or "do" anything? To say that society caused a problem leaves us helpless to correct the situation because we haven't the faintest notion where to begin. If, for example, society is the cause of juvenile delinquency, how do we tackle the problem? Must we change society? If so, how?

"If the coach and horses and the footmen and the beautiful clothes all turned back into the pumpkin and the mice and the rags, then how come the glass slipper didn't turn back too?"

The point is that "society" is an abstraction, a concept that refers to a group of people who interact in particular ways. To *attribute social problems to an abstraction* like "society" does not help us resolve the problems. Sometimes people who attribute the cause of a particular problem to society intend to *deny individual responsibility*. To say that society causes delinquency may be a way of saying that the delinquent child is not responsible for his or her behaviour. Still, we can recognize the social causes of problems without either attributing them to an abstraction like society or relieving the individual of responsibility for his or her behaviour.

For example, we could talk about the family problems that contribute to delinquency. A family is a concrete phenomenon. Furthermore, we could say that the family itself is a victim of some kind of societal arrangement, such as government regulations that tend to perpetuate poverty and cause stress and disruption in many families. In that case, we could say that families need to be helped by changing the government regulations that keep some of them in poverty and, thereby, facilitate delinquent behaviour.

Society, in short, does not cause anything. Rather, problems are caused by that which the concept of society represents—people acting in accord with certain social arrangements and within a particular cultural system.

• Fallacy of "Personal Attack"

A tactic among debaters is to *attack the opponent personally* when one can't support one's position by reason, logic, or facts. This diverts attention from the issue and focuses it on the personality. We will call this the **fallacy of personal attack** (philosophers call it *ad hominem*). It can be remarkably effective in avoiding the application of reason or the consideration of facts in a discussion of a social problem. We will extend the meaning when applying this fallacy to the analysis of social problems: we will use it to mean either attacking the opponent in a debate about a problem or *attacking the people who are the victims* of the problem.

Historically, the poor have suffered from this approach to their problem. Matza (1966) detailed how the poor of many nations in many different times have been categorized as "disreputable." Instead of offering sympathy or being concerned for the poor, people tend to label the poor as disreputable and, consequently, deserving of or responsible for their plight. This means, of course, that those of us who are not poor are relieved of any responsibility....

The meaning and seriousness of any social problem may be sidestepped by attacking the intelligence or character of the victims of the problem or of those who call attention to the problem. We need only recall a few of the many labels that have been thrown at victims to recognize how common this approach is: deadbeats, draft dodgers, niggers, kikes, bums, traitors, perverts and so forth.

The myth that immigrants are a burden on the Canadian economy can help to foster racial prejudice.

• Fallacy of "Appeal to Prejudice"

In addition to attacking the opponent, a debater may try to support an unreasonable position by using another technique: **fallacy of appeal to prejudice**. (Philosophers call it argument *ad populum*.) It involves using popular prejudices or passions to convince others of the correctness of one's position. When the topic is social problems, this means using *popular slogans* or *popular myths* to sway people emotionally rather than using reasoning from systematic studies.

For example, a popular slogan that appeared as a car bumper sticker during the early 1970s read, "I fight poverty; I work." This appeal to popular prejudice against "freeloaders" used the popular myth that the poor are those who are unwilling to work. This kind of appeal is doubly unfortunate because it assaults the character of the poor unfairly, and it is based upon and helps to perpetuate a myth. As we will see, the poverty problem is not a problem of work. Jobs for the unemployed will not eliminate poverty from America.

Some slogans or phrases last for decades and are revived to oppose efforts to resolve social problems. "Creeping socialism" has been used to describe many government programs designed to aid the underdogs of our society. The term is not used when the programs are designed to help business or industry, or when the affluent benefit from the programs. It has been remarked, "What the government does for me is progress; what it does for you is socialism."

In some cases, the slogans use general terms that reflect *traditional values*. Thus, the various advances made in civil rights legislation–voting, public accommodations, open housing–have been resisted in the name of "rights of the individual." Such slogans help to perpetuate the myth that legislation that benefits Blacks infringes on the constitutional rights of the white majority.

Myths, in turn, help to perpetuate social problems. In the absence of other evidence, we all tend to rely upon popular notions. Many Americans continue to assume that rape is often the woman's fault because she has sexually provoked the man. These Americans either have seen no evidence to the contrary or have dismissed that evidence as invalid. And, unfortunately, myths tend to become so deeply rooted in our thinking that when we are confronted by new evidence, we may have difficulty accepting it.

Myths are hard to break down. But if we want to understand social problems, we must abandon the popular ideas and assumptions and resist the popular slogans and prejudices that cloud our thinking, and we must choose instead to make judgements based on evidence.

• Fallacy of "Circular Reasoning"

The ancient Greek physician Galen reportedly praised the healing qualities of a certain clay by pointing out that all who drink the remedy recover quickly–except those whom it does not help. The latter die and are not

The world is for thousands a freak show; the images flicker past and vanish; the impressions remain flat and unconnected in the soul. Thus they are easily led by the opinions of others, are content to let their impressions be shuffled and rearranged and evaluated differently.

Johann Wolfgang Von Goethe

helped by any medicine. Obviously, according to Galen, the clay fails only in incurable cases. This is an example of the **fallacy of circular reasoning**: using conclusions to support the assumptions that were necessary to make the conclusions.

Circular reasoning often creeps into analyses of social problems. A person might argue that Blacks are inherently inferior and assert that their inferiority is evident in the fact that they can hold only menial jobs and are not able to do intellectual work. In reply, one might point out that Blacks are not doing more intellectual work because of discriminatory hiring practices. The person might then reply that Blacks could not be hired for such jobs anyway because they are inferior.

Similarly, one may hear the argument that homosexuals are sex perverts. This assumption is supported by the observation that homosexuals commonly have remained secretive about their sexual preference. But, one might counter, the secrecy is due to the general disapproval of homosexuality. No, comes the retort, homosexuality is kept secret because it is a perversion.

Thus, in circular reasoning we bounce *back and forth between assumptions and conclusions*. Circular reasoning leads nowhere in our search for understanding of social problems.

• Fallacy of "Appeal to Authority"

Virtually everything we know is based on some *authority*. We know comparatively little from personal experience or personal research. The authority we necessarily rely on is someone else's experience or research or belief. We accept notions of everything from the nature of the universe to the structure of the atom, from the state of international relationships to the doctrines of religion—all on the basis of some authority. Most people accept a war as legitimate on the authority of their political leaders. Many accept the validity of capital punishment on the authority of law enforcement officers. Some accept the belief of religious authority that use of contraceptives is morally wrong in spite of the population problem. (They may even deny that there really is a population problem.)

This knowledge that we acquire through authority can be inaccurate, and the beliefs can exacerbate rather than resolve or ameliorate social problems. The **fallacy of appeal to authority** means an *illegitimate appeal to authority*. Such an appeal obtrudes into thinking about social problems in at least three ways.

First, the *authority may be ambiguous*. Appeal is made to the Bible by both those who support and those who oppose capital punishment and by both those who castigate and those who advocate help for the poor. Supporters of capital punishment point out that the Bible, particularly the Old Testament, decreed death for certain offenses. Opponents counter that the death penalty contradicts New Testament notions of Christian love. Those who castigate the poor call attention to St. Paul's idea that he who does not work should not eat. Those who advocate help for the poor refer us to Christ's words about ministering to the needy and feeding the hungry. Consequently, an appeal to this kind of authority is really an appeal to a particular interpretation of the authority. Because the interpretations are contradictory, we must find other bases for making our judgments.

Second, the *authority may be irrelevant to the problem.* The fact that a man is a first-rate physicist does not mean he can speak with legitimate authority about race relations. We tend to be impressed with people who have made significant accomplishments in some area, but their accomplishments should not overwhelm us if those people speak about a problem outside their area of achievement or expertise. Nor would we be overwhelmed by the wisdom of our forebears. Benjamin Franklin was a remarkable man, and his advice on how to acquire wealth has been heard, in part at least, by millions of Americans throughout history. But whatever the value of that advice for Franklin's contemporaries, it is of little use for most of America's poor today.

Finally, the *authority may be pursuing a bias* rather than studying a problem. To say that someone is pursuing a bias is not necessarily to disparage that person, because pursuing a bias is part of the job for many people. For example, military officers analyze the problem of war from a military rather than a moral, political, or economic perspective. That is their job. And that is why decisions about armaments, defense, and war should not be left solely to the military. From a military point of view, one way to prevent war is to be prepared to counter any enemy attack. We must be militarily strong, according to this argument, so that other nations will hesitate to initiate an attack upon us....

Authority can be illegitimately or arbitrarily assumed and illegitimately or inaccurately used. Both represent the fallacy of appeal to authority.

• Fallacy of "Composition"

That the whole is equal to the sum of its parts appears obvious to many people. That what is true of the part is also true of the whole likewise seems to be a reasonable statement. But the former is debatable, and the latter is the **fallacy of composition**. As economists have illustrated for us, *what is valid for the part is also valid for the whole* is not necessarily true. Consider, for example, the relationship between work and income. If a particular farmer works hard and the weather is not adverse, his income may rise. But if every farmer works hard and the weather is favourable, and a bumper crop results, the total farm income may fall. The latter case is based upon supply and demand, while the former case assumes that a particular farmer outperforms other farmers.

In thinking about social problems, we *cannot assume that what is true for the individual is also true for the group.* An individual may be able to resolve a problem insofar as it affects him or her, but that resolution is not available to all members of the group. For example, a man who is unemployed and living in poverty may find work that enables him to escape poverty by moving, by concentrated effort, or by working for less than someone else.

> The unleashed power of the atom has changed everything save our modes of thinking and we thus drift toward unparalleled catastrophe.
>
> *Albert Einstein*

Hiroshima, 1945. Military officers in positions of authority do not always consider the moral implications.

REVIEW

1. What examples can be drawn from Canadian society to illustrate each of the nine fallacies of thinking?

2. What problems could result when quick, though seemingly logical, conclusions are drawn?

3. "Numerous logical conclusions can be drawn from any particular set of data." How does this qualification complicate the interpretation of facts?

As we will see in our discussion of poverty, that solution is not possible for most of the nation's poor. Something may be true for a particular individual or even a few individuals and yet be inapplicable or counterproductive for the entire group of which the individuals are members (as in the example of farmers).

• The Fallacy of "Non Sequitur"

A number of the fallacies already discussed involve non sequitur, but we need to look at this way of thinking separately because of its importance. Literally, non sequitur means "*it does not follow.*" This **fallacy of non sequitur** is commonly found when people interpret statistical data....

Daniel Bell (1960) showed how statistics on crime can be misleading. In New York one year, reported assaults were up 200 percent, robberies were up 400 percent, and burglaries were up 1,300 percent! Those are the "facts," but what is the meaning? We might conclude that a crime wave occurred that year. Actually, the larger figures represented a new method of crime reporting that was much more effective in determining the total amount of crime. An increase in reported crime rates can mean different things, but it does not necessarily signify an actual increase in the amount of crime.

One other example involves studies of women who work. Some employers have been convinced that women are not desirable as workers because they are less committed to the job than men are. One of the facts that appears to support that notion is the higher turnover rate of women. Women do indeed have a higher rate of leaving jobs than men have. But what is the meaning of that fact? Are women truly less committed to their jobs? Does the employer run the risk of having to find a replacement sooner if a woman rather than a man is hired for a job? When we look at the situation more closely, we find that the real problem is that women tend to be concentrated in lower level jobs. Also, women who quit a job tend to find another one very quickly. Thus, women may be uncommitted to a particular–low-level–job, but they are strongly committed to work. Furthermore, if we look at jobs with the same status, the turnover rate is no higher for women than men....

INTERPRETING "FACTS"

These illustrations are not meant to discourage anyone from drawing conclusions. Instead, they are another reminder of the need for thorough study and the need to avoid quick conclusions, even when those conclusions seem logical on the surface.

Contrary to popular opinion, *"facts" do not necessarily speak for themselves.* They usually must be *interpreted,* and they must be interpreted in the light of the complexity of social life. Furthermore, numerous logical conclusions usually can be drawn from any particular set of data.

LITTLE RED RIDING HOOD—REVISITED

"MODERN ENGLISH"

RUSSELL BAKER

In an effort to make the classics accessible to contemporary readers, Russell Baker is translating them into modern "English." Here, then, is the translation of "Little Red Riding Hood."

Once upon a point in time, a small person named Little Red Riding Hood initiated plans for the preparation, delivery and transportation of foodstuffs to her grandmother, a senior citizen residing at a place of residence in a wooded area of indeterminate dimension.

In the process of implementing this program, her incursion into the area was in mid-transportation process when it attained interface with an alleged perpetrator. This individual, a wolf, made inquiry as to the whereabouts of Little Red Riding Hood's goal, as well as inferring that he was desirous of ascertaining the contents of Little Red Riding Hood's foodstuffs basket, and all that.

"It would be inappropriate to lie to me," the wolf said, displaying his huge jaw capability. Sensing that he was a mass of repressed hostility intertwined with acute alienation, she indicated.

"I see you indicating," the wolf said, "but what I don't see is whatever it is you're indicating at, you dig?"

Little Red Riding Hood indicated more fully, making one thing perfectly clear–to wit, that it was to her grandmother's residence and with a consignment of foodstuffs that her mission consisted of taking her to and with.

At this point in time the wolf moderated his rhetoric and proceeded to grandmother's residence. The elderly person was then subjected to the disadvantages of total consumption and transferred to residence in the perpetrator's stomach.

"That will raise the old woman's consciousness," the wolf said to himself. He was not a bad wolf, but only a victim of an oppressive society, a society that not only denied wolves' rights, but actually boasted of its capacity for keeping the wolf from the door. An interior malaise made itself manifest inside the wolf.

"Is that the national malaise I sense within my digestive tract?" wondered the wolf. "Or is it the old person seeking to retaliate for her

PREVIEW

Much of the "official" English found in government documents and company reports is better described as "bureaucratese." Such writing is notoriously made up of indirect expression and excessively complicated vocabulary. By parodying this writing in his translation of a well-known fairy tale, Baker (a journalist, humourist and winner of two Pulitzer prizes) reveals its misapplications and its power to distort.

consumption by telling wolf jokes to my duodenum?" It was time to make a judgement. The time was now, the hour had struck, the body lupine cried out for decision. The wolf was up to the challenge. He took two stomach powders right away and got into bed.

The wolf had adopted the abdominal distress recovery posture when Little Red Riding Hood achieved his presence.

"Grandmother," she said, "your ocular implements are of an extraordinary order of magnitude."

"The purpose of this enlarged viewing capability," said the wolf, "is to enable your image to register a more precise impression upon my sight systems."

"In reference to your ears," said Little Red Riding Hood, "it is noted with the deepest respect that far from being underprivileged, their elongation and enlargement appear to qualify you for unparalleled distinction."

"I hear you loud and clear, kid," said the wolf, "but what about these new choppers?"

"If it is not inappropriate," said Little Red Riding Hood, "it might be observed that with your new miracle masticating products you may even be able to chew taffy again."

This observation was followed by the adoption of an aggressive posture on the part of the wolf and the assertion that it was also possible for him, due to the high efficiency ratio of his jaw, to consume little persons, plus, as he stated, his firm determination to do so at once without delay and with all due process and propriety, notwithstanding the fact that the ingestion of one entire grandmother had already provided twice his daily recommended cholesterol intake.

There ensued flight by Little Red Riding Hood accompanied by pursuit in respect to the wolf and a subsequent intervention on the part of a third party, heretofore unnoted in the record.

Due to the firmness of the intervention, the wolf's stomach underwent axe-assisted aperture with the result that Little Red Riding Hood's grandmother was enabled to be removed with only minor discomfort.

The wolf's indigestion was immediately alleviated with such effectiveness that he signed a contract with the intervening third party to perform with grandmother in a television commercial demonstrating the swiftness of this dramatic relief for stomach discontent.

"I'm going to be on television," cried grandmother.

And they all joined her happily in crying, "What a phenomena!"

REVIEW

1. What does Baker's translation teach us about the function of words? What literary device do they serve in this piece?

2. What members of modern society, other than writers, is Baker targeting?

3. How does Baker's choice of vocabulary affect your experience of the story?

RULES FOR WRITERS

A Few "Do's" and "Don'ts"

Now-retired hockey star Wayne Gretzky claims he had no outstanding physical abilities. He simply liked to practice. Good writing is the same. Here are some tips, written in tongue-in-cheek form, to get you started.

1. Verbs **has** to agree with their subjects.
2. Prepositions are not words to end sentences **with**.
3. **And** don't start a sentence with a conjunction.
4. It is wrong **to ever split** an infinitive.
5. Avoid cliches **like the plague**. (They're **old hat**.)
6. Be **more or less** specific.
7. Parenthetical remarks **(however relevant)** are **(usually)** unnecessary.
8. Also **too**, never, **ever** use **repetitive** redundancies.
9. **No sentence fragments.**
10. Contractions **aren't** necessary and **shouldn't** be used.
11. Foreign words and phrases are not **apropos**.
12. Do not use more words than necessary; **it's highly superfluous**.
13. **Don't use no** double negatives.
14. Eschew ampersands **&** abbreviations, **etc.**
15. One-word sentences? **Eliminate.**
16. The passive voice **is to be ignored**.
17. Eliminate commas, that are, not necessary. Parenthetical words **however** should be enclosed in commas.
18. Never use a big word when a **diminutive** one would **suffice**.
19. Use words correctly, **irregardless** of how others use them.
20. Understatement is always the **absolute best** way to put forth **earth-shaking** ideas.
21. Use the apostrophe in **it's** proper place and omit it when **its** not needed.
22. Resist hyperbole; not one writer **in a million** can use it correctly.
23. Exaggeration is a **billion times worse** than understatement.

    And finally…

24. Proofread carefully to see if **you any** words out.

If English is spoken in heaven … God undoubtedly employs Cranmer as his speechwriter. The angels of the lesser ministries probably use the language of the New English Bible and the Alternative Service Book for internal memos.

Charles, Prince of Wales

Benjamin West, *Benjamin Franklin Discovering Electricity* (c. 1816-17). Courtesy of Philadelphia Museum of Art.

PART 2

Science and Technology

Science is an integral part of culture. It's not this foreign thing, done by an arcane priesthood. It's one of the glories of the human intellectual tradition.

Stephen Jay Gould

The "Canadarm" has been Canada's important contribution to the space program.

Science and Technology

An Introduction

Young adults today are reminded constantly that an understanding of "science and technology" is the key to living and prospering in the twenty-first century. But what exactly is "science and technology" all about, and why is it so important?

Perhaps the first important distinction to make is between "science," on the one hand, and "technology," on the other. The two are obviously related, but they are not the same. **Technology** refers to the machines and devices that do things–for example, trains, planes and automobiles (theoretically, even the household hammer). **Science** normally refers to "basic" science–that is, research designed to explain fundamental processes (for example, particle physics, biochemical reactions, etc.). Science, in other words, has to do with knowledge proper; technology, with the tools.

This simple distinction is clear, but the issue gets more complicated. At the frontiers of science, which is the science we usually hear about when there is a breakthrough, highly sophisticated technological tools are employed (e.g., particle accelerators). These tools are often based on advanced scientific knowledge and frequently are experimental. At these extremes, what is science and what is merely a tool of science is sometimes hard to fathom. The distinction is still more complex, since much of what is nowadays referred to as "new technology" is not of the "material objects" variety, but rather streams and streams of "invisible" computer codes–that is, **software technology**. Finally, to make matters more complicated still, new scientific research is now applied so quickly that it is difficult to know which came first, the knowledge or the tool.

THE SCIENTIFIC METHOD

To make sense of the distinction between science and technology, it may be helpful to shift over and examine what is meant by "the scientific method," which is a concept commonly associated with science (but not really with technology). **The scientific method** is merely an approach to doing scientific research that allows the researcher to get a little closer to the truth. It involves testing **hypotheses** (or propositions) under controlled experimental conditions such that if, under such conditions, one variable is shown to affect another, then there is good reason to believe that the two are definitely connected in some way. From many such **empirical findings**, scientists can go on to further lines of inquiry and eventually elaborate scientific **theories and scientific laws**. The hypothesis may range from the mundane, such as the conductivity of copper wire, to the remarkable, such as the theoretical work of Hawking, featured in this section, on black holes. But no matter, the rules are the same: predict and then subject the prediction to rigorous testing. This is the method or approach that has come down to us over hundreds of years of scientific inquiry and has allowed scientists to make fundamental discoveries and, subsequently, for this knowledge to be used to create many technological devices that enhance our daily lives.

KEY TERMS

- Technology
- Science
- Software technology
- Scientific method
- Hypotheses
- Empirical findings
- Theories and scientific laws
- Ethical questions
- Cloning

WHAT'S ALL THE FUSS ABOUT?

Why, then, is any of this important? One fairly obvious reason is that science and technology affect on our daily lives enormously. The rapid development in this field has affected everything from kitchen blenders to biotechnology, from snack foods to chaos theory. However, not only do we live in a technological world (see, for example, the selection on MP3 music files), but the high-tech world is where the jobs and therefore our livelihoods are.

But "knowledge is power" in the areas of science and technology for another very important reason as well. Paradoxically, the rapid scientific advances pose new **ethical questions** that do not lend themselves to "scientific" solutions. Such ethical questions involve social values and moral judgements. For example, as biologists and geneticists delve deeper into the chemistry of life, who is to decide how far such research should go; for example, in **cloning** animals and humans or determining the sex of a yet-to-be-conceived child? And what about the ethics of experimenting on animals or the genetic modification of foods to make them more resilient to disease and give them a longer shelf life? Understanding and influencing these kinds of ethical decisions, as we certainly must, requires a knowledge of science and technology.

This unit begins to explore these kinds of questions. The selections are written by some of the world's best-known scientists and writers–scientists such as Stephen Hawking, Carl Sagan, David Suzuki and Marie Curie. Keep in mind the important science/technology distinction, as well as the potential ethical problems and concerns, and it should make the reading easier. It is hoped that the reader will come away with a better understanding of these issues and their importance to each and every one of us.

Hello, Dolly! The recent "cloning" of a sheep raises serious ethical questions. What or who is next?

Science as a Way of Thinking

Can We Know the Universe?

CARL SAGAN

Our universe includes much that is unknown and, at the same time, much that is knowable. Therein lies the joy for the scientist. A universe in which everything is known would be static and dull.

PREVIEW

Why can't we travel faster than the speed of light? In this article, astronomer, popular science writer, and TV host Carl Sagan discusses science and scientific knowledge in general. He also considers the limits of human knowledge.

Science is a way of thinking much more than it is a body of knowledge. Its goal is to find out how the world works, to seek what regularities there may be, to penetrate to the connections of things—from subnuclear particles, which may be the constituents of all matter, to living organisms, the human social community, and thence to the cosmos as a whole. Our **intuition** is by no means an infallible guide. Our perceptions may be distorted by training and prejudice or merely because of the limitations of our sense organs, which, of course, perceive directly but a small fraction of the phenomena of the world. Even so straightforward a question as whether in the absence of friction a pound of lead falls faster than a gram of fluff was answered incorrectly by Aristotle and almost everyone else before the time of Galileo. **Science** is based on **experiment**, on a willingness to challenge old dogma, on an openness to see the universe as it really is. Accordingly, science sometimes requires courage—at the very least the courage to question the conventional wisdom.

Beyond this the main trick of science is to *really* think of something; the shape of clouds and their occasional sharp bottom edges at the same altitude everywhere in the sky; the formation of a dewdrop on a leaf; the origin of a name or a word—Shakespeare, say, or "philanthropic"; the reason for human social customs—the incest taboo, for example; how it is that a lens in sunlight can make paper burn; how a "walking stick" got to look so much like a twig; why the Moon seems to follow us as we walk; what prevents us from digging a hole down to the centre of the Earth; what the definition is of "down" on a spherical Earth; how it is possible for the body to convert yesterday's lunch into today's muscle and sinew; or how far is up—does the universe go on forever, or if it does not, is there any meaning to the question of what lies on the other side? Some of these questions are pretty easy. Others, especially the last, are mysteries to which no one even today knows the answer. They are natural questions to ask. Every culture has posed such questions in one way or another. Almost always the proposed answers are in the nature of "Just So Stories," attempted explanations divorced from experiment, or even from careful comparative observations.

But the **scientific cast of mind** examines the world critically as if many alternative worlds might exist, as if other things might be here which are not. Then we are forced to ask why what we see is present and not something else. Why are the Sun and the Moon and the planets spheres? Why not pyramids, or cubes, or dodecahedra? Why not irregular, jumbly shapes? Why so symmetrical, worlds? If you spend any time spinning **hypotheses**, checking to see whether they make sense, whether they conform to what else we know, thinking of tests you can pose to substantiate or deflate your hypotheses, you will find yourself doing science. And as you come to practice this habit of thought more and more you will get better and better at it. To penetrate into the heart of the thing–even a little thing, a blade of grass, as Walt Whitman said–is to experience a kind of exhilaration that, it may be, only human beings of all the beings on this planet can feel. We are an intelligent species and the use of our intelligence quite properly gives us pleasure. In this respect the brain is like a muscle. When we think well, we feel good. Understanding is a kind of ecstasy....

Human beings are, understandably, highly motivated to find regularities, natural laws. The search for rules, the only possible way to understand such a vast and complex universe, is called science. The universe forces those who live in it to understand it. Those creatures who find everyday experience a muddled jumble of events with no predictability, no regularity, are in grave peril. The universe belongs to those who, at least to some degree, have figured it out.

It is an astonishing fact that there *are* laws of nature, rules that summarize conveniently–not just qualitatively but quantitatively–how the world works. We might imagine a universe in which there are no such laws, in which the 10^{80} elementary particles that make up a universe like our own behave with utter and uncompromising abandon. To understand such a universe we would need a brain at least as massive as the universe. It seems unlikely that such a universe could have life and intelligence, because beings and brains require some degree of internal stability and order. But even if in a much more random universe there were such beings with an intelligence much greater than our own, there could not be much knowledge, passion or joy.

Fortunately for us, we live in a universe that has at least important parts that are knowable. Our **common-sense experience** and our evolutionary history have prepared us to understand something of the workaday world. When we go into other realms, however, common sense and ordinary intuition turn out to be highly unreliable guides. It is stunning that as we go close to the speed of light our mass increases indefinitely, we shrink toward zero thickness in the direction of motion, and time for us comes as near to stopping as we would like. Many people think that this is silly, and every week or two I get a letter from someone who complains to me about it. But

Nothing is rich but the inexhaustible wealth of nature. She shows us only surfaces, but she is a million fathoms deep.
Ralph Waldo Emerson

Sagan's international best-selling book, *Cosmos,* based on his award-winning TV series.

KEY TERMS

- Intuition
- Science
- Experimentation in science
- Scientific cast of mind
- Hypotheses
- Common-sense experience
- Special Theory of Relativity
- Quantum mechanics
- Laws of nature

REVIEW

1. How does Sagan draw the distinction between science and non-science?

2. How does Sagan treat the verb "to know" when he asks "can we know the universe?"

3. Why does Sagan suppose that humans are driven to find natural, regular laws governing our universe? Could the same thing be said of people 1,000 years ago, or have technological developments altered this drive?

it is a virtually certain consequence not just of experiment but also of Albert Einstein's brilliant analysis of space and time called the **Special Theory of Relativity**. It does not matter that these effects seem unreasonable to us. We are not in the habit of travelling close to the speed of light. The testimony of our common sense is suspect at high velocities.

Or consider an isolated molecule composed of two atoms shaped something like a dumbbell—a molecule of salt, it might be. Such a molecule rotates about an axis through the line connecting the two atoms. But in the world of **quantum mechanics**, the realm of the very small, not all orientations of our dumbbell molecule are possible. It might be that the molecule could be oriented in a horizontal position, say, or in a vertical position, but not at many angles in between. Some rotational positions are forbidden. Forbidden by what? By the **laws of nature**. The universe is built in such a way as to limit, or quantize, rotation. We do not experience this directly in everyday life; we would find it startling as well as awkward in sitting-up exercises, to find arms outstretched from the sides or pointed up to the skies permitted but many intermediate positions forbidden. We do not live in the world of the small, on the scale of 10^{-13} centimetres, in the realm where there are twelve zeros between the decimal place and the one. Our common-sense intuitions do not count. What does count is experiment—in this case observations from the far infrared spectra of molecules. They show molecular rotation to be quantized.

The idea that the world places restrictions on what humans might do is frustrating. Why *shouldn't* we be able to have intermediate rotational positions? Why *can't* we travel faster than the speed of light? But so far as we can tell, this is the way the universe is constructed. Such prohibitions not only press us toward a little humility; they also make the world more knowable. Every restriction corresponds to a law of nature, a regularization of the universe. The more restrictions there are on what matter and energy can do, the more knowledge human beings can attain. Whether in some sense the universe is ultimately knowable depends not only on how many natural laws there are that encompass widely divergent phenomena, but also on whether we have the openness and the intellectual capacity to understand such laws. Our formulations of the regularities of nature are surely dependent on how the brain is built, but also, and to a significant degree, on how the universe is built.

For myself, I like a universe that includes much that is unknown and, at the same time, much that is knowable. A universe in which everything is known would be static and dull, as boring as the heaven of some weak-minded theologians. A universe that is unknowable is no fit place for a thinking being. The ideal universe for us is one very much like the universe we inhabit. And I would guess that this is not really much of a coincidence.

FROM THE BIG BANG TO BLACK HOLES

OUR PICTURE OF THE UNIVERSE

STEPHEN HAWKING

The eventual goal of science is to provide a single theory that describes the whole universe. It has been a long time coming. But humanity's deepest desire for knowledge is justification enough for our continuing quest.

PREVIEW

Despite being afflicted with the debilitating ALS, or "Lou Gehrig's Disease," physicist Stephen Hawking is often mentioned in the same breath as such figures as Aristotle, Copernicus, Galileo, Newton and Einstein. In this selection, taken from his famous book **A Brief History of Time** (also turned into a popular film of the same name), Hawking describes highlights in the history of his science and its goal of nothing less than a complete description of the universe we live in, a single theory that describes the whole universe.

A well-known scientist (some say it was Bertrand Russell) once gave a public lecture on astronomy. He described how the earth orbits around the sun and how the sun, in turn, orbits around the centre of a vast collection of stars called our galaxy. At the end of the lecture, a little old lady at the back of the room got up and said: "What you have told us is rubbish. The world is really a flat plate supported on the back of a giant tortoise." The scientist gave a superior smile before replying, "What is the tortoise standing on?" "You're very clever young man, very clever," said the old lady. "But it's turtles all the way down!"

Most people would find the picture of our universe as an infinite tower of tortoises rather ridiculous, but why do we think we know better? What do we know about the universe, and how do we know it? Where did the universe come from, and where is it going? Did the universe have a beginning, and if so, what happened *before* then? What is the nature of time? Will it ever come to an end? Recent breakthroughs in physics, made possible in part by fantastic new technologies, suggest answers to some of these long-standing questions. Someday these answers may seem as obvious to us as the earth orbiting the sun—or perhaps as ridiculous as a tower of tortoises. Only time (whatever that may be) will tell.

As long ago as 340 B.C. the Greek philosopher Aristotle, in his book *On the Heavens*, was able to put forward two good arguments for believing that the earth was a round sphere rather than a flat plate. First, he realized that eclipses of the moon were caused by the earth coming between the sun and the moon. The earth's shadow on the moon was always round, which would be true only if the earth was spherical. If the earth had been a flat disk, the shadow would have been elongated and elliptical, unless the eclipse always occurred at a time when the sun was directly under the centre of the disk. Second, the Greeks knew from their travels that the North Star appeared lower in the sky when viewed in the south than it did in more northerly regions. (Since the North Star lies over the North Pole, it appears to be directly above an observer at the North Pole, but to someone looking from the equator, it appears to lie just at the horizon.) From the difference in the apparent position of the North Star in Egypt and Greece, Aristotle even quoted an estimate that the distance around the earth was 400,000 stadia. It is not known exactly what length a stadium was, but it may have been about 200 yards, which would make Aristotle's estimate about twice the currently accepted figure. The Greeks even had a third argument that the earth must be round, for why else does one first see the sails of a ship coming over the horizon, and only later see the hull?

Aristotle thought that the earth was stationary and that the sun, the moon, the planets, and the stars moved in circular orbits about the earth. He believed this because he felt, for mystical reasons, that the earth was the centre of the universe, and that circular motion was the most perfect. This idea was elaborated by Ptolemy in the second century A.D. into a complete **cosmological model**. The earth stood at the centre, surrounded by eight spheres that carried the moon, the sun, the stars, and the five planets known at the time, Mercury, Venus, Mars, Jupiter, and Saturn. The planets themselves moved on smaller circles attached to their respective spheres in order to account for their rather complicated observed paths in the sky. The outermost sphere carried the so-called fixed stars, which always stay in the same positions relative to each other but which rotate together across the sky. What lay beyond the last sphere was never made very clear, but it certainly was not part of mankind's observable universe.

Ptolemy's model provided a reasonably accurate system for predicting the positions of heavenly bodies in the sky. But in order to predict these positions correctly, Ptolemy had to make an assumption that the moon followed a path that sometimes brought it twice as close to the earth as at other times. And that meant that the moon ought sometimes to appear twice as big as at other times! Ptolemy recognized this flaw, but nevertheless his model was generally, although not universally, accepted. It was adopted by the Christian church as the picture of the universe that was in accordance with Scripture, for it had the great advantage that it left lots of room outside the sphere of fixed stars for heaven and hell.

A simpler model, however, was proposed in 1514 by a Polish priest, **Nicholas Copernicus**. (At first, perhaps for fear of being branded a heretic by his church, Copernicus circulated his model anonymously.) His idea was that the sun was stationary at the centre and that the earth and the planets moved in circular orbits around the sun. Nearly a century passed before this idea was taken seriously. Then two astronomers—the German, Johannes Kepler, and the Italian, Galileo Galilei—started publicly to support the Copernican theory, despite the fact that the orbits it predicted did not quite match the ones observed. The death blow to the Aristotelian/Ptolemaic theory came in 1609. In that year, Galileo started observing the night sky with a telescope, which had just been invented. When he looked at the planet Jupiter, Galileo found that it was accompanied by

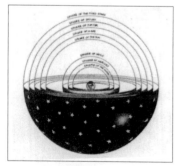

Ptolemy's cosmological model (with the earth at the centre) was revised by Copernicus in 1514.

several small satellites or moons that orbited around it. This implied that everything did *not* have to orbit directly around the earth, as Aristotle and Ptolemy had thought. (It was, of course, still possible to believe that the earth was stationary at the centre of the universe and that the moons of Jupiter moved on extremely complicated paths around the earth, giving the *appearance* that they orbited Jupiter. However, Copernicus' theory was much simpler.) At the same time, Johannes Kepler had modified Copernicus' theory, suggesting that the planets moved not in circles but in ellipses (an ellipse is an elongated circle). The predictions now finally matched the observations.

As far as Kepler was concerned, elliptical orbits were merely an ad hoc hypothesis, and a rather repugnant one at that, because ellipses were clearly less perfect than circles. Having discovered almost by accident that elliptical orbits fit the observations well, he could not reconcile them with his idea that the planets were made to orbit the sun by magnetic forces. An explanation was provided only much later, in 1687, when Sir Isaac Newton published his *Philosophiae Naturalis Principia Mathematica*, probably the most important single work ever published in the physical sciences. In it Newton not only put forward a theory of how bodies move in space and time, but he also developed the complicated mathematics needed to analyze those motions. In addition, Newton postulated a law of universal gravitation according to which each body in the universe was attracted toward every other body by a force that was stronger the more massive the bodies and the closer they were to each other. It was this same force that caused objects to fall to the ground. (The story that Newton was inspired by an apple hitting his head is almost certainly apocryphal. All Newton himself ever said was that the idea of gravity came to him as he sat "in a contemplative mood" and "was occasioned by the fall of an apple.") Newton went on to show that, according to his law, gravity causes the moon to move in an elliptical orbit around the earth and causes the earth and the planets to follow elliptical paths around the sun.

The Copernican model got rid of Ptolemy's celestial spheres, and with them, the idea that the universe had a natural boundary. Since "fixed stars" did not appear to change their positions apart from a rotation across the sky caused by the earth spinning on its axis, it became natural to suppose that the fixed stars were objects like our sun but very much farther away.

Newton realized that, according to his theory of gravity, the stars should attract each other, so it seemed they could not remain essentially motionless. Would they not all fall together at some point? In a letter in 1691 to Richard Bentley, another leading thinker of his day, Newton argued that this would indeed happen if there were only a finite number of stars distributed over a finite region of space. But he reasoned that if, on the other hand, there were an infinite number of stars, distributed more or less uniformly over infinite space, this would not happen, because there would not be any central point for them to fall to.

I cannot believe that God plays dice with the cosmos.

Albert Einstein

Isaac Newton. His idea of gravity was prompted "by the fall of an apple"!

This argument is an instance of the pitfalls that you can encounter in talking about infinity. In an infinite universe, every point can be regarded as the centre, because every point has an infinite number of stars on each side of it. The correct approach, it was realized only much later, is to consider the finite situation, in which the stars all fall in on each other, and then to ask how things change if one adds more stars roughly uniformly distributed outside this region. According to Newton's law, the extra stars would make no difference at all to the original ones on average, so the stars would fall in just as fast. We can add as many stars as we like, but they will still always collapse in on themselves. We now know it is impossible to have an infinite static model of the universe in which gravity is always attractive.

It is an interesting reflection on the general climate of thought before the twentieth century that no one had suggested that the universe was expanding or contracting. It was generally accepted that either the universe had existed forever in an unchanging state, or that it had been created at a finite time in the past more or less as we observe it today. In part this may have been due to people's tendency to believe in eternal truths, as well as the comfort they found in the thought that even though they may grow old and die, the universe is eternal and unchanging....

When most people believed in an essentially static and unchanging universe, the question of whether or not it had a beginning was really one of **metaphysics** or theology. One could account for what was observed equally well on the theory that the universe had existed forever or on the theory that it was set in motion at some finite time in such a manner as to look as though it had existed forever. But in 1929, Edwin Hubble made the landmark observation that wherever you look, distant galaxies are moving rapidly away from us. In other words, the universe is expanding. This means that at earlier times objects would have been closer together. In fact, it seemed that there was a time, about ten or twenty thousand million years ago, when they were all at exactly the same place and when, therefore, the density of the universe was infinite. This discovery finally brought the question of the beginning of the universe into the realm of science.

Hubble's observations suggested that there was a time, called the **big bang**, when the universe was infinitesimally small and infinitely dense. Under such conditions all the laws of science, and therefore all ability to predict the future, would break down. If there were events earlier than this time, then they could not affect what happens at the present time. Their existence can be ignored because it would have no observational consequences. One may say that time had a beginning at the big bang, in the sense that earlier times simply would not be defined. It should be emphasized that this beginning in time is very different from those that had been considered previously. In an unchanging universe a beginning in time is something that has to be imposed by some being outside the universe; there is no physical necessity for a beginning. One can imagine that God created the universe at literally any time in the past. On the other hand, if the universe is expanding, there may be physical reasons why there had to be a beginning. One could still imagine that God created the universe at the instant of the big bang, or even afterwards in just such a way as to make it look as though there had been a big bang, but it would be meaningless to suppose that it was created *before* the big bang. An expanding universe does not preclude a creator, but it does place limits on when he might have carried out his job!

In order to talk about the nature of the universe and to discuss questions such as whether it has a beginning or an end, you have to be clear about what a **scientific theory** is. I shall take the simpleminded view that a theory is just a model of the universe, or a restricted part of it, and a set of rules that relate quantities in the model to observations that we make. It exists only in our minds and does not have any other reality (whatever that might mean). A theory is a good theory if it satisfies two requirements: It must accurately describe a large class of observations on the basis of a model that contains only a few arbitrary elements, and it must make definite predictions about the results of future observations. For example, **Aristotle's theory** that everything was made out of four elements, earth, air, fire, and water, was simple enough to qualify, but it did not make any definite predictions. On the other hand, Newton's theory of gravity was based on an even simpler model, in which bodies attracted each other with a force that was proportional to a quantity called their mass and inversely proportional to the square of the distance between them. Yet it predicts the motions of the sun, the moon, and the planets to a high degree of accuracy.

Any physical theory is always provisional, in the sense that it is only a **hypothesis**: you can never prove it. No matter how many times the results of experiments agree with some theory, you can never be sure that the next time the result will not contradict the theory. On the other hand, you can disprove a theory by finding even a single observation that disagrees with the predictions of the theory. As philosopher of science Karl Popper has emphasized, a good theory is characterized by the fact that it makes a number of predictions that could in principle be disproved or **falsified by observation**. Each time new experiments are observed to agree with the predictions the theory survives, and our confidence in it is increased; but if ever a new observation is found to disagree, we have to abandon or modify the theory. At least that is what is supposed to happen, but you can always question the competence of the person who carried out the observation.

In practice, what often happens is that a new theory is devised that is really an extension of the previous theory. For example, very accurate observations of the planet Mercury revealed a small difference between its motion and the predictions of Newton's theory of gravity. Einstein's general theory of relativity predicted a slightly different motion from Newton's theory. The fact that Einstein's predictions matched what was seen, while Newton's did not, was one of the crucial confirmations of the new theory. However, we still use Newton's theory for all practical purposes because the difference between its predictions and those of general relativity is very small in the situations that we normally deal with. (Newton's theory also

> *I seem to have been only like a boy playing on the seashore, and diverting myself in now and then finding a smoother pebble or a prettier shell than ordinary, whilst the great ocean of truth lay all undiscovered before me.*
>
> Sir Isaac Newton

"Look, an apple is about to land on him—he's got a great future ahead of him in physics!"

has the great advantage that it is much simpler to work with than Einstein's!)

The eventual goal of science is to provide a single theory that describes the whole universe. However, the approach most scientists actually follow is to separate the problem into two parts. First, there are the laws that tell us how the universe changes with time. (If we know what the universe is like at any one time, these physical laws tell us how it will look at any later time.) Second, there is the question of the initial state of the universe. Some people feel that science should be concerned with only the first part; they regard the question of the initial situation as a matter for metaphysics or religion. They would say that God, being omnipotent, could have started the universe off any way he wanted. That may be so, but in that case he also could have made it develop in a completely arbitrary way. Yet it appears that he chose to make it evolve in a very regular way according to certain laws. It therefore seems equally reasonable to suppose that there are also laws governing the initial state.

It turns out to be very difficult to devise a theory to describe the universe all in one go. Instead, we break the problem up into bits and invent a number of partial theories. Each of these partial theories describes and predicts a certain limited class of observations, neglecting the effects of other quantities, or representing them by simple sets of numbers. It may be that this approach is completely wrong. If everything in the universe depends on everything else in a fundamental way, it might be impossible to get close to a full solution by investigating parts of the problem in isolation. Nevertheless, it is certainly the way that we have made progress in the past. The classic example again is the Newtonian theory of gravity, which tells us that the gravitational force between two bodies depends only on one number associated with each body its mass, but is otherwise independent of what the bodies are made of. Thus one does not need to have a theory of the structure and constitution of the sun and the planets in order to calculate their orbits.

Today scientists describe the universe in terms of two basic partial theories—the general theory of relativity and quantum mechanics. They are the great intellectual achievements of the first half of this century. The general theory of relativity describes the force of gravity and the large-scale structure of the universe, that is, the structure on scales from only a few miles to as large as a million million million million (1 with twenty-four zeros after it) miles, the size of the observable universe. Quantum mechanics, on the other hand, deals with phenomena on extremely small scales, such as a millionth of a millionth of an inch. Unfortunately, however, these two theories are known to be inconsistent with each other—they cannot both be correct. One of the major endeavors in physics today, and the major theme of this book, is the search for a new theory that will incorporate them both—a quantum theory of gravity. We do not yet have such a theory, and we may still be a long way from having one, but we do already know many of the properties that it must have. And we shall see … that we already know a fair amount about the predictions a quantum theory of gravity must make.

Now, if you believe that the universe is not arbitrary, but is governed by definite laws, you ultimately have to combine the partial theories into a complete unified theory that will describe everything in the universe. But there is a fundamental paradox in the search for such a complete unified theory. The ideas about scientific theories outlined above assume we are rational beings who are free to observe the universe as we want and to draw logical deductions from what we see. In such a scheme it is reasonable to suppose that we might progress ever closer toward the laws that govern our universe. Yet if there really is a complete unified theory, it would also presumably determine our actions. And so the theory itself would determine the outcome of our search for it! And why should it determine that we come to the right conclusions from the evidence? Might it not equally well determine that we draw the wrong conclusion? Or no conclusion at all?

The only answer that I can give to this problem is based on Darwin's principle of **natural selection**. The idea is that in any population of self-reproducing organisms, there will be variations in the genetic material and upbringing that different individuals have. These differences will mean that some individuals are better able than others to draw the right conclusions about the world around them and to act accordingly. These individuals will be more likely to survive and reproduce and so their pattern of behaviour and thought will come to dominate. It has certainly been true in the past that what we call intelligence and scientific discovery has conveyed a survival advantage. It is not so clear that this is still the case: our scientific discoveries may well destroy us all, and even if they don't, a complete unified theory may not make much difference to our chances of survival. However, provided the universe has evolved in a regular way, we might expect that the reasoning abilities that natural selection has given us would be valid also in our search for a complete unified theory, and so would not lead us to the wrong conclusions.

Because the partial theories that we already have are sufficient to make accurate predictions in all but the most extreme situations, the search for the ultimate theory of the universe seems difficult to justify on practical grounds. (It is worth noting, though, that similar arguments could have been used against both relativity and quantum mechanics, and these theories have given us both nuclear energy and the microelectronics revolution!) The discovery of a complete **unified theory**, therefore, may not aid the survival of our species. It may not even affect our life-style. But ever since the dawn of civilization, people have not been content to see events as unconnected and inexplicable. They have craved an understanding of the underlying order in the world. Today we still yearn to know why we are here and where we came from. Humanity's deepest desire for knowledge is justification enough for our continuing quest. And our goal is nothing less than a complete description of the universe we live in.

KEY TERMS

- Ptolemy's cosmological model
- Nicholas Copernicus
- Johannes Kepler
- Isaac Newton
- Metaphysics
- The big bang
- Scientific theory
- Aristotle's theory of the elements
- Hypotheses
- Falsification by observation
- Natural selection
- Unified theory of the universe

REVIEW

1. What key connection does Hawking make between theory and technology in his discussion of the early astronomers? How has this connection been strengthened over time?

2. What is Hawking's definition of a theory? What are the advantages for a theoretical physicist such as Hawking of approaching theories in this way?

3. How does Hawking make the connection between theoretical physics and Darwinian evolution? Is this connection convincing?

UNEXPECTED VISTAS

"EUREKA" MOMENTS IN SCIENCE

JAMES TREFIL

About 250 B.C., it is said, the Greek mathematician Archimedes shouted "Eureka! Eureka!" ("I've got it, I've got it!") after stumbling on a way to distinguish gold from an alloy. Unexpected breakthroughs in science and other areas frequently result from someone applying their own unique vista on the world.

PREVIEW

Science is rigorous and exacting work. But there would be no body of scientific knowledge at all without the creative process that conceived the scientific propositions to begin with. In this article prolific science writer James Trefil discusses the creative process in science.

One of the great rewards of hiking or backpacking is to follow a trail and, suddenly and without warning, top a hill or come to a break in the trees and see the panorama of the countryside laid out before you. The view of the distant waterfall or rolling hills is often remembered as the high point of the entire excursion.

Such experiences occur in intellectual life, too. The moment of the "Aha!"–which cartoonists usually render by showing a light bulb coming on above someone's head–is an analogous happening. So too is the unexpected discovery that two things seemingly unconnected with each other are in fact intimately related. But while every hiker on a given trail will see the same view, the **intellectual vista** has the property that each person who comes to it can see something entirely different.

For example, imagine a line of motorists at a traffic light. Each of them is looking at the same thing, a rectangular yellow box with three coloured lights in it. But it is possible, even likely, that each of them *sees* something very different from the others. Suppose that the first person in line is an electrical engineer. To him, the traffic light is just one appendage of a large computer-operated grid that regulates the movement of vehicles throughout the downtown area. If you pressed him to go on–to describe the far reaches of his view–he might start musing about the light as one example of control systems and eventually wind up talking about the best-designed control system of them all, the human brain.

The driver of the second car in line is the representative of a large manufacturing firm. He sees the traffic light as an item that is built in a factory and sold to the city. After thinking for a while, he might go on to talk about the vast interconnecting web of economic activity, from mining to maintenance work, that has to be in place before something like a traffic signal is possible. He might even end with some general speculations about human beings as tool-making animals.

In the third car is an attorney. To him the traffic light might symbolize the set of laws human beings have developed. The mechanical or economic aspect of the device would be much less important than the rules of conduct it symbolizes. After all, at any given moment there are thousands of cars being driven in a city, and almost every driver obeys the traffic signals. Behind this display of mass obedience, our attorney may see the vast structure of the modern legal system, from legislators to courts to police officers. If pressed, he might go on to speculate about those aspects of the human character that require such a system to allow large groups of people to live together in relative harmony.

Each of our motorists sees the traffic light as part of a large interconnected network. The simple apparatus is seen to be just one aspect of an important system that governs some aspect of our lives. In a sense, the traffic light is like an object in the foreground of some marvellous medieval landscape painting, a device the artist uses to induce us to look further and see the rich tapestry of nature and civilization that lies behind it. I will call each driver's view of the traffic light a *vista*, a term that carries with it the connotation of wide-ranging view.

So the traffic light teaches us several important lessons. It tells us that the breadth and scope of the vista really have very little to do with the object that starts us looking. Whether the traffic light is seen as just a self-contained mechanical device or as part of a much larger system is primarily a function of the individual looking at it, and, more importantly, of that individual's training and **habits of thought**.

The traffic light also teaches us that two individuals looking at the same thing need not see the same vista. It's almost as if two hikers reach the same point in a trail, from which one sees a waterfall while the other sees a shady forest. We can often get an entirely different view of the world just by talking to people whose backgrounds lead them to see vistas different from our own.

Like other professionals, scientists have their unique vistas. It would be a mistake, however, to assume that all scientists share a common view of things. I was frequently surprised during the several years I spent as part of an interdisciplinary team in cancer research by just how much the training of the other team members affected the way they looked at our work. To a biologist a cell is part of an evolving, growing, living system; to a physicist it is a "**black box**" that processes energy and produces an ordered system; to a statistician it is one more bit of data to put into a computer program. Clearly, there is no such thing as a single, monolithic "**scientific**" **vista**.

KEY TERMS

- "Eureka!" moment
- Intellectual vista
- Habits of thought
- Black box
- Scientific vista

REVIEW

1. Trefil states that "every hiker on a given trail will see the same view." Is this true? How does the perception of the pastoral vista differ from that of the intellectual vista?

2. According to Trefil, the traffic lights teach us several important lessons. What are these?

3. In what way does our personal background affect what we see?

The Discovery of Radium

Science—for Science's Sake?

MARIE CURIE

Contrary to popular belief, scientific research (like art) must be done "for itself," for the beauty of science, and then there is always the chance that the discovery may become, like the radium, a benefit for humanity. So argues physicist Marie Curie who, with her husband, discovered radium.

PREVIEW

The following short article is from an address by one of the world's greatest experimental physicists. Marie Curie gave this presentation to an audience at Vassar College in New York State, acknowledging a gift by American women to her of a gram of radium for use in her research. Radium was (and is) extremely expensive and difficult to produce. In this article she describes the general course of her work on radiation.

I could tell you many things about radium and **radioactivity** and it would take a long time. But as we cannot do that, I shall give you only a short account of my early work about radium. Radium is no more a baby; it is more than twenty years old, but the conditions of the discovery were somewhat peculiar, and so it is always of interest to remember them and to explain them.

We must go back to the year 1897. Professor Curie and I worked at that time in the laboratory of the School of Physics and Chemistry where Professor Curie held his lectures. I was engaged in some work on uranium rays which had been discovered two years before by Professor Becquerel. I shall tell you how these uranium rays may be detected. If you take a photographic plate and wrap it in black paper and then on this plate, protected from ordinary light, put some uranium salt and leave it a day, and the next day the plate is developed, you notice on the plate a black spot at the place where the uranium salt was. This spot has been made by special rays which are given out by the uranium and are able to make an impression on the plate in the same way as ordinary light. You can also test those rays in another way, by placing them on an electroscope. You know what an electroscope is. If you charge it, you can keep it charged several hours and more, unless uranium salts are placed near to it. But if this is the case the electroscope loses its charge and the gold or aluminum leaf falls gradually in a progressive way. The speed with which the leaf moves may be used as a measure of the intensity of the rays; the greater the speed, the greater the intensity.

I spent some time in studying the way of making good **measurements** of the uranium rays, and then I wanted to know if there were other elements, giving out rays of the same kind. So I took up a work about all known elements and their compounds and found that uranium compounds are active and also all thorium compounds, but other elements were not found active, nor were their compounds. As for the uranium and thorium compounds, I found that they were active in proportion to their uranium or thorium content. The more uranium or thorium, the greater the activity, the activity being an **atomic property** of the elements, uranium and thorium.

Then I took up measurements of minerals and I found that several of those which contain uranium or thorium or both were active. But then the activity was not what I would expect; it was greater than for uranium or thorium compounds, like the oxides which are almost entirely composed of these elements. Then I thought that there should be in the minerals some unknown element having a much greater radioactivity than uranium or thorium. And I wanted to find and to separate that element, and I settled to that work with Professor Curie. We thought it would be done in several weeks or months, but it was not so. It took many years of hard work to finish that task. There was not *one* element; there were several of them. But the most important is radium, which could be separated in a **pure state**.

All the tests for the separation were done by the method of electrical measurements with some kind of electroscope. We just had to make chemical separations and to examine all products obtained, with respect to their activity. The product which retained the radioactivity was considered as that one which had kept the new element; and, as the radioactivity was more strong in some products, we knew that we had succeeded in concentrating the new element. The radioactivity was used in the same way as a spectroscopical test.

The difficulty was that there is not much radium in a mineral; this we did not know at the beginning. But we now know that there is not even one part of radium in a million parts of good ore. And, too, to get a small quantity of pure radium salt, one is obliged to work up a huge quantity of ore. And that was very hard in a laboratory.

We had not even a good **laboratory** at that time. We worked in a hangar where there were no improvements, no good chemical arrangements. We had no help, no money. And because of that, the work could not go on as it would have done under better conditions. I did myself the numerous crystallization which were wanted to get the radium salt separated from the barium salt, with which it is obtained, out of the ore. And in 1902 I finally succeeded in getting pure radium chloride and determining the atomic weight of the new element, radium, which is 226, while that of barium is only 137.

Later I could also separate the metal radium, but that was a very difficult work; and, as it is not necessary for the use of radium to have it in this state, it is not generally prepared that way.

Now, the special interest of radium is in the intensity of its rays, which is several million times greater than the uranium rays. And the effects of the rays make the radium so important. If we take a practical point of view, then the most important property of the rays is the production of physiological effects on the cells of the human organism. These effects may be used for the cure of several diseases. Good results have been obtained in

Science may be described as the art of systematic over-simplification.

Karl Popper, philosopher

Marie Curie, co-discoverer of radium, was the first female recipient of a Nobel Prize.

REVIEW

1. Radium rays produce effects that are beneficial in the treatment of physical diseases. What harmful effects were revealed by the widespread use of such treatment, which were unknown to Marie Curie?

2. Why do you think that Marie Curie was so interested in radioactivity that she would devote so many years of strenuous work, and ultimately her life, to isolating and measuring radium?

3. Describe the "beauty of science" that Curie refers to. What do you think are some of the "beautiful" aspects of her research work, as she might have seen them?

many cases. What is considered particularly important is the treatment of cancer. The medical utilization of radium makes it necessary to get that element in sufficient quantities. And so a factory of radium was started, to begin with, in France, and later in America, where a big quantity of ore named carnotite is available. America does not produce many grams of radium every year but the price is still very high because the quantity of radium contained in the ore is so small. The radium is more than a hundred thousand times dearer than gold.

But we must not forget that when radium was discovered no one knew that it would prove useful in hospitals. The work was one of **pure science**. And this is a proof that scientific work must not be considered from the point of view of the direct usefulness of it. It must be done for itself, **for the beauty of science,** and then there is always the chance that a scientific discovery may become, like the radium, a benefit for humanity.

But science is not rich; it does not dispose of important means; it does not generally meet recognition before the material usefulness of it has been proved. The factories produce many grams of radium every year, but the laboratories have very small quantities. It is the same for my laboratory, and I am very grateful to the American women who wish me to have more of radium, and give me the opportunity of doing more work with it.

The scientific history of radium is beautiful. The properties of the rays have been studied very closely. We know that particles are expelled from radium with a very great velocity, near to that of light. We know that the atoms of radium are destroyed by expulsion of these particles, some of which are atoms of helium. And in that way it has been proved that the radioactive elements are constantly disintegrating, and that they produce, at the end, ordinary elements, principally helium and lead. That is, as you see, a theory of transformation of atoms, which are not stable, as was believed before, but may undergo spontaneous changes.

Radium is not alone in having these properties. Many having other radioelements are known already: the polonium, the mesothorium, the radiothorium, the actinium. We know also radioactive gases, named emanations. There is a great variety of substances and effects in radioactivity. There is always a vast field left to **experimentation** and I hope that we may have some beautiful progress in the following years. It is my earnest desire that some of you should carry on this scientific work, and keep for your ambition the determination to make a permanent contribution to science.

How Did Life Begin?

Three Scientific Hypotheses

JAMES TREFIL

Scientists now have several "hypotheses" about how the first living cell emerged 4-5 billion years ago. Modern cells have had billions of years of Darwinian "natural selection" to sharpen their ability to deal with their environments.

Four and a half billion years ago the earth was a hot ball of molten rock. Today there is no spot on its surface where you can't find evidence of life. How did we get from there to here?

We already know a large part of the answer to this question. Anyone who has been to a natural history museum probably remembers the dinosaur fossils—exact replicas in stone of the bones of now extinct monsters. In fact, fossils have been formed in abundance over the past 600 million years, preserving the life stories not only of dinosaurs but of many other life forms as well. Before this period, animals had no bones or other hard parts from which fossils could form, but impressions of **complex life forms** (think of them as jellyfish) have been found going back several hundred million years more. And from the time before that, believe it or not, pretty clear evidence for the existence of single-celled organisms has been found.

It may come as a surprise to learn that we can detect fossil evidence of organisms as microscopic as bacteria, but paleontologists have been doing just that for some time. The technique works like this: you find a rock formed from the ooze on an ocean bottom long ago, cut it into slices, and examine the slices under an ordinary microscope. If you're lucky (and highly skilled) you will find impressions left by long-dead cells. Using precisely this technique, scientists have been able to follow the trail of life back to fairly complex colonies of blue-green algae some 3.5 billion years old. Life on earth must have started well before that.

We also know that the early stages of the solar system coincided with a massive rain of cosmic debris on the newly formed planets. Astronomers call this period the "**Great Bombardment**," and it lasted for something like the first half billion years of the earth's history. Had life formed during this period, any massive impact would have wiped it out (it would, for example, take an asteroid only the size of Ohio to bring in enough energy to boil all the water in the oceans). Thus we are coming to realize that there is a

PREVIEW

How was the earth transformed from a barren place of molten rock to one that is teeming with life? In this piece, science writer James Trefil discusses three hypotheses that seek to explain the missing step that gave rise to the first living cell.

Sooner or later, someone is going to reproduce the elementary forms of life in the laboratory.

REVIEW

1. What scientific bases underlie the three hypotheses outlined by Trefil?

2. What "situation" do scientists assume gave rise to a self-contained, reproducing cell?

3. What role have fossils played in the development of these hypotheses?

narrow window in time—perhaps 500 million years—during which life not only must have arisen from **inanimate matter** but developed into a fairly complex ecosystem of algae.

Scientists have known since the 1950s that it is possible, by adding energy in the form of heat or electrical discharges to materials believed to have been present in the earth's early atmosphere, to produce molecules of the type found in living systems. They also know that in a relatively short time (geologically speaking) such processes would turn the world's oceans into a stew of energy-rich molecules—so-called **Primordial Soup**. Research today centres on trying to understand how this situation gave rise to a self-contained, reproducing cell.

Here are a few of the current ideas about how this could have happened:

• **RNA World**—RNA, a close cousin of the more familiar DNA, plays a crucial role in the chemical machinery of cells. Recently scientists have been able to create short stretches of RNA that, placed in the right sort of nutrient broth, can copy itself. Was this the first step on the road to life?

• **Clay World**—certain kinds of clays have static electrical charges on their surfaces. These charges may have attracted molecules from the soup and bound them together. Once the molecules were formed, they would float away, carrying only indirect evidence of their origin.

• **Primordial Oil Slick**—my favourite. The same chemical reactions that created the Primordial Soup would have made the kinds of molecules that form droplets of fat in a pot of soup. Each droplet would enclose a different mix of chemicals, and each would be, in effect, a separate experiment in the formation of life. In this theory, the first globule whose chemicals were able to replicate themselves grew, split, and became the ancestor of us all.

Whichever of these (or other) theoretical processes actually occurred, it had to produce that **first living cell** within a few hundred million years. And this fact, in turn, gives rise to the most intriguing idea of all. If primitive life is really that easy to produce, sooner or later (and I suspect it will be sooner) someone is going to reproduce the process in the laboratory. The product of such an experiment won't look impressive compared to even the simplest cells today, although it will have the same basic biochemistry. Modern cells, after all, have had 4 billion years of **natural selection** to sharpen their ability to deal with their environments. The experiments will most likely produce a sluggish blob of chemicals surrounded by fat molecules that will take in energy and materials from the environment and reproduce itself. But that blob will forge the last link in the chain between the barren earth of 4 billion years ago and us.

UNSCRAMBLING LIFE

WHITHER THE HUMAN GENOME PROJECT?

JAMES TREFIL

The human genome contains about 50,000 to 100,000 genes, of which 4,000 may be associated with disease. The colossal Human Genome Project is seeking to determine which genes are good and which are bad.

At the end of the 1980s there was a major debate in the scientific community over the **Human Genome Project** (HGP), whose purpose was to produce a complete reading of human DNA (the sum total of any organism's DNA is called its genome). Some scientists objected to the project on the grounds that it would be too boring to attract good minds, among other things. Others raised ethical and political issues. Despite these objections, the Human Genome Project was founded by Congress in 1990 as a fifteen-year, multi-billion-dollar enterprise. I'm happy to report that now, better than one-third of the way into the project, none of the objections have turned out to be valid. Advances in technology have allowed most of the boring work to be handed off to machines, and many of the best scientific minds in the country are involved in the HGP in one way or another.

Here's what the project is about: the DNA of every cell in every human being contains the blueprint for turning a single cell into a functioning adult. One human differs from another by only a fractional percentage of that blueprint, which means that you only have to "read" the DNA blueprint once, and then you have the information forever. Furthermore, as we are now beginning to realize, virtually every human disease has a genetic component, so being able to read the blueprint will have enormous medical payoffs.

The easiest way to picture **DNA** is as a long, flexible ladder, with each rung made up of two molecules (called bases) locked together. If you take that ladder and give it a little twist, it procures the familiar **double-helix** structure of DNA. Certain stretches of DNA–anywhere from a few thousand to a few hundred thousand bases long–are called **genes**. The sequence of bases on these genes contains the instructions for the production of proteins that will control the chemical reactions in the cell. In human cells, the DNA is wrapped in bundles called **chromosomes**. Most cells contain

PREVIEW

In the early 1950s, Francis Crick, a British biophysicist, and James Watson, an American biochemist, disclosed the three-dimensional structure of deoxyribonucleic acid (DNA)—the famous "double helix." DNA is the substance that transmits genetic characteristics from one generation to the next. Knowledge of its structure led to rapid advances in genetics. Now, scientists involved in the Human Genome project have taken on the daunting task of unravelling the entire genetic make-up of humans.

KEY TERMS

- Human Genome Project
- Human DNA
- Double-helix structure
- Genes
- Chromosomes
- Gene mapping
- Gene sequencing
- Gene therapies
- Genetic propensity

REVIEW

1. What scientific processes are involved in reading the "blueprint" of human DNA?

2. What steps are necessary to establish whether a particular defect in a particular gene is responsible for a particular disease?

3. What ethical problems are generated by the knowledge that certain diseases are genetically based?

forty-six chromosomes: twenty-three from the mother and twenty-three from the father.

There are two ways to explore DNA. A process called "**mapping**" involves finding the placement of specific genes on specific chromosomes. You can think of mapping as a rough first exploration of the genome—something like the Lewis and Clark expedition to the American Northwest. Another process, called "**sequencing**," involves specifying the actual rung-by-rung order of base pairs in the DNA "ladder"—rather like the National Geological Survey that followed Lewis and Clark. The goal of the HGP is to produce both an exhaustive map and a complete sequencing of human DNA.

To establish that a particular kind of defect in a particular gene is responsible for a particular disease, it is necessary to (1) find which chromosome the gene is on, (2) find the exact location of the gene on that chromosome, (3) sequence the gene, and (4) identify the "misspelling" associated with the disease. For example, in 1989, the cause of the most common form of cystic fibrosis was identified as the absence of three specific base pairs on a specific gene of chromosome seven, and this knowledge has already led to experimental [gene] **therapies** for the disease. This is a good example of what we can expect from the HGP.

But once the Genome Project is completed, we will be faced with a new set of problems. If, for example, conditions like alcoholism and propensities for any number of diseases are genetically based, what should we do with that information? Most people (myself included) would want to know if they had a **genetic propensity** for a disease if they could do something about it. For example, someone with a known propensity for a particular cancer could arrange to have regular tests so that if the cancer did develop it could be caught early, with a high chance of successful outcome. On the other hand, suppose someone analyzed your genome and told you that no matter what you did, you had a fairly strong chance of contracting an incurable disease before your fiftieth birthday. Would you want to know that? I certainly wouldn't. And then there are the questions of who owns the information on the genome.

In any case, the Genome Project is moving along. In 1995 the first complete genome of a living organism (a simple bacterium) was published; in 1996, the 12-million-base genome of brewer's yeast. The main points of discussion these days are, as you might expect, cost (current goals are in the range of 20-30 cents per base) and accuracy (the goal is 99.99 percent). New automated techniques capable of meeting these goals are expected to produce sequences of about 3 percent of the human genome by 1999. But the work will go steadily forward, and sometime after the turn of the century, we will have the reading of the entire human blueprint. Before that time maybe we should start thinking about what we're going to do with it.

CONSCIOUSNESS—THE FINAL FRONTIER

COGITO ERGO SUM

JAMES TREFIL

The true "reductionist" might think that all our subjective experience is nothing more than "the behaviour of a vast assembly of nerve cells and their associated molecules." Popular science writer James Trefil begs to differ.

"I THINK, therefore I am." With these words, the French philosopher Rene Descartes (1596-1650) set the stage for one of the great debates of modern times—a debate that is no closer to resolution now than it was in his lifetime. This is the debate over what, exactly, it means for a human being to be conscious, to think, to feel emotions, to have a subjective experience of the world. I include it on my Top Ten list [of important issues in science] for two reasons: first, it is the only major question in the sciences that we don't even know how to ask and, second, I see techniques developing and schools of thought forming that lead me to believe that this will become *the* scientific question of the twenty-first century.

In all other areas of science, we have a sense of the basic concepts and categories, which allow us to pose the questions in useful terms (by which I mean terms that suggest how to go about finding an answer). In cosmology, for example, we may not have a fully unified Theory of Everything, but we have a pretty good sense of what one would took like and how to go about finding it.

In the area of mind/brain/consciousness, however, we really don't know what the categories are, what the important questions are, or how to go about asking them. Should we be concentrating on the workings of cells in the brain? On large-scale brain functions? On deeper metaphysical or philosophical questions? Right now scientists are groping around trying to sort out these issues. There are numerous approaches to the problem, but my sense is that the researchers are starting to snake out into three broad groups, which I will call the neurophysiologists, the quantum mechanics, and the mystics.

The best known of the neurophysiologists is Francis Crick, Nobel laureate and codiscoverer of the structure of DNA. He argues that the way to understand consciousness is to look at single neurons or collections of neurons in the brain, that all our subjective experience is nothing more than

PREVIEW

The answer to the question of what it means for a human being to be conscious remains unresolved in our modern times. At issue is how this question should be approached. In this article, Trefil explores the preferred approaches of neurophysiologists, quantum mechanics and mystics as researchers seek to find an answer.

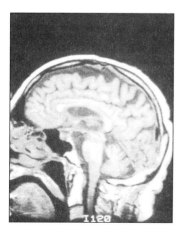

Is human consciousness merely "a vast assembly of nerve cells and their associated molecules"?

KEY TERMS

• Schools of thought
• Consciousness
• Neurophysiological model
• Quantum mechanical model
• Mystics model
• Emergent property of complex systems

REVIEW

1. Why does Trefil see the question of the meaning of human consciousness as becoming "the scientific question of the twenty-first century"?

2. What aspects of this question pose problems for scientists?

3. What do you think of the statement, credited to the mystics, that "there are some things that science was never meant to know"?

"the behaviour of a vast assembly of nerve cells and their associated molecules." Your feelings of joy and sorrow, in other words, are nothing more than the firing of billions of neurons in your brain. People who follow this track study the details of brain functioning (particularly of vision) and try to understand the rich panorama of human experience in those terms. Although you might think that as a physicist I would favour a reductionist approach, I have to say that I hope that these guys are wrong, although in my dark moments I think they may be right.

The **quantum mechanics**, whose most prominent spokesman is the English mathematician Roger Penrose, argue that the laws of physics underlying ordinary electrical circuits (and the brain as pictured by neurophysiologists) fail to capture the full unpredictability and nonlinearity of the brain. In their view, we won't understand the brain until we have a fundamentally new understanding of the behaviour of matter at the atomic level. It is here, they argue, that the origin of consciousness and feelings must be sought, for this last great gap in our understanding of the universe lies at the boundary between the large-scale world (ruled by Newtonian physics) and the small-scale world of the atom (ruled by quantum mechanics). If we can fill in this gap, they argue, we will eventually have a true theory of the mind. Penrose, in fact, argues that this understanding will come from a quantum theory of gravity.

When I think about the third group—the **mystics**—I picture a stereotypical scene from a 1950s grade-B science fiction movie (a genre to which I must confess a mild addiction). There is often a white-haired, pipe-smoking scientist in these movies, sort of an Albert Einstein clone, who at some crucial moment delivers himself of the opinion: "There are some things, my boy, that science was never meant to know." In the same way, some people (mainly philosophers) argue that human beings either will not, should not, or cannot gain an understanding of consciousness. In some cases the arguments are based on old arguments about the impossibility of deriving a purely mental state from a purely physical system. Other arguments, based on analogies to evolution, state that because humans have never had to understand consciousness, they don't have the mental equipment to do so. But all of them come to the same conclusion: the methods of science alone can never solve this problem.

So how will this question be answered? My own guess is that consciousness will turn out to be an **emergent property of complex systems**. I suspect we will discover that in the process of hooking up lots of neurons to make a brain, there comes a point where "more" becomes "different." And while this point of view could be accommodated within either the neurophysiological or the quantum mechanical framework, my hope is that when all is said and done, human beings will be found to be something more than "a vast assembly of nerve cells and their associated molecules."

Do NOT Use the F-Word ...

A New Spectre is Haunting Europe

TOM POLLARD

The word "Frankenstein," first coined by Mary Shelley in her 1818 novel by the same name, refers to any creation that ultimately destroys its own creator. There is now concern about genetically altered "Frankenstein" foods and whether they (like Frankenstein's monster) might not consume us all.

Frankenstein was a fictional scientist who created a fictional monster, but today *real* scientists are meddling with the *real* genetic make-up of whole food groups and the results are frightening many people throughout the world.

"**Frankenstein foods,**" as they are known by their opponents, are food products that have been genetically altered by scientists to maximize their yield or protect them from disease—all worthy causes. But the progress of science and technology has once again brought humanity smack up against a dilemma of human proportions: are safeguards in place to protect the human species from these new "Frankenstein foods"? So far, the response of the scientists is not reassuring.

PREVIEW

"You are what you eat," the old saying goes. Nowadays, however, it is not always obvious what you are eating. Canadian writer Tom Pollard argues that the issue is not so much whether human intervention in "raw nature" is desirable, since clearly there are benefits, but whether all the necessary precautions have been taken and nature itself will not respond with a vengeance.

HARD TO SWALLOW

Undoubtedly, part of the public apprehension in Europe is due to the scare over **Mad Cow Disease** (BCE), which pretty well decimated the British beef industry. In the face of serious health concerns, the British government failed to act quickly, then tried to cover up, and only subsequently slaughtered British cow herds to eradicate the disease. The Mad Cow scare is not too far from the surface of the debates around the merits of genetically modified food. The seven largest grocery chains in Britain have committed themselves to getting rid of genetically modified organisms in food.

Activists in the **environmental movement** are in the forefront of those concerned about the genetic modification of food crops-splicing genes from another organism into their chromosomes to prolong shelf life or help ward off insects and disease. The fear is that genes transferred between species might then move to another crop, possibly resulting in superweeds or

Frankenstein foods. Ripe for the eating? Environmental activists are not convinced.

REVIEW

1. British grocery chains are determined to eliminate genetically modified organisms in food. Compare their plan for action with the stance taken by the food industry in Canada.

2. Given the sheer number of products in Canada that contain GMOs, is it reasonable to now expect the food industry to include such information in their labels? When should this issue have been addressed?

3. How can we make the Canadian government more accountable for keeping us informed about biotechnological research in this country?

indestructible bacteria. If this happens, the human health consequences could be enormous.

Already, the amount of food Canadians eat that contains **genetically modified organisms** (GMOs) is startling. CBC Radio's "This Morning" series on Frankenstein foods noted that it is not only modified potatoes and tomatoes but basic products such as soya oil, which is used in processed foods of all types. Estimates of the amount of food now containing GMOs range as high as 30,000 different products. In part, the problem is that the foods are not labelled as containing GMOs even though they are now present in foods of all types—canned soups, baked items, oils and margarine, sugar and even french fries.

While the first **gene splicing** occurred in 1982, it was only in 1996 that genetic manipulation of eatable food was given the green light. At this pace, what the future holds is anybody's guess.

Possibly it is Canadians, rather than Europeans, who should be more worried about the amount of research that is currently underway. According to Martin Mittelstaed in the *Globe and Mail,* the number of field trials in Canada is more than that of the entire European Union, and Canada is becoming recognized throughout the world as a centre for biotechnology. Biotech firms and agricultural researchers have conducted more than 4,200 field trials in the past ten years. The Canadian figures were obtained under access to information legislation by the Green Party of Canada, which is loosely affiliated to the environmental movement (the "**Green Movement**") worldwide. According to Joan Russow, the party's national leader, Canadians are generally unaware of the nature and extent of biotechnology research in this country.

The fact that ordinary Canadians have not been kept well informed, if true, may be most of the problem. For who is ensuring that the driving force behind biotechnological research is not profit-gauging national and multinational companies that are less concerned about the environment and health than about profit margins? And who is watching the politicians if the public is not informed? **Democratic societies** depend not only on "one person, one vote" but on an informed public, and one of the jobs of elected figures is to ensure that the public is well informed.

Underlying all this, of course, is the relentless march of scientific inquiry, now plumbing the depths of life itself, or at least its biological aspects. Is all this progress? It is hard to ignore the enormous potential of genetic research—not the least of which is an abundance of food in a food-starved world.

Yet on the other side is Mary Shelley's mad scientist and the monster he created. Good novels, like some genetically modified foods, have a long shelf life.

THE PAIN OF ANIMALS

SACRED TRUTHS

DAVID SUZUKI

Chimpanzees, along with the gorilla, are our closest relatives—they share 99 percent of our genes. Ironically, this is why scientists experiment on them. But inflicting pain on any animal poses big ethical problems—our inhumanity to other species. How can we reconcile our need to know with our moral obligations as the dominant species?

Medical technology has taken us beyond the normal barriers of life and death and thereby created unprecedented choices in *human* lives. Until recently, we have taken for granted our right to use other species in any way we see fit. Food, clothing, muscle power have been a few of the benefits we've derived from this exploitation. This tradition has continued into scientific research where animals are studied and "sacrificed" for human benefit. Now serious questions are being asked about our right to do this.

Modern biological research is based on a shared evolutionary history of organisms that enables us to extrapolate from one organism to another. Thus, most fundamental concepts in heredity were first shown in fruit flies, **molecular genetics** began using bacteria and viruses and much of physiology and psychology has been based on studies in mice and rats. But today, as extinction rates have multiplied as a result of human activity, we have begun to ask what right we have to use all other animate forms simply to increase human knowledge or for profit or entertainment. Underlying the **"animal rights" movement** is the troubling question of where we fit in the rest of the natural world.

When I was young, one of my prized possessions was a BB gun. Dad taught me how to use it safely and I spent many hours wandering through the woods in search of prey. It's not easy to get close enough to a wild animal to kill it with a BB gun, but I did hit a few pigeons and starlings. I ate everything I shot. Then as a teenager, I graduated to a .22 rifle and with it, I killed rabbits and even shot a pheasant once.

One year I saw an ad for a metal slingshot in a comic book. I ordered it, and when it arrived, I practised for weeks shooting marbles at a target. I got to be a pretty good shot and decided to go after something live. Off I went to the woods and soon spotted a squirrel minding its own business doing whatever squirrels do. I gave chase and began peppering marbles at it until

PREVIEW

David Suzuki is a Canadian geneticist, columnist and popular host of television and radio programs on science. In this article, he deplores the degradation of our environment. He sees part of the explanation for this deterioration in our blind adherence to "sacred truths" that have no basis in reality.

Canadian geneticist David Suzuki hosts the popular CBC televison program, *The Nature of Things*.

finally it jumped onto a tree, ran to the top and found itself trapped. I kept blasting away and grazed it a couple of times so it was only a matter of time before I would knock it down. Suddenly, the squirrel began to cry—a piercing shriek of terror and anguish. That animal's wail shook me to the core and I was overwhelmed with horror and shame at what I was doing—for no other reason than conceit with my prowess with a slingshot, I was going to *kill* another being. I threw away the slingshot and my guns and have never hunted again.

All my life, I have been an avid fisherman. Fish have always been the main source of meat protein in my family, and I have never considered fishing a sport. But there is no denying that it is exciting to reel in a struggling fish. We call it "playing" the fish, as if the wild animal's desperate struggle for survival is some kind of game....

I studied the genetics of fruit flies for twenty-five years and during that time probably raised and killed tens of millions of them without a thought. In the early seventies, my lab discovered a series of mutations affecting behaviour of flies, and this find led us into an investigation of nerves and muscles. I applied for and received research funds to study behaviour in flies on the basis of the *similarity* of their neuromuscular systems to ours. In fact, psychologists and neurobiologists analyze behaviour, physiology and neuroanatomy of guinea pigs, rats, mice and other animals as *models* for human behaviour. So our nervous systems must closely resemble those of other mammals.

These personal anecdotes raise uncomfortable questions. What gives us the right to exploit other living organisms as we see fit? How do we know that these other creatures don't feel pain or anguish just as we do? Perhaps there's no problem with fruit flies, but where do we draw the line? I used to rationalize angling because fish are cold-blooded, as if warm-bloodedness indicates some kind of demarcation of brain development or greater sensitivity to pain. But anyone who has watched a fish's frantic fight to escape knows that it exhibits all the manifestations of pain and fear.

I've been thinking about these questions again after spending a weekend in the Queen Charlotte Islands watching grey whales close up. The majesty and freedom of these magnificent mammals contrasted strikingly with the appearance of whales imprisoned in aquariums. Currently, the Vancouver Public Aquarium is building a bigger pool for some of its whales. In a radio interview, an aquarium representative was asked whether even the biggest pool can be adequate for animals that normally have the entire ocean to rove. Part of her answer was that if we watched porpoises in the pool, we'd see that "they are quite happy."

That woman was projecting human perceptions and emotions on the porpoises. Our ability to empathize with other people and living things is one of our endearing qualities. Just watch someone with a beloved pet, an avid gardener with plants or, for that matter, even an owner of a new car and you will see how readily we can personalize and identify with another living organism or an object. But are we justified in our inferences about captive animals in their cages?

Most wild animals have evolved with a built-in need to move freely over vast distances, fly in the air or swim through the ocean. Can a wild animal imprisoned in a small cage or pool, removed from its habitat and forced to conform to the impositions of our demands, ever be considered "happy"?

Animal rights activists are questioning our right to exploit animals, especially in scientific research. Scientists are understandably defensive, especially after labs have been broken into, experiments ruined and animals "liberated." But just as I have had to question my hunting and fishing, scientists cannot avoid confronting the issues raised, especially in relation to our closest relatives, the primates.

People love to watch monkeys in a circus or zoo and a great deal of the amusement comes from the recognition of ourselves in them. But our relationship with them is closer than just superficial similarities. When doctors at Loma Linda hospital in California implanted the heart of a baboon into the chest of Baby Fae, they were exploiting our close *biological* relationship.

Any reports on **experimentation** with familiar mammals like cats and dogs are sure to raise alarm among the lay public. But the use of **primates** is most controversial. In September 1987, at the Wildlife Film Festival in Bath, England, I watched a film shot on December 7, 1986, by a group of animal liberationists who had broken into SEMA, a biomedical research facility in Maryland. It was such a horrifying document that many in the audience rushed out after a few minutes. There were many scenes that I could not watch. As the intruders entered the facility, the camera followed to peer past cage doors, opened to reveal the animals inside. I am not ashamed to admit that I wept as baby monkeys deprived of any contact with other animals seized the fingers of their liberators and clung to them as our babies would to us. Older animals cowered in their tin prisons, shaking from fear at the sudden appearance of people.

The famous chimpanzee expert, Jane Goodall, also screened the same film and as a result asked for permission to visit the SEMA facility. This is what she saw (*American Scientist*, November-December 1987):

> Room after room was lined with small, bare cages, stacked one above the other, in which monkeys circled round and round and chimpanzees sat huddled, far gone in depression and despair.

> Young chimpanzees, three or four years old, were crammed, two together into tiny cages measuring 57 cm by 57 cm and only 61 cm high. They could hardly turn around. Not yet part of any experiment, they had been confined to these cages for more than three months.

> The chimps had each other for comfort, but they would not remain together for long. Once they are infected, probably with hepatitis, they will be separated and placed in another cage. And there they will remain, living in conditions of severe sensory deprivation, for the next several years. During that time they will become insane.

Goodall's horror sprang from an intimate knowledge of chimpanzees in their native habitat. There, she has learned, chimps are nothing like the captive animals that we know. In the wild, they are highly social, requiring

The scientific mind does not so much provide the right answers as ask the right questions.

Claude Lévi-Strauss, anthropologist

Gorillas and chimps share 99% of our genes, thereby posing ethical questions for researchers.

REVIEW

1. Why are serious questions being raised now about our right to exploit other species as we see fit? What historical influences resulted in our assuming this "right"?

2. What human ability allows us to enjoy seeing another being in a caged environment? Do you agree, with Suzuki, that the inferences we draw are erroneous?

3. Do the results of scientific research on primates justify the avoidance by researchers of the issues raised by animal rights activists?

constant interaction and physical contact. They travel long distances, and they rest in soft beds they make in the trees. Laboratory cages do not provide the conditions needed to fulfil the needs of these social, emotional and highly intelligent animals.

Ian Redmond (*BBC Wildlife*, April 1988) gives us a way to understand the horror of what lab conditions do to chimps:

> Imagine locking a two- or three-year-old child in a metal box the size of an isolette—solid walls, floor and ceiling, and a glass door that clamps shut, blotting out most external sounds—and then leaving him or her for months, the only contact, apart from feeding, being when the door swings open and masked figures reach in and take samples of blood or tissue before shoving him back and clamping the door shut again. Over the past 10 years, 94 young chimps at SEMA have endured this procedure.

Chimpanzees, along with the gorilla, are our closest relatives, sharing 99 percent of our genes. And it's that **biological proximity** that makes them so useful for research—we can try out experiments, study infections and test vaccines on them as models for people. And although there are only about 40,000 chimps left in the wild, compared to millions a few decades ago, the scientific demand for more has increased with the discovery of AIDS.

No chimpanzee has ever contracted **AIDS**, but the virus grows in them, so scientists argue that chimps will be invaluable for testing vaccines. On February 19, 1988, the National Institute of Health in the U.S. co-sponsored a meeting to discuss the use of chimpanzees in research. Dr. Maurice Hilleman, Director of the Merck Institute for Therapeutic Research, reported:

> We need more chimps.... The chimpanzee is certainly a threatened species and there have been bans on importing the animal into the United States and into other countries, even though ... the chimpanzee is considered to be an agricultural pest in many parts of the world where it exists. And secondly, it's being destroyed by virtue of environmental encroachment—that is, destroying the natural habitat. So these chimpanzees are being eliminated by virtue of their being an agricultural pest and by the fact that their habitat is being destroyed. So why not rescue them? The number of chimpanzees for AIDS research in the United States [is] somewhere in the hundreds and certainly, we need thousands.

Our **capacity to rationalize** our behaviour and needs is remarkable. Chimpanzees have occupied their niche over tens of millennia of biological evolution. *We* are newcomers who have encroached on *their* territory, yet by defining them as *pests* we render them expendable. As Redmond says, "The fact that the chimpanzee is our nearest zoological relative makes it perhaps the unluckiest animal on earth, because what the kinship has come to mean is that we feel free to do most of the things to a chimp that we mercifully refrain from doing to each other."

And so the impending epidemic of AIDS confronts us not only with our inhumanity to each other but to other species.

Obligation to Endure

Backward to a Chemically Sterile, Insect-Free World

RACHEL CARSON

Our chemical assault on our very own environment seems to be unrelenting. No one has pressed this issue more than Rachel Carson, who imbued her work with the idea that humans were but one part of nature, distinguished primarily by their power to alter it, in some cases irreversibly.

The history of life on earth has been a history of interaction between living things and their surroundings. To a large extent, the physical form and the habits of the earth's vegetation and its animal life have been molded by the environment. Considering the whole span of earthly time, the opposite effect, in which life actually modifies its surroundings, has been relatively slight. Only within the moment of time represented by the present century has one species—man—acquired significant power to alter the nature of his world.

During the past quarter century this power has not only increased to one of disturbing magnitude but it has changed in character. The most alarming of all man's **assaults upon the environment** is the contamination of air, earth, rivers, and sea with dangerous and even lethal materials. This pollution is for the most part irrecoverable; the chain of evil it initiates not only in the world that must support life but in living tissues is for the most part irreversible. In this now universal contamination of the environment, chemicals are the sinister and little recognized partners of radiation in changing the very nature of the world—the very nature of its life. Strontium 90, released through nuclear explosions into the air, comes to earth in rain or drifts down as fallout, lodges in soil, enters into the grass or corn or wheat grown there, and in time takes up its abode in the bones of a human being, there to remain until his death. Similarly, chemicals sprayed on croplands or forests or gardens lie long in soil, entering into living organisms, passing from one to another in a chain of poisoning and death. Or they pass mysteriously by underground streams until they emerge and, through the alchemy of air and sunlight, combine into new forms that kill vegetation, sicken cattle, and work unknown harm on those who drink from once pure wells. As Albert Schweitzer has said, "Man can hardly even recognize the devils of his own creation."

PREVIEW

In a short span of time humans have altered the very nature of life on earth, which took millions of years to develop. In this essay, biologist and activist Rachel Carson (1907-64) describes the results and warns us of the risks of our indiscriminate use of chemical insecticides—which includes possible gene mutations. In her famous book, "Silent Spring" (1962) Carson challenged the practices of agricultural scientists and the U.S. Government and called for a change in the way humankind viewed the world. She was attacked by the chemical industry and by some in the government as an alarmist but courageously continued her fight to protect the living world.

It took hundreds of millions of years to produce the life that now inhabits the earth—eons of time in which that developing and evolving and diversifying life reached a state of adjustment and balance with its surroundings. The environment, rigorously shaping and directing the life it supported, contained elements that were hostile as well as supporting. Certain rocks gave out dangerous radiation; even within the light of the sun, from which all life draws its energy, there were shortwave radiations with power to injure. Given time—time not in years but in millennia—life adjusts, and a balance has been reached. For time is the essential ingredient; but in the modern world there is no time.

The rapidity of change and the speed with which new situations are created follow the impetuous and heedless pace of man rather than the deliberate pace of nature. Radiation is no longer merely the background radiation of rocks, the bombardment of cosmic rays, the ultraviolet of the sun that have existed before there was any life on earth; radiation is now the unnatural creation of man's tampering with the atom. The chemicals to which life is asked to make its adjustment are no longer merely the calcium and silica and copper and all the rest of the minerals washed out of the rocks and carried in rivers to the sea; they are the synthetic creations of man's inventive mind, brewed in his laboratories, and having no counterparts in nature.

To adjust to these chemicals would require time on the scale that is nature's; it would require not merely the years of a man's life but the life of generations. And even this, were it by some miracle possible, would be futile, for the new chemicals come from our laboratories in an endless stream; almost five hundred annually find their way into actual use in the United States alone. The figure is staggering and its implications are not easily grasped—500 new chemicals to which the bodies of men and animals are required somehow to adapt each year, chemicals totally outside the limits of biologic experience.

Among them are many that are used in man's war against nature. Since the mid-1940s over 200 basic chemicals have been created for use in killing insects, weeds, rodents, and other organisms described in the modern vernacular as "pests": and they are sold under several thousand different brand names.

These sprays, dusts, and aerosols are now applied almost universally to farms, gardens, forests, and homes—nonselective chemicals that have the power to kill every insect, the "good" and the "bad," to still the song of birds and the leaping of fish in the streams, to coat the leaves with a deadly film, and to linger on in soil—all this though the intended target may be only a few weeds or insects. Can anyone believe it is possible to lay down such a barrage of poisons on the surface of the earth without making it unfit for all life? They should not be called "insecticides," but "biocides."

The whole process of spraying seems caught up in an endless spiral. Since DDT was released for civilian use, a process of escalation has been going on in which ever more toxic materials must be found. This has

The damage to the environment is sometimes obvious; unfortunately, we seldom do anything about it.

happened because insects, in a triumphant vindication of Darwin's principle of the survival of the fittest, have evolved super races immune to the particular insecticide used, hence a deadlier one has always to be developed—and then a deadlier one than that. It has happened also because, for reasons to be described later, destructive insects often undergo a "flareback," or resurgence, after spraying, in numbers greater than before. Thus the chemical war is never won, and all life is caught in its violent crossfire.

Along with the possibility of the extinction of mankind by nuclear war, the central problem of our age has therefore become the contamination of man's total environment with such substances of incredible potential for harm—substances that accumulate in the tissues of plants and animals and even penetrate the germ cells to shatter or alter the very material of heredity upon which the shape of the future depends.

Some would-be architects of our future look toward a time when it will be possible to alter the human germ plasm by design. But we may easily be doing so now by inadvertence, for many chemicals, like radiation, bring about **gene mutations**. It is ironic to think that man might determine his own future by something so seemingly trivial as the choice of an insect spray.

All this has been risked—for what? Future historians may well be amazed by our distorted sense of proportion. How could intelligent beings seek to control a few unwanted species by a method that contaminated the entire environment and brought the threat of disease and death even to their own kind? Yet this is precisely what we have done. We have done it, moreover, for reasons that collapse the moment we examine them. We are told that the enormous and expanding use of pesticides is necessary to maintain farm production. Yet is our real problem not one of *overproduction*? Our farms, despite measures to remove acreages from production and to pay farmers not to produce, have yielded such a staggering excess of crops that the American taxpayer in 1962 is paying out more than one billion dollars a year as the total carrying cost of the surplus-food storage program. And is the situation helped when one branch of the Agriculture Department tries to reduce production while another states, as it did in 1958, "It is believed generally that reduction of crop acreages under provisions of the Soil Bank will stimulate interest in use of chemicals to obtain maximum production on the land retained in crops."?

All this is not to say there is no insect problem and no need of control. I am saying, rather, that control must be geared to realities, not to mythical situations, and that the methods employed must be such that they do not destroy us along with the insects....

Much of the necessary knowledge is now available but we do not use it. We train **ecologists** in our universities and even employ them in our governmental agencies but we seldom take their advice. We allow the chemical death rain to fall as though there were no alternative, whereas in fact there

That which is not good for the beehive cannot be good for the bees.

Marcus Aurelius, Roman emperor

Rachel Carson called for new policies to protect human health and the environment.

REVIEW

1. According to Carson, how has man changed the "very nature of the world"? In what time span has this taken place?

2. Give examples from other areas of science to which the idea expressed by Albert Schweitzer, that "man can hardly even recognize the devils of his own creation," is applicable.

3. Carson posits that the public is responsible for the decision to continue use of chemical insecticides. What changes in attitude must take place before we accept this responsibility? What measures could we take to implement our decision to discontinue use?

are many, and our ingenuity could soon discover many more if given opportunity.

Have we fallen into a mesmerized state that makes us accept as inevitable that which is inferior or detrimental, as though having lost the will or the vision to demand that which is good? Such thinking, in the words of the ecologist Paul Shepard, "idealizes life with only its head out of water, inches above the limits of toleration of the corruption of its own environment.... Why should we tolerate a diet of weak poisons, a home in insipid surroundings, a circle of acquaintances who are not quite our enemies, the noise of motors with just enough relief to prevent insanity? Who would want to live in a world which is just not quite fatal?"

Yet such a world is pressed upon us. The crusade to create a chemically sterile, insect-free world seems to have engendered a fanatic zeal on the part of many specialists and most of the so-called control agencies. On every hand there is evidence that those engaged in spraying operations exercise a ruthless power. "The regulatory entomologists ... function as prosecutor, judge and jury, tax assessor and collector and sheriff to enforce their own orders," said Connecticut entomologist Neely Turner. The most flagrant abuses go unchecked in both state and federal agencies.

It is not my contention that **chemical insecticides** must never be used. I do contend that we have put poisonous and biologically potent chemicals indiscriminately into the hands of persons largely or wholly ignorant of their potentials for harm. We have subjected enormous numbers of people to contact with these poisons, without their consent and often without their knowledge. If the Bill of Rights contains no guarantee that a citizen shall be secure against lethal poisons distributed either by private individuals or by public officials, it is surely only because our forefathers, despite their considerable wisdom and foresight, could conceive of no such problem.

I contend, furthermore, that we have allowed these chemicals to be used with little or no advance investigation of their effect on soil, water, wildlife, and man himself. Future generations are unlikely to condone our lack of prudent concern for the integrity of the natural world that supports all life.

There is still very limited awareness of the nature of the threat. This is an **era of specialists**, each of whom sees his own problem and is unaware of or intolerant of the larger frame into which it fits. It is also an era dominated by industry, in which the right to make a dollar at whatever cost is seldom challenged. When the public protests, confronted with some obvious evidence of damaging results of pesticide applications, it is fed little tranquilizing pills of half truth. We urgently need an end to these false assurances, to the sugar coating of unpalatable facts. It is the public that is being asked to assume the risks that the insect controllers calculate. The public must decide whether it wishes to continue on the present road, and it can do so only when in full possession of the facts. In the words of Jean Rostand, "The **obligation to endure** gives us the right to know."

The Origin of Species

Illustration of the Action of "Natural Selection"

CHARLES DARWIN

Charles Darwin (1809-1882) was the major exponent of the theory of evolution. In this short extract from his famous book, "On the Origin of Species," Darwin gives an easy-to-understand example of the "action of natural selection." Darwinian theory is the unifying basis of biological science.

In order to make it clear how, as I believe, natural selection acts, I must beg permission to give one or two imaginary illustrations. Let us take the case of a wolf, which preys on various animals, securing some by craft, some by strength, and some by fleetness; and let us suppose that the fleetest prey, a deer for instance, had from any change in the country increased in numbers, or that other prey had decreased in numbers, during that season of the year when the wolf is hardest pressed for food.

I can under such circumstances see no reason to doubt that the swiftest and slimmest wolves would have the best chance of surviving, and so be preserved or selected–provided always that they retained strength to master their prey at this or at some other period of the year, when they might be compelled to prey on other animals.

Even without any change in the proportional numbers of the animals on which our wolf preyed, a cub might be born with an innate tendency to pursue certain kinds of prey. Nor can this be thought very improbable; for we often observe great differences in the natural tendencies of our domestic animals; one cat, for instance, taking to catch rats, another mice; one cat, according to Mr. St. John, bringing home winged game, another hares or rabbits, and another hunting on marshy ground and almost nightly catching woodcocks or snipes.

Now, if any slight innate change of habit or of structure benefited an individual wolf, it would have the best chance of surviving and of leaving offspring. Some of its young would probably inherit the same habits or structure, and by the repetition of this process, a new variety might be formed which would either supplant or coexist with the parent-form of wolf. Or, again, the wolves inhabiting a mountainous district, and those frequenting the lowlands, would naturally be forced to hunt different prey; and from the continued preservation of the individuals best fitted for the two sites, two varieties might slowly be formed...."

PREVIEW

Darwin's voyages to the Galapagos islands and his examination of the fossil record convinced him that species had evolved over millions of years through a mechanism that he called natural selection. (The key terms and review for this article are included with the following selection "Why Sex Works" by Nicholas Wade.)

Charles Darwin's theory of natural selection provides the unifying basis of modern biology.

Why Sex Works

The Dismal Answer

NICHOLAS WADE

Why are there two sexes rather than just one or three? According to evolutionary biologists, sexual reproduction (which results in a mixing of genes in later generations) may just be a "successful" evolutionary outcome, a billion years or so ago, to avoid extinction. In other words, Charles Darwin's theory of natural selection may apply here as well. Killjoy biologists!

PREVIEW

Charles Darwin's celebrated "theory of natural selection" (according to which more favourable genetic traits of living species are "selected" over generations for their "fit" with a particular environment—hence the immense variety of natural species and lineages) may have an even more basic application to the emergence of two sexes. Was sex itself, a billion or so years ago, a mere Darwinian "adaptation"? We may never know the answer for sure, of course, but this article by science writer Nicholas Wade provides an interesting context to review the basics of Darwinian theory.

It is hard to see why economics is called the dismal science when the title is so much better deserved by **evolutionary biology**. For biologists, the human race is being loaded down with **bad mutations**, the more so as medical advances thwart the scythe of natural selection from culling the weak.

Another thing that bugs biologists is sex. Like James Thurber, they have long asked why it is necessary. Yeah, babies, but you could make them much more easily by **parthenogenesis**–virgin birth–the mode of procreation favoured by stick insects and other sensible creatures. When it comes to sexual intercourse, the biologists stand foursquare with Lord Chesterfield, who advised his son that "the pleasure is momentary, the position ridiculous and the expense damnable."

The biologists' two interests, doom and sex, have intersected in a new report that shows there is indeed a purpose to sex: to sweep away the bad mutations that would otherwise drag us toward terminal degeneracy. Two British biologists, Adam Eyre Walker and Peter D. Keightley, came up with an ingenious way of estimating the number of bad mutations that have flowed in and out of the **human genome** during the six million years since we and chimpanzees stopped calling each other cousins. They found that at least 1.6 and probably 3 mutations per person must have been eliminated in each generation. This is an amazing number when you consider that a mutation can only disappear through a "genetic death"–when its owner, or child or grandchild, dies without progeny.

"That implies three genetic deaths per person!" said the **population geneticist** James F. Crow of the University of Wisconsin in a commentary on the new study, "Why aren't we extinct?"

Evidently we manage to beat the odds somehow or other. Last week Service Corporation International, a major operator of funeral homes and cemeteries, forecast meagre earnings because of reduced mortality rates, a

The peacock's tail. This flamboyant tail belongs to the male peacock and is biologists' favourite example of "sexual selection." Sexual selection is a special type of natural selection in which competition for mates can, over generations, favour individuals with certain hereditary traits. Sexual selection results in "sexual dimorphism" because one sex is selected for traits that are not required by the other. Examples include antlers on male deer and the brightly coloured patterns on male birds (such as the peacock).

KEY TERMS

- Natural selection (Darwin's theory)
- Evolutionary biology
- Bad mutations
- Parthenogenesis
- The human genome
- Population genetics
- Genes
- Biological extinction (in Darwinian theory)

REVIEW

1. In your own words, explain the basic idea behind the theory of natural selection as elaborated in this article by Nicholas Wade and the previous article by Charles Darwin.

2. What does Wade mean when he says that medical advances have thwarted "the scythe of natural selection from culling the weak"?

3. What does Wade mean when he says that it seems that "the gamble of sex beats death"?

grim outlook that resulted in a 44 percent tumble in its stock price. What magic draught cleanses us of bad mutations without demanding one life for each?

Now you begin to see how sex works. If we bred like stick insects, our children would have the exact same faults as their parents, knowledge of which would destroy all respect between generations.

In sex, however, life's biggest non-regulated lottery, one's **genes** first get shuffled among themselves and a random assortment is then cut into someone else's deck. Bad mutations get left on the cutting room floor, or if they combine in a fetus, their synergistic effect will probably cause a speedy death, eliminating many mutations at once.

The fact is, the gamble of sex beats death. By not acting like stick insects, we escape **extinction**. Maybe those evolutionary biologists aren't such dismal killjoys after all.

Posture Maketh the Man

From Ape to Humans

STEPHEN JAY GOULD

Which came first, our superior brain size or our upright posture? The higher status accorded to the fruits of the mind over the labour of the body has infiltrated all aspects of Western culture, including the field of anthropology.

PREVIEW

Social prejudice led to the assumption that increasing brain size propelled our evolution, according to Stephen Jay Gould. Gould explores the origins of this bias and the political context of scientific research. Gould is a professor of biology, geology and the history of science at Harvard University and a popular writer on natural evolution.

No event did more to establish the fame and prestige of The American Museum of Natural History than the Gobi Desert expeditions of the 1920s. The discoveries, including the first dinosaur eggs, were exciting and abundant, and the sheer romance fit Hollywood's most heroic mold. It is still hard to find a better adventure story than Roy Chapman Andrews's book (with its chauvinistic title): *The New Conquest of Central Asia.* Nonetheless, the expeditions utterly failed to achieve their stated purpose: to find in Central Asia the ancestors of man. And they faded for the most elementary of reasons—we evolved in Africa, as Darwin had surmised fifty years earlier.

Our African ancestors (or at least our nearest cousins) were discovered in cave deposits during the 1920s. But these australopithecines failed to fit preconceived notions of what a "missing link" should look like, and many scientists refused to accept them as bona fide members of our lineage. Most anthropologists had imagined a fairly harmonious transformation from ape to human, propelled by increasing intelligence. A missing link should be intermediate in both body and brain—Alley Oop or the old (and false) representations of stoopshouldered Neanderthals. But the australopithecines refused to conform. To be sure, their brains were bigger than those of any ape with comparable body size, but not much bigger. Most of our evolutionary increase in brain size occurred after we reached the australopithecine level. Yet these small-brained australopithecines walked as erect as you or I. How could this be? If our evolution was propelled by an enlarging brain, how could upright posture—another "hallmark of hominization," not just an incidental feature—originate first? In a 1963 essay, George Gaylord Simpson used this dilemma to illustrate

the sometimes spectacular failure to predict discoveries even when there is a sound basis for such prediction. An evolutionary example is the failure to predict discovery of a "missing link," now known [*Australopithecus*], that was upright and tool-making but had the physiognomy and cranial capacity of an ape.

We must ascribe this "spectacular failure" primarily to a subtle prejudice that led to the following, invalid extrapolation: We dominate other animals by **brain power** (and little else); therefore, an increasing brain must have propelled our own evolution at all stages. The tradition for subordinating upright posture to an enlarging brain can be traced throughout the history of anthropology. Karl Ernst von Baer, the greatest embryologist of the nineteenth century (and second only to Darwin in my personal pantheon of scientific heroes) wrote in 1828: "Upright posture is only the consequence of the higher development of the brain ... all differences between men and other animals depend upon construction of the brain." One hundred years later, the English anthropologist G.E. Smith wrote: "It was not the adoption of the erect attitude or the invention of articulate language that made man from an ape, but the gradual perfecting of a brain and the slow building of the mental structure, of which erectness of carriage and speech are some of the incidental manifestations."

Against this chorus of emphasis upon the brain, a very few scientists upheld the **primacy of upright posture**. Sigmund Freud based much of his highly idiosyncratic theory for the origin of civilization upon it. Beginning in his letters to Wilhelm Fliess in the 1890s and culminating in his 1930 essay on *Civilization and Its Discontents*, Freud argued that our assumption of upright posture had reoriented our primary sensation from smell to vision. This devaluation of olfaction shifted the object of sexual stimulation in males from cyclic odors of estrus to the continual visibility of female genitalia. Continual desire of males led to the evolution of continual receptivity in females. Most mammals copulate only around periods of ovulation; humans are sexually active at all times (a favourite theme of writers on sexuality). Continual sexuality has cemented the human family and made civilization possible; animals with strongly cyclic copulation have no strong impetus for stable family structure. "The fateful process of civilization," Freud concludes, "would thus have set in with man's adoption of an erect posture."

Although Freud's ideas gained no following among anthropologists, another minor tradition did arise to stress the primacy of upright posture. (It is, by the way, the argument we tend to accept today in explaining the morphology of australopithecines and **the path of human evolution**.) The brain cannot begin to increase in a vacuum. A primary impetus must be provided by an altered mode of life that would place a strong, selective premium upon intelligence. Upright posture frees the hands from locomotion and for manipulation (literally, from *manus* = "hand"). For the first time, tools and weapons can be fashioned and used with ease. Increased intelligence is largely a response to the enormous potential inherent in free hands for manufacture—again, literally. (Needless to say, no anthropologist has ever been so naive as to argue that brain and posture are completely independent in evolution, that one reached its fully human status before the

Biologically the species is the accumulation of the experiments of all its successful individuals since the beginning.

H.G. Wells, British author

Stephen Jay Gould, zoologist, geologist and popular author in the field of natural evolution.

other began to change at all. We are dealing with interaction and mutual reinforcement. Nevertheless, our early evolution did involve a more rapid change in posture than in brain size; complete freeing of our hands for using tools preceded most of the evolutionary enlargement of our brain.)

In another proof that sobriety does not make right, von Baer's mystical and oracular colleague Lorenz Oken hit upon the "correct" argument in 1809, while von Baer was led astray a few years later. "Man by the upright walk obtains his character," writes Oken, "the hands become free and can achieve all other offices.... With the freedom of the body has been granted also the freedom of the mind." But the champion of upright posture during the nineteenth century was Darwin's German bulldog Ernst Haeckel. Without a scrap of direct evidence, Haeckel reconstructed our ancestor and even gave it a scientific name, *Pithecanthropus alalus*, the upright, speechless, small-brained ape-man. (*Pithecanthropus*, by the way, is probably the only scientific name ever given to an animal before it was discovered. When Du Bois discovered Java Man in the 1890s, he adopted Haeckel's generic name but he gave it the new specific designation *Pithecanthropus erectus*. We now usually include this creature in our own genus as *Homo erectus*.)

But why, despite Oken and Haeckel's demurral, did the idea of cerebral primacy become so strongly entrenched? One thing is sure; it had nothing to do with direct evidence—for there was none for any position. With the exception of Neanderthal (a geographic variant of our own species according to most anthropologists), no fossil humans were discovered until the closing years of the nineteenth century, long after the dogma of cerebral primacy was established. But debates based on no evidence are among the most revealing in the history of science, for in the absence of factual constraints, the **cultural biases** that affect all thought (and which scientists try so assiduously to deny) lie nakedly exposed.

Indeed, the nineteenth century produced a brilliant exposé from a source that will no doubt surprise most readers—Friedrich Engels. (A bit of reflection should diminish surprise. Engels had a keen interest in the natural sciences and sought to base his general philosophy of dialectical materialism upon a "positive" foundation. He did not live to complete his "dialectics of nature," but he included long commentaries on science in such treatises as the *Anti-Dühring*.) In 1876, Engels wrote an essay entitled, *The Part Played by Labor in the Transition from Ape to Man*. It was published posthumously in 1896 and, unfortunately, had no visible impact upon Western science.

Engels considers three essential features of human evolution: speech, a large brain, and upright posture. He argues that the first step must have been a descent from the trees with subsequent evolution to upright posture by our ground-dwelling ancestors. "These apes when moving on level ground began to drop the habit of using their hands and to adopt a more and more erect gait. This was the decisive step in the transition from ape to man." Upright posture freed the hand for using tools (labour, in Engels's terminology); increased intelligence and speech came later.

Thus the hand is not only the organ of labor, it is also the product of labor. Only by labor, by adaptation to ever new operations … by the ever-renewed employment of these inherited improvements in new, more and more complicated operations, has the human hand attained the high degree of perfection that has enabled it to conjure into being the pictures of Raphael, the statues of Thorwaldsen, the music of Paganini.

Engels presents his conclusions as though they followed deductively from the premises of his **materialist philosophy**, but I am confident that he cribbed them from Haeckel. The two formulations are almost identical, and Engels cites the relevant pages of Haeckel's work for other purposes in an earlier essay written in 1874. But no matter. The importance of Engels's essay lies, not in its substantive conclusions, but in its trenchant political analysis of why Western science was so hung up on the **a priori assertion** of cerebral primacy.

As humans learned to master their material surroundings, Engels argues, other skills were added to primitive hunting–agriculture, spinning, pottery, navigation, arts and sciences, law and politics, and finally, "the fantastic reflection of human things in the human mind: religion." As wealth accumulated, small groups of men seized power and forced others to work for them. Labour, the source of all wealth and the primary impetus for human evolution, assumed the same low status of those who laboured for the rulers. Since rulers governed by their will (that is, by feats of mind), actions of the brain appeared to have a motive power of their own. The profession of philosophy followed no unsullied ideal of truth. Philosophers relied on state or religious patronage. Even if Plato did not consciously conspire to bolster the privileges of rulers with a supposedly abstract philosophy, his own class position encouraged an emphasis on thought as primary, dominating, and altogether more noble and important than the labour it supervised. This **idealistic tradition** dominated philosophy right through to Darwin's day. Its influence was so subtle and pervasive that even scientific, but apolitical, materialists like Darwin fell under its sway. A bias must be recognized before it can be challenged. Cerebral primacy seemed so obvious and natural that it was accepted as given, rather than recognized as a deep-seated social prejudice related to the class position of professional thinkers and their patrons. Engels writes:

> All merit for the swift advance of civilization was ascribed to the mind, to the development and activity of the brain. Men became accustomed to explain their actions from their thoughts, instead of from their needs…. And so there arose in the course of time that idealistic outlook on the world which, especially since the downfall of the ancient world, has dominated men's minds. It still rules them to such a degree that even the most materialistic natural scientists of the Darwinian school are still unable to form any clear idea of the origin of man, because under that ideological influence they do not recognize the part that has been played therein by labor.

The importance of Engels's essay does not lie in the happy result that *Australopithecus* confirmed a specific theory proposed by him–via Haeckel–but rather in his perceptive analysis of the political role of science and of the social biases that must affect all thought.

Indeed, Engels's theme of the separation of head and hand has done much to set and limit the course of science throughout history. Academic

Freud concluded that the process of civilization began with "man's adoption of an erect posture."

KEY TERMS

- Australopithecines
- The "missing link"
- Primacy of "brain power"
- Primacy of "upright posture"
- The path of human evolution
- Cultural biases
- Materialist philosophy
- Idealistic philosophy
- A priori assertions
- Social prejudice

science, in particular, has been constrained by an ideal of "pure" research, which in former days barred a scientist from extensive experimentation and empirical testing. Ancient Greek science laboured under the restriction that patrician thinkers could not perform the manual work of plebeian artisans. Medieval barber-surgeons who had to deal with battlefield casualties did more to advance the practice of medicine than academic physicians who rarely examined patients and who based their treatment on a knowledge of Galen and other learned texts. Even today, "pure" researchers tend to disparage the practical, and terms such as "aggie school" and "cow college" are heard with distressing frequency in academic circles. If we took Engels's message to heart and recognized our belief in the inherent superiority of pure research for what it is—namely **social prejudice**—then we might forge among scientists the union between theory and practice that a world teetering dangerously near the brink so desperately needs.

REVIEW

1. Why did scientists refuse to accept australopithecines as a "missing link" in the lineage of man?

2. Why was the idea of cerebral primacy so readily accepted despite the lack of physical evidence to support it? With whom did this idea originate?

3. Gould asserts that the most revealing debates in the history of science are those that are based on a lack of factual evidence. Is this true of debates in other disciplines?

The Body in the Bog

There, But for the Grace of God, Lie We

GEOFFREY BIBBY

The world of superstition, in which the spirits had to be bought off and placated, ended scarcely a thousand years ago in Europe with the coming of Christianity. The price to be paid for prosperity or victory in war during this period? Human sacrifice.

The business of the **archaeologist** is the digging up of the past, the reconstruction of remote history. He does his best to find out what our remote ancestors did and thought and felt from the material remains they left in the ground. A distinguished archaeologist has unflatteringly described himself and his colleagues as surgeons probing into the workings of the human brain with picks, shovels, and builders' trowels. "Fortunately," he adds "our patients are already dead."

This comparison must not be taken too literally. When Sir Mortimer Wheeler describes the archaeologist as investigating people who are dead, he means, I am afraid, that we are trying to find out about these dead-and-gone people by studying the things they left behind them, their implements and weapons and coins and pots and pans. The nearest we normally get to the people themselves is their skeletons, and there is a limit to what can be deduced from dry bones.

I wish to tell an archaeological detective story that is different—a detective story that begins with a body and no artifacts.

My part in the story began on Monday, April 28, 1952, when I arrived at the Prehistoric Museum of Aarhus, in mid-Denmark, to find a dead body on the floor of my office. On an iron sheet stood a large block of peat, and at one end of it the head and right arm of a man protruded, while one leg and foot stuck out from the other end. His skin was dark brown, almost chocolate coloured, and his hair was a brownish red.

He had been found on Saturday afternoon by workers cutting peat in a little bog near Grauballe, about twenty miles away. He lay a yard below the surface, but peat had been dug for generations there so that the "surface" had lain much higher, even within living memory. The finders had informed the local doctor of their discovery, not so much because he was a doctor but because he was known to be an antiquary of repute. And he had informed Professor Peter Glob, who was the director of our museum.

PREVIEW

In this article, British archaeologist Geoffrey Bibby leads us through an "archaeological detective story" that begins with the finding of a body in the peat bogs of Denmark. The mystery deepens with the evidence of other murdered "bog bodies," all dating from the same period of Danish prehistory. An investigation supports Bibby's conclusion that all were victims of ritual human sacrifice.

This was not Professor Glob's first "bog body"; he knew what to expect and made preparations accordingly. The next day he drove out to the bog, cut a section through the peat exposing the lie of the body, drew and photographed that section, took samples of the peat surrounding the body, and then cut out the whole block in which the body lay and brought it in to the museum in a truck.

That Monday we carefully dug away the peat covering the body, taking samples every two inches. The body lay face down, with one leg drawn up and the arms twisted somewhat behind it. It was completely naked. When we removed the peat from below the body (after turning it over in a plaster cast to preserve its original position), we still found nothing, no trace of clothing, no artifacts—nothing except the naked body.

At this point we turned for help to the professor of forensic medicine at Aarhus University, who carried out a thorough autopsy and presented us with a lengthy and detailed report:

"This most unusually well-preserved body has, as a result of the particular composition of the earth in which it has lain, undergone a process of conservation which appears to resemble most closely a tanning. This has made the skin firm and resistant, and has to a high degree counteracted the various processes of decay which normally commence soon after death ... the subject is an adult male, and the condition of the teeth suggests that he was of somewhat advanced age.... On the front of the throat was found a large wound stretching from ear to ear.... This wound may with certainty be interpreted as an incised lesion, probably caused by several cuts inflicted by a second person. The direction of the wound and its general appearance make it unlikely that it could be self-inflicted or accidentally inflicted after death.... The investigation of the hair suggests that the subject was dark-haired. The reddish coloration is presumably accounted for by the body having lain in peat."

So the man from Grauballe had had his throat cut, and we had a murder mystery on our hands.

The investigation went on. The police expert reported: "There is nothing unusual about the fingerprints obtained. I myself possess the same type of pattern on the right thumb and middle finger—without therefore claiming any direct descent from Grauballe Man. Among the present-day Danish population the two patterns occur with a frequency of, respectively, 11.2 and 68.3 percent."

More important were the results we got from the peat samples and from a portion of the liver region that we had excised and sent to the radioactive-carbon laboratory.

It happens that the botanists of Scandinavia have worked out in great detail the changing composition of the vegetation of the region since the last ice age ended more than ten thousand years ago. They do this by means of the thousands of infinitesimal grains of pollen to be found in any cubic centimeter of peat. The time within this sequence when any particular specimen of peat was formed is shown by the proportion of certain types of pollen grains, particularly of tree pollen. And the pollen analysts could tell us that the peat immediately below Grauballe Man had been formed early in the period the Danes call the Roman Iron Age, a period extending from the beginning of the Christian Era to about A.D. 300.

But they could tell us more. The peat *above* the body was of *earlier* date than that directly below and around the body, and the peat at a little distance to either side of the body was earlier still. The body had clearly been buried in a hole cut in the peat–but not in a hole cut to receive it. The only explanation to fit the facts was that a hole had been cut, probably to obtain peat for fuel, had stood open for some years (long enough for new peat to form in the water at the bottom of the hole), and then Grauballe Man had been thrown into this new peat and the hole had been filled in with peat from the surface layers.

The radio-carbon laboratory–which determines the age of organic substances by measuring the residual carbon-14 in the specimen–could tell us that this had occurred and that Grauballe Man had died in A.D. 310, with a possible error of a hundred years in either direction. This did not surprise us; for, though local newspapers and gossip had made much of a certain "Red Christian," a drunkard farmhand who was said to have disappeared one night some sixty years before, not far from the Grauballe peat bog, we should have been very surprised indeed if the pollen laboratory and the radio-carbon laboratory had *not* given us a date in the region of 100 B.C.-A.D. 300.

For Grauballe Man was far from being an isolated example. Bodies have always been turning up in the peat bogs of Denmark–and not only in Denmark. They are frequently found in northwest Germany and even as far south as Holland. In that area there are records of something like two hundred bog bodies. Since the earlier records are not very detailed, sometimes merely an entry in a parish registry of the "body of a poor man drowned in such and such a bog," the statistics are far from exact. The earliest doubtful record of this nature is from 1450, at Bonstorf in Germany. And the first detailed report is from 1773, when a completely preserved body of a man was found three feet deep in the peat at Ravnholt on the Danish island of Fünen. The body lay on its back with its arms crossed behind it–"as though they had been bound," says the parish clerk. Apart from a sheepskin around the head, it was naked. When the sheepskin was removed, it could be seen that the man had had his throat cut.

In 1797, in southwest Jutland, another well-preserved male body was found, naked save for one oxhide moccasin but covered with two calfskin cloaks. The cause of death is not recorded, and the body was hurriedly buried in a nearby churchyard when it began to dry out and decompose.

And so it went. Every few years a body would be found, would be a nine-day wonder in its immediate locality because of its surprising state of preservation, and would be buried again when it began to smell.

A few of the bodies achieved more than local fame. In 1853, about fifty miles south of Copenhagen a body was found, probably that of a woman, though there was little left besides the skeleton and the long, fair hair. The body was noteworthy because it was accompanied by a bronze brooch and seven glass beads, which even then could be dated to the Iron Age and which we can now date to about A.D. 300.

Eight years earlier a much more complete female body had been found at Haraldskaer, in south Jutland, not far from the burial mounds of Gorm, the last heathen king of Denmark and his queen, nor from the site of the first Christian church in Denmark, built about A.D. 950 by Gorm's son, Harald Bluetooth. The body lay in the peat with its hands and feet held down by forked sticks, and it achieved some notoriety in Denmark because some learned antiquaries claimed that it was Queen Gunhild of Norway, who, according to legend, had been enticed to Denmark by Harald Bluetooth and drowned by him in a morass. Even at the time of discovery, though, the evidence for this identification was regarded as too slender.

The first photograph of a peat-bog body dates from 1873 and is of a body found near Kiel. It was a man's body with a triangular hole in the forehead. He was naked except for a piece of leather bound around the left shin, but his head was covered with a large square woollen blanket and a sewn skin cape. An attempt was made to preserve him for exhibition by smoking, and several photographs were taken, some extravagantly posed. The first photograph of a body *in situ* was taken in 1892. The body was found not many miles away from the place where Grauballe Man was discovered sixty years later, and very close indeed to another recent find, the Tollund Man.

The list could be continued almost indefinitely. But it is only within recent years that pollen analysis has been developed to a stage where the bodies can be accurately dated. And all the bodies found since have proved to date to the same restricted period of Danish prehistory, the first three centuries of the Christian era. This fact makes it possible—indeed essential—to regard them as a single "case."

Apart from Grauballe Man, four bodies have been found in the peat bogs of Denmark since World War II, and all have been subjected to the same thorough analysis that we gave Grauballe Man. Three came from the same bog, the large peat area of Borremose in north Jutland. The first was a man, naked like so many of the others but with two cloaks of skin beside him. Around his neck was a rope noose, which may have been the cause of death, although the body was too badly preserved to be certain. There were odd features about the noose; it had been knotted at the neck, and both of the fairly short ends had been bent over and lashed with leather thongs to prevent them from unraveling, surely an unduly elaborate treatment for an ordinary hangman's noose.

The second body was that of a woman, again poorly preserved. The upper part of the body appeared to have been naked, while the lower part was covered with a blanket, a shawl, and other bits of clothing. There was a leather cord around the neck, but the cause of death was apparently a crushing blow on the skull.

The third body was also a woman's, a rather stout lady who lay face downward in the peat with only a blanket wrapped around her middle and held in place by a leather strap. She was no sight for squeamish archaeologists–she had been scalped and her face battered to pieces, though perhaps after death.

It is with quite unjustified relief that one turns from the rather macabre Borremose bodies to the well-known **Tollund Man** whose portrait has been in the press of the world and who has had the honour of appearing on British television. Tollund Man was discovered in 1950, two years before Grauballe Man and under the same circumstances, by farmers cutting peat. The discovery was reported to the police, and they called in Professor Glob, who described what he saw:

"In the peat cut, nearly seven feet down, lay a human figure in a crouched position, still half-buried. A foot and a shoulder protruded, perfectly preserved but dark-brown in color like the surrounding peat which had dyed the skin. Carefully we removed more peat, and a bowed head came into view.

"As dusk fell, we saw in the fading light a man take shape before us. He was curled up, with legs drawn under him and arms bent, resting on his side as if asleep. His eyes were peacefully shut; his brows were furrowed, and his mouth showed a slightly irritated quirk as if he were not overpleased by this unexpected disturbance...."

Tollund Man was found to be naked except for a leather belt around his waist and a leather cap upon his head, a cap made of eight triangular gussets of leather sewn together. There was one other item. Around his neck was the elaborately braided leather rope with which they had hanged him.

It is clear, I think, that we have a case of mass murder. There are too many points of similarity between the killings for it to be possible to consider each independently of the others. I should point out, though, that their generally fantastic state of preservation is not one of these points of similarity. It is merely our good fortune. The preservation is due the fact that the peat bogs contain sufficient humic acid and tannic acid to halt the processes of decay and start a **tanning process** that can preserve the body. (This process, incidentally, we have carried to its logical conclusion with Grauballe Man. Eighteen months in an oak vat in a concentrated solution based on oak shavings has completed the tanning process that nature commenced some eighteen hundred years ago. Grauballe Man, on exhibition at the Prehistoric Museum in Aarhus, needs only a little linseed oil now and then in order to last indefinitely.)

Tollund Man. Around his neck was the elaborately braided rope with which they had hanged him.

There is one condition for preservation, however, for otherwise the peat bogs would be full of the bodies of every animal that falls into them. The body must be *buried* in the peat, deep enough down to be below the oxygen-containing surface levels. And this–the fact that all these bodies were disposed of in old cuttings in the peat–*is* one of the common factors that cause us to regard all the killings as a single phenomenon.

Another is the fact that all the bodies are naked. Though it is the rule rather than the exception for articles of clothing to be found with the bodies, and sometimes wrapped around the bodies, they are never regularly clothed in the garments. But the most obvious similarity is that all have died violent deaths and that all are found in bogs.

And that leads to the next step in the inquiry: the question of motive. Why are these bodies there at all?

These are not ordinary burials. Archaeologists are very well acquainted with the burials of this period of Danish prehistory. They were elaborate, clearly showing evidence of belief in an afterlife in which the dead would have need of material things. The graves are large and edged with stones. The body lies carefully arranged on its side, together with a whole set of pottery vessels, or in the case of the wealthy, with glass and silver ware imported from the Roman Empire. The vessels must have held provisions for the journey to the afterworld, for there is often a leg of pork or of mutton with the rest of the provisions, and even a knife to carve the joint.

It is clear that whatever it was that resulted in the deaths of the bodies in the bogs also deprived them of regular, ritual burial.

We must dismiss the most obvious explanation—that the bodies were victims of robbery with violence. All are dated to the comparatively short period of three hundred years at the beginning of our era. It may have been a lawless time—though farther south it is the period of the Pax Romana—but certainly it was no more lawless than many other periods: the period before, of the great Celtic and Germanic wanderings; or the period after, when the Roman Empire was breaking up and all the vultures flocked to the kill; or the Viking period; or much of the Middle Ages. We should expect a much greater spread in date if the bodies are to be explained as the victims of robber bands.

We must widen our scope and look not so much at the bodies as at the bogs. What do we find there?

Any Danish archaeologist can answer that question at length. And he can illustrate his answer at the Danish National Museum in Copenhagen, where room after room is full of things found in bogs. More than half of the best treasures of Danish prehistory have been found in bogs, and the archaeologist will tell you that these treasures were offerings to the gods.

Now, archaeologists have often been accused of calling in hypothetical gods and cult practices whenever they find anything they cannot explain by obvious mundane means. A theory of offerings in the peat bogs must not be accepted uncritically. But how else is one to explain why a Stone Age farmer, some four thousand years ago, very carefully laid seven large, new, unused stone axes side by side in a row in a peat bog? How is one to explain why several pairs of the big bronze trumpets known as lurs, the finest known products of the Danish Bronze Age, have been found in the bogs in good working order?

It begins to look as though anything of prehistoric date found in the bogs of Denmark is a priori likely to be an offering to the gods. If we move forward to the actual period of the bog bodies, we find the offerings in the bogs getting more numerous and more varied and richer. In the early 1950s I spent three years a few miles south of our museum, helping to dig out an immense offering of weapons—several thousand iron swords and spearheads and arrowheads and shield bosses—all of them burned, bent, hacked to pieces, and then deposited in a lake in the middle of a peat bog. They had been deposited at various times—it was a regular place of offering—but all during the period A.D. 150-300. Among the weapons lay the skeletons of two horses—and here perhaps we approach quite close in spirit to the bog bodies, for the horses had been beheaded before they were offered, and marks on the bones showed quite clearly where spears had been stuck into the carcasses, before or after death.

We are entering a dark region. Our probings into the minds of our distant ancestors are lifting a corner of a veil that seems to cover an area of deep superstition, a time when the peat bogs were the abodes of gods and spirits, who demanded sacrifice. When we look now at the bodies in the bogs it seems by no means impossible that they, too, were offerings; that the sacrifices to the gods also included human sacrifices.

We must ask ourselves what we know about the gods and goddesses of this period.

At the northern end of that very bog at Borremose in which three of the bodies were found, there was discovered in 1897 a large caldron of solid silver. In itself the Gundestrup caldron is far and away the most intrinsically valuable of all the bog offerings. But it is more than that; it is a picture book of European religion around the beginning of the Christian era. Its sides are decorated, inside and out, with a series of panels bearing pictures, in relief, of gods and goddesses, of mythical animals, and of ritual scenes. Admittedly the caldron is believed to have been manufactured in southeast Europe and to have been brought to Denmark as booty, but the deities portrayed are like the native Danish gods of the period.

It is particularly noteworthy that each one of these deities, although otherwise naked, bears a torque, or broad necklet, at the throat, which appears to have been a symbol of kingship and of divinity. It has even been suggested—perhaps not entirely fancifully—that the oddly elaborate nooses around the necks of Tollund and Borremose Man in some way set them apart as consecrated to the gods. We know from the sagas, not many hundreds of years later, that in Viking times hanged men were sacred to Odin, the chief god of the Viking pantheon.

One of the interior caldron panels shows clearly that the idea of human sacrifice was not alien to the religion of the time. It is admittedly a different ceremony of sacrifice, with the victim dropped headfirst into, or perhaps slaughtered above, a caldron, perhaps the Gundestrup caldron itself. The cutting of the throats of animal victims and the draining of their blood into a caldron was not unknown even among the civilized Greeks and Romans—and Grauballe Man, like many of the victims in the Danish bogs, had had his throat cut.

Speculation concerning details of ritual, though fascinating, can hardly be justified by the slender evidence at our disposal. But the general picture cannot be questioned: the Danes of the early Christian centuries worshipped torque-bearing gods and goddesses; they were not averse to human sacrifice; and the holy places of the divinities were the peat bogs.

There is one source of information that we have not yet tapped. The historians and geographers of the Roman Empire wrote books, some of which describe the manners and customs of peoples beyond the imperial frontiers. The books must be used with caution; few of the authors had visited the regions they describe, and their accounts may well be as full of misunderstandings and fanciful explanations as anything the modern archaeologist can invent to explain what he finds.

But there is a passage in Tacitus's *Germania*, an account of the peoples beyond the Rhine written in A.D. 98, that bears on our study of the Danish bog bodies. Tacitus names seven tribes to the north of Germany, including the Angles, who are known to have lived in south Jutland before they invaded England in the fifth century together with the Saxons and Jutes. And he says:

> these people ... are distinguished by a common worship of Nerthus, or Mother Earth. They believe that she interests herself in human affairs and rides through their peoples. In an island of Ocean stands a sacred grove, and in the grove stands a car draped with a cloth which none but the priest may touch. The priest can feel the presence of the goddess in this holy of holies, and attends her, in deepest reverence, as her car is drawn by oxen. Then follow days of rejoicing and merrymaking in every place that she honors with her advent and stay. No-one goes to war, no-one takes up arms; every object of iron is locked away; then, and only then, are peace and quiet known and prized, until the goddess is again restored to her temple by the priest, when she has had her fill of the society of men. After that, the car, the cloth and, believe it if you will, the goddess herself are washed clean in a secluded lake. This service is performed by slaves who are immediately afterwards drowned in the lake. Thus mystery begets terror and a pious reluctance to ask what that sight can be which is allowed only to dying eyes.

Here we may be getting close to an answer. Nerthus—Mother Earth—is clearly a goddess of fertility; she may be the "goddess with the torque." And the time of peace and rejoicing when the goddess is driven around the countryside in her draped carriage will be the time of sowing, the vernal equinox. **Pagan survivals** of this spring festival still exist in many parts of Europe, in mummers' plays and Maypole dancing and Queens of the May. And in the National Museum in Copenhagen may be seen one of the ox-drawn carriages that almost certainly was used to carry the image of the fertility goddess around the fields. It was found—inevitably—in a peat bog, Dejbjerg in east Jutland, in the 1880s. Richly carved and decorated with ornaments of bronze, it is far too fine a wagon to have been used for mundane purposes. Upon it stands a palanquin, a carrying chair with a canopy, within which the image of the goddess must have rested.

A final point brings the evidence full circle to the bodies in the bogs. Microscopic examination of the stomach contents of the men from Borremose, Tollund, and Grauballe shows that their food for several days before death had been vegetarian. It seems to have consisted of some sort of porridge or mash composed of various kinds of corn, or sorrel and heart's ease (both cultivated during the Iron Age), and of the seeds of such weeds as were accidentally harvested along with the corn. It has been suggested that this was a ritual diet, part of the ceremony needed to make the corn grow. Be that as it may, it is significant that there was no trace of any of the edible plants or fruits of summer in the stomach contents. So whatever our uncertainty about the precise year of death, we can say with confidence that the season of the year was winter or early spring.

Further we cannot go. We have been probing, with our picks and shovels and builders' trowels, not merely into the brains but perhaps also into the souls of men, and we must be content if our diagnosis is imprecise and inconclusive. But it does take us a little way beyond the conventional archaeological picture of the material lives of the simple peasants of **barbarian Europe**. Behind the material life, interleaved with it and perhaps dominating it, was the world of taboos and magic and superstition, the spirits of the earth and of the heavens, who had to be bribed or placated or bought off. One of the occupational risks of Iron Age Europe, right up to the end of the Viking period scarcely a thousand years ago, was that of being chosen as victim, as the price to be paid for prosperity in the next harvest or victory in the next war. It was only with the coming of Christianity that human sacrifice ceased in Europe; looking on the bodies from the Danish bogs we should do well to realize that there, but for the grace of God, lie we.

KEY TERMS

- Archaeology
- Bog body
- Radio-carbon laboratory
- Grauballe Man and Tollund Man
- Tanning process (preservation)
- Offerings to the gods
- Human sacrifices
- The Christian era
- Pagan survivals
- Barbarian Europe

REVIEW

1. What medical treatments were standard in the early part of this century? How effective were they in treating serious illness?

2. What evidence led Bibby to conclude that the bodies had been the victims of mass murder?

3. What information was imparted by the decorations on the Gundestrup caldron? How did this information feature in the solution to the mystery of the bog bodies?

Mind-Boggling Medical Milestones

Better Living with Technology

DANIEL Q. HANEY

Modern medicine has undergone revolutionary changes in this century. Technological advances have allowed medicine to retool itself, and discoveries as far-reaching as DNA have been made. It has become less art and more science, making this the best time in history to get sick.

PREVIEW

The question of what has changed in medicine in this century is responded to by journalist Daniel Haney with, What hasn't? Haney reminds us of how risky the practice of medicine once was and describes the recent and significant advances in medical science, from the use of antibiotics and vaccines to organ transplants, that have revolutionized this field.

A century ago, the standard medicines in a doctor's bag included arsenic, mercury and other substances that could kill before they cured. When these didn't work, doctors might recommend mustard poultices to draw out imaginary poisons. A physical exam often amounted to little more than looking at the patient's tongue.

Undoubtedly, healers often made people feel better, then as now. Wise practitioners have never underestimated the restorative powers of a reassuring touch. Nevertheless, a trip to the doctor in those days was a dicey business at best.

Despite all the shortcomings of modern medicine—the cost, the impersonal reliance on technology, the many ills still beyond its reach—there has never been a better time to get sick than right now. The revolution in medicine during the 20th century is mind-bending.

What's changed? The real question is: What hasn't?

Alfred Gilman, a Nobel winner from the University of Texas Southwestern Medical Center, counted the medicines used at the turn of century that are still given today. He found only about 15—digitalis, morphine, Aspirin, quinine, iron and a few other minerals and such.

"Somewhere between 1910 and 1912, a random patient with a random disease consulting a doctor chosen at random had for the first time in the history of mankind a better than 50-50 chance of profiting from the encounter."

The quote is attributed to Lawrence J. Henderson, a Harvard biochemist who died in 1942. But even in his time, medicines that now tame infections, high blood pressure and so much else were unimagined.

Dr. Michael DeBakey, Baylor College of Medicine's renowned heart surgeon, finished medical school in 1932—still a decade before antibiotics—and one of his earliest memories as a doctor is sitting up all night watching a patient die of an abdominal infection.

"When I graduated," he remembers, "there was virtually nothing you could do for heart disease. If a patient came in with a heart attack, it was up to God."

Slowly at first and then accelerating at mid-century, medicine retooled itself. It became less art, more science. Purges and placebos gave way to things that actually worked.

Here are some essential landmarks of this metamorphosis.

Antibiotics

Many argue this is the single most impressive medical achievement of the century. The discovery began in the 1920s, when Alexander Fleming at St. Mary's Hospital in London found that a mold, which he identified as Penicillium rubrum, killed staphylococci bacteria growing in a lab dish.

Ten years later, scientists from Oxford came across his write-up and set about purifying the key substance. By D-Day in 1944, there was plenty of penicillin to treat allied soldiers.

Soon streptomycin and other antibiotics followed. A new class of medicines, appropriately labelled miracle drugs, had been created. Suddenly, such implacable killers as tuberculosis, diphtheria, pneumonia, syphilis and tetanus were treatable.

X-Rays

German scientist Wilhelm Roentgen demonstrated the power of the X-ray in 1895 when he took a picture of the bones of his wife's left hand. This profoundly important innovation did not make its way into routine care until the 1920s. The shadowy grey pictures literally opened a window into the body. Now doctors could see fractures, tumours, congested lungs.

Much more followed—ultrasound, CT scans, PET scans, MRIs—each offering a different internal view of the body without actually invading it.

"The imaging technology has probably had a bigger role than anything else in changing the way we think about the human body," says Dr. Joel Howell of the University of Michigan.

Maternal and Infant Care

In 1900, life expectancy in the United States was 48. Now it is 76. Much of this gain came in the first half of the century, before many of the big research breakthroughs occurred. The major reason was vast improvements in public health—clean water, plumbing, refrigeration and especially an understanding of the importance of sanitation during childbirth.

Women today are only about one-tenth as likely to die while giving birth as they were at the turn of the century. Childhood mortality plunged as well. Today, only about 1 percent of babies die before age 5 in well-off parts of the world.

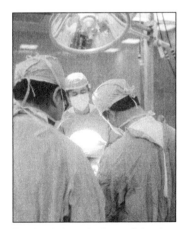

The breakthroughs in medicine in the last 100 years make this the best time ever to get ill.

• Insulin

In the late 1800s, scientists realized the pancreas made something the body needed to burn sugar. In 1921, Frederick Banting and Charles Best of the University of Toronto isolated the active material in dogs. They gave it to a dog near death with diabetes, and the animal quickly got better.

The next year, they tried a similar experiment on a dying 14-year-old boy. Almost immediately his blood sugar level fell; within a few weeks he was able to go home, though dependent on injections of the newly isolated substance, insulin.

Large-scale production of the hormone followed. Though it did not cure diabetes, it proved to be an important lifesaver.

• Heart Disease Treatments

From the invention of the electrocardiograph in 1903 to the prescription of cholesterol-lowering statin drugs in the 1990s, the understanding and treatment of diseases of the heart and circulatory system have been among medicine's outstanding successes.

High blood pressure, heart failure, irregular heartbeats and heart attacks all became treatable conditions. Much of this is the result of a stunning increase in heart medicines—diuretics, beta blockers, ACE inhibitors, calcium channel blockers, clot busters and more—used in various combinations to keep diseased and damaged hearts pumping.

The bypass operation Dr. DeBakey developed in the 1960s, along with angioplasty, became routine for opening clogged arteries in the heart.

Perhaps as important as the medical breakthroughs were science's new understanding of the role of cholesterol, fat, smoking and exercise in this disease.

• Mental-Illness Treatments

One of the most important insights of the 20th century is the understanding that serious mental disease results from disruptions in the chemistry of the brain. It has led to the development and acceptance of medicines for illnesses of the mind.

The first truly effective drug was lithium, used to control manic depression in 1949. In the 1950s came chlorpromazine and other medicines for schizophrenia. Then followed treatments for depression.

• Vaccines

Edward Jenner administered the first vaccine for smallpox in 1796, but the broad use of vaccines is a 20th-century development.

Certainly the century's most famous was the polio vaccine. With its power to paralyze children, polio was one of the most feared of diseases. Jonas Salk of the University of Pittsburgh developed a vaccine made from killed virus, and it was declared safe and effective in 1955. Five years later, Albert Sabin's more effective oral vaccine was introduced.

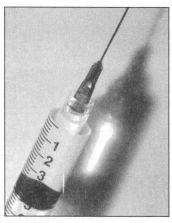

We take medical care for granted, yet in much of the Third World, basic medical care does not exist.

Now vaccines are used to control a long list of once-common diseases—mumps, flu, chicken pox, diphtheria, Haemophilus influenzae, hepatitis A and B, whooping cough, tetanus and many more.

• Transplants

In 1954 in Boston, Drs. J. Hartwell Harrison and Joseph Murray performed the first successful kidney transplant. To get around the biggest problem—the body's tendency to reject foreign tissue—the operation was done on identical twins.

In 1963, doctors attempted lung and liver transplants. Then came heart transplants, first by Dr. Christiaan Barnard in South Africa and next by Americans Norman Shumway and Denton Cooley.

Organ transplants did not become routine until the late 1970s with the development of cyclosporine, a drug that suppresses the body's tendency to attack the new organ. Today, about 70 percent of recipients survive at least four years.

• AIDS Treatments

AIDS, discovered in 1981, turned out to be one of medicine's toughest challenges, a disease targeting the body in ways never before seen and caused by a virus, a class of microbe that medicine was virtually powerless against.

In short order, scientists identified the virus and developed tests to diagnose infection and prevent transmission through the blood supply. However, the real breakthrough came in the mid-1990s with the development of combinations of drugs that keep the virus from multiplying. While a cure and a vaccine are still elusive, the dramatic effect of these therapies raises hopes that AIDS at least has been turned into a manageable disease.

• DNA

The biggest discovery of the century? "It's DNA. No question at all," says Dr. Meyer Friedman of the University of California, San Francisco.

It started with the discovery by James Watson of the U.S. and Francis Crick of Britain in 1953 of the rope-ladder structure of deoxyribonucleic acid. Each rung of the ladder is a unit of genetic code, and together they contain all the construction plans of life.

Now, an understanding of genes' role in triggering cancer has revolutionized the way scientists think about new therapies.

Still, many believe this is barely the start. Like the discovery of X-rays at the end of the 19th century, the harnessing of genes at the end of the 20th is likely to pay off in powerful new ways to control human ills in the century to come.

KEY TERMS

- Antibiotics
- X-rays
- Maternal and infant care
- The discovery of insulin
- Heart disease treatments
- Mental-illness treatments
- Vaccines
- Transplantation of body organs
- AIDS treatments
- DNA

REVIEW

1. What features does the Internet have that make it a suitable subject for the study of human behaviour?

2. How did the discovery of antibiotics affect health care? How is the discovery of DNA likely to affect health care in the future?

3. What do you think is the single most impressive advance in medical science? Why?

MP3—Profiting from Technology

Musicians Love It

THE ECONOMIST

The spread of pirate audio in the form of "MP3" music files on the World Wide Web is forcing the record industry to find better ways of getting recorded music to the public. Meanwhile, the downloading fun continues.

PREVIEW

MP3-compressed bootlegged music and free software packages for playing it are widely accessible through the Internet. An MP3 player has been inexpensively retailed. This report, taken from "The Economist" (a weekly newsmagazine from Britain), informs us that the resultant loss of sales has caused members of the Recording Industry Association of America to produce MP3 players of their own and to attempt to impose an improved standard in order to limit duplication and address the issue of copy protection.

Much has happened to the distribution of music over the Internet since the **MP3 phenomenon** took campuses around the world by storm two years ago. Short for Motion Picture Expert Group-1/Level-3, MP3 is widely used in the digital TV and multimedia business for compressing the audio part of a video programme. Though it is a "lossy" form of **digital compression** (sounds masked by other sounds are discarded or "lost"), an MP3 music track scrunched to a twelfth its size on a CD sounds to an ordinary ear every bit as good as the original when played back.

A CD holds more than 600 megabytes of digitized music, with a typical five-minute track accounting for around 50 megabytes. To transmit all the digital bits in a single CD track on the net would take two hours with even the zippiest modern modem; to transmit the whole CD would take more than a day. But if you compress a music file using MP3, it takes little more than ten minutes to download. And it takes up only four megabytes, not 50 megabytes, of hard-drive space on the downloader's computer.

What has infuriated the record industry is the way MP3 has made it possible for computer-savvy teenagers to distribute CD-quality music free over the Internet—and so allow pristine digital copies of the original to proliferate. Though widely used, transmitting copies of music titles in this way is generally illegal. Most of the MP3-compressed songs posted on websites are **bootlegged material** belonging to major record companies, music publishers and recording artists.

Thousands of websites now exist on the Internet where fans can not only locate the music titles they want, but also get all the software tools needed to play the MP3 songs they have downloaded. A minority of MP3 websites are legitimate, offering only music that the **copyright owners** (typically "garage bands" hoping to be discovered) have agreed to distribute in this way. But even respectable websites feel no compunction about helping visitors find the MP3 titles they want to download. Lycos, one of the most popular sites on the World Wide Web, has recently installed a database listing more than 500,000 MP3-formatted songs. A San Diego distributor of free music gets more than 200,000 visitors a day to its website.

Pundits from the industry claim that more than 15m copies of free software packages (WinAmp, FreeAmp and Sonique) for playing MP3 music files on personal computers have been downloaded from the Internet so far. If only one in ten of them is used regularly, the record industry could already be losing sales worth hundreds of millions of dollars annually—equivalent to its losses caused by pirate CD plants in China, Mexico and elsewhere.

It is not just the speed and ease with which web audio can be banded around the globe that is driving the Recording Industry Association of America (RIAA) nuts. It was bad enough when college kids downloaded bootlegged MP3 tracks and played them back through clunky sound systems attached to their personal computers in college dormitories. But then, in October 1998, along came the Rio PMP300, a pocket-sized MP3 player costing $199 that can store dozens of tracks and play them back, Walkman-style, through headphones while on the move.

> *Reality is 80m polygons.*
> Alvy Ray Smith, computer guru

IF YOU CAN'T BEAT THEM

The RIAA has tried every trick in the book to prevent Diamond Multimedia Systems of San Jose, California, from selling its Rio player. To no avail. Diamond has shipped more than 150,000 units and cannot keep up with demand. Envious of its success, a dozen other makers are about to plunge in with MP3 players of their own. Industry pundits expect 2m portable players to be on the streets by next Christmas. With that many players in circulation, MP3 could become the industry standard for web audio. Although there is nothing wrong with MP3 technically, it works without any form of copy protection. And that is anathema to the RIAA.

The record companies and film studios have grudgingly accepted that banning digital recording is not an option. But they have managed instead to get all the big consumer-electronics firms to include encryption circuitry in their digital recorders so the machines cannot make "serial copies"—i.e., produce a copy from an existing copy. Although a first-generation recording can be made from any digital source, be it a CD, DVD (digital video disc) or satellite TV broadcast, the serial encryption circuitry ensures that the recording is effectively a mule—i.e., incapable of breeding second-generation copies.

Unable to beat the bootleggers, the RIAA now plans to join them—by offering a better standard of its own called Secure Digital Music Initiative (SDMI), which will include some form of copy protection to prevent or limit duplication of the record companies' music.

The music industry has replied with its own "standard," and a prayer that the copying will stop.

REVIEW

1. How does the use of MP3 technology affect the time it takes to download digitized music?

2. How does "encryption circuitry" in digital recorders limit the copying of bootlegged music?

3. Is the posting and copying of MP3-compressed bootlegged music an ethical act? Who will benefit from the introduction of a digital recording standard designed to limit the illegal duplication of copyrighted music?

In early March, executives from more than 100 entertainment and electronics companies gathered in Los Angeles to hammer out details for the new audio compression standard. All the big names were there—from Sony, Toshiba and IBM to Time-Warner, Bertelsmann and EMI. Unfortunately, many of the participants saw the RIAA's pitch for a new audio standard as a chance to get their own proprietary compression technique adopted—so they can ask **royalties** for its use. Sony is pressing the SDMI group to adopt its MagicGate, while Toshiba is doing all it can to push its ID system as a replacement for MP3. Nippon Telegraph and Telephone is lobbying hard for the InfoBind system it has developed with Kobe Steel. Yet another proprietary compression technique is being proposed by Texas Instruments.

The good news is that Leonardo Chiariglione of Telecom Italia has been put in charge of the SDMI standards-setting body. Mr. Chiariglione was the brains behind MP3. If he can work the technical magic a second time, fans will be able to get their hands on music collections from even the most obscure of artists who have little chance of getting distributed today—all courtesy of the Internet. And the really funny thing is that the Luddites of the record industry will be all the richer for it.

SHALL I COMPARE THEE TO A SWARM OF INSECTS?

SEARCHING FOR THE ESSENCE OF THE WORLD WIDE WEB

GEORGE JOHNSON

How can one describe the web—as an ecosystem, a rock concert, a thunderstorm? Researchers are seriously thinking about such things.

Gazing through a computer screen onto the vast expanse of the World Wide Web, one feels like an explorer perched at the edge of an endless wilderness. It's a bit of a letdown, then, to learn how very finite the whole place really is.

Researchers at a company called Alexa Internet, using computers to automatically plumb the depths of this ocean of information, recently estimated that, as of last summer, the Web was three terabytes in size–three trillion bytes of information, about 5,000 CD-ROM's. Just about the whole thing would fit onto Sun Microsystem's top-of-the-line StorEdge A7000 Intelligent Storage Server, an array of speedy hard-disk drives occupying less than 150 cubic feet. This **cyberspace** that people have been romping around in could be squeezed inside a bedroom closet.

But it's not the size of the Web that matters. As the world is increasingly coming to appreciate, physical space and cyberspace operate according to different rules. In what they describe as a new science of Webology, computer scientists at the Xerox Palo Alto Research Center in Silicon Valley recently funnelled a large portion of the Web, about 55 million pages (leaving out the pictures), onto 400 billion bytes of disk space. Held in captivity in Palo Alto, this Web in a Box is poked and prodded, studied like a great beast–or, to use the metaphor the researchers prefer, like an **ecosystem**.

With the help of this simulation, and by probing the real, living Web with electronic signals, they seek laws by which the members of the planetary community of Internet foragers compete and cooperate in the constant search for information. The **Internet** has become a living laboratory, a place to study mass human behaviour with a precision and on a scale never possible before.

"No central authority has cultivated the Web as a beautiful garden," said Dr. Bernardo Huberman, an Internet ecologist at Xerox PARC. "It grows on its own, like an ecosystem." **Informavores** hunting down an interesting

PREVIEW

Having estimated the size of the seemingly endless Web, researchers are now probing it to discern laws of mass human behaviour. In a new science called "Webology," journalist George Johnson informs us, computer scientists are studying the activity of information seekers as they compete and cooperate in the "living laboratory" of the Internet.

site link it to their own; and that site is soon linked to others, forming a vast spider web of connections.

"The sheer reach and structural complexity of the Web makes it an ecology of knowledge, with relationships, information 'food chains,' and dynamic interactions that could soon become as rich as, if not richer than, many natural ecosystems," Dr. Huberman wrote in a paper last year with his colleagues Peter Pirolli, James Pitkow and Rajan Lukose.

But it is hard to find the right metaphor for something so strange. Viewed in real time, with data seekers buzzing from site to site, the Web can seem like a swarm of virtual insects, one whose flutterings (in the form of mouse clicks) can be recorded and sifted for clues to behavioural laws.

"We are not doing computer science," Dr. Huberman said, "but something more akin to social science." What strategies do people use to hunt down information? Why, for no apparent reason, do storms of activity suddenly surge through the Internet, causing the whole thing to grind to a halt? And why, just as mysteriously, do these information fronts suddenly subside?

Ever since the Web began to burgeon, barely under human control, people have been straining to relate it to something familiar—an ecosystem, the weather, an unruly crowd at a rock concert. The Web is a great ocean on which you surf from site to site. It's a cyberspace with a topology of its own: Two points distant in physical space can be adjacent in cyberspace, a single mouse click away. But an E-mail message sent in an instant to a neighbour next door might be routed through a maze of links extending thousands of miles.

Lada Adamic, a Stanford University graduate student working on Xerox PARC's Internet ecology project, recently found that cyberspace, like the world described in the John Guare play *Six Degrees of Separation*, is a small place indeed. Just as any two people on Earth are said to be connected by a human chain of acquaintance with no more than a few links, so can you pick two Web sites at random and get from one to the other with about four clicks.

The research quantifies what Web users intuitively know: Because of the high density of connections, it can be surprisingly easy to find information in what amounts to a library without a card catalog, filled with unindexed books.

The thunderstorms of congestion on the Net, another study found, can be analyzed in terms of **crowd behaviour**. (Meteorology, sociology—the metaphors inevitably clash.) Sudden clots of congestion can sometimes be traced to obvious causes, like the recent virtual lingerie show of Victoria's Secret. More often they arise and quickly dissipate for obscure reasons best understood using what social scientists call game theory.

You log on to the Internet and find the playing field uncrowded. With Web sites popping up as quickly as you touch their links, you click more and more, downloading video files and sound tracks with little regard for the capacity, or "**bandwidth**," you are consuming. Millions of other players

"The Net" is based on millions of microchips, but it is more than just the sum of its parts.

are selfishly doing the same. Inevitably the activity reaches a threshold and connection speeds start to crawl.

Should you stay around, knowing that others will soon give up in frustration, leaving you more room? Or will you gain in the long run if you help relieve the congestion, logging off until the storm has probably blown by? You must decide, in terms of game theory, whether to defect from the common good or cooperate.

The result is a classic social dilemma, a vastly larger-scale version of what happens when you are confronted with a steady busy signal at the theater box office and must decide whether to call back later or set your phone on constant redial. Short spikes of congestion are followed by lulls–a pattern that can be predicted statistically and verified by "pinging" the Net, as the engineers say, bouncing thousands of packets of information off a particular site and timing in milliseconds how long they take to return.

From measuring millions of mouse clicks, another study has derived a mathematical "law of surfing" predicting how many pages one typically visits within a single Web site–about 1-1/2, a finding that has been of keen interest to Internet entrepreneurs.

As the Web continues to grow exponentially (with everyone someday as likely to have a Web page as a street address), it will become an ever richer distillation of human behaviour. Even the dead, discontinued pages will be around for scholars to scrutinize. A group called the Internet Archive in San Francisco has collected and stored on disks and tapes over a billion Web pages, exceeding 13 terabytes. (The entire Library of Congress has been estimated to contain 20 terabytes of text.) The plan is to provide snapshots, year by year, of just what the great terrestrial brain has been thinking.

KEY TERMS

- Cyberspace
- Ecosystem (the Internet as)
- Internet
- Informavores
- Crowd behaviour model
- Bandwidth
- Game theory

REVIEW

1. According to researchers, what is the size of the Web? How much physical storage space would it require?

2. List the metaphors used to describe the World Wide Web. Why is it difficult to find the "right" metaphor?

3. How important is it to record the activity of the Web? Of what value might archival material be to future scholars?

Nathan Petroff, *Modern Times* (1917). Courtesy of the National Gallery of Canada, Ottawa.

PART 3

The Social Sciences

Part of the federalist campaign during the 1995 Quebec referendum.

The circumstances of human society are too complicated to be submitted to the rigour of mathematical calculation.

Marquis de Custine, author

The Social Sciences

An Introduction

"Philosophers have only interpreted the world," wrote the young Karl Marx, more than 150 years ago, "the point is to change it." Part of changing the world involves understanding it, and that is the task that social scientists have set for themselves. They have been more or less successful.

The second article in this unit describes Stanley Milgram's famous "obedience experiments" in the 1960s. Miligram was puzzled, as are we all, by the ease with which otherwise normal people, in the right conditions, can carry out atrocities against other people. The examples are far too many—from **genocide** against six million Jews in Nazi Germany to recent **ethnic cleansing** in Ruanda and more recently in Bosnia and Kosovo. Other selections in this unit note the generous "other side" of the human character—the **selfless behaviour** of Black leader Martin Luther King, Jr., the efforts of a very young woman to bring McDonalds' fast-food workers under a bargaining agreement and the plea for a more forgiving political system by Bob Rae.

These two themes—human cruelty and human generosity—are nevertheless linked. All the selections in this unit underline the fundamental point that our behaviour, even at its seemingly most individualistic and even chaotic state, is more than a programmed response, and that the ever-changing patterns of human relationship are much more complex than any superficial investigation might suggest. The task of the **social sciences** (psychology, sociology, economics and political science, to take just the main disciplines) is to help us understand these connections better. It is only by understanding them (through hypotheses and theories) that we can possibly shape the world to everyone's advantage.

NATURE AND NURTURE

This unit, then, focuses on the individual and his or her relation to the wider social world. That is, it examines not only the individual personality but the nature of **society** as well (i.e., its social institutions, politics and economy).

The first article examines, a little provocatively, whether or not our individual actions are simply "programmed" (similar to the proverbial rats in a psychologist's cage) by forces beyond our immediate control. Social scientists, of course, agree that "**nurture**" (i.e., upbringing and the wider social environment) plays a big part in how we behave as individuals and as groups, that there is more to human behaviour than the blueprint left by "**nature**." But how the social environment influences behaviour, and by how much, is certainly not agreed upon nor are the social and psychological dimensions of human behaviour well understood.

This unit also covers more controversial ground. For example, several selections examine the way women traditionally have been, and still are, often regarded as second-class citizens and how this is beginning to change, partly as a result of the organized **women's movement**. Other articles examine the question of racial discrimination against visible minorities and the significance of **multiculturalism** in Canada, which makes it rather unique. Still other articles examine our politics ("Living Together") and changes in our working life ("Mac Attack" and "Life in a Fast-Food Factory"). Most of the selections are interesting, sometimes even amusing (for example, "Body Ritual among the 'Nacirema'" and "It's a Small World"), but they all make the point that, as individuals, we are all interrelated and in very complex ways.

THE IDEA OF SOCIAL SCIENCE

The social sciences differ from the physical and natural sciences in that the subject matter is not "objective" physical and natural forces but the seemingly "less disciplined" actions of individuals and groups. This presents two problems for social researchers. The first is that individuals do not behave like mindless particles (though sometimes they may appear to behave mindlessly); the second is that social scientists themselves are a part of the very unit they are investigating (and therefore social scientists are open to introducing personal **bias** into their research).

In choosing the selections for this unit we have tried to avoid bias or opinions that might suggest favouritism in this or that debate or controversy or this or that view of social science. The purpose is not to influence opinions or advocate any particular cause, but rather to give a sense of what social science is all about (compared to the physical sciences or the humanities). However, it needs to be said that a close reading will probably uncover some biases—for example, a bias in favour of full equality between the sexes and among all races and religions, a bias in favour of peace, and a bias in favour of free and open debate. These biases we could not avoid.

The unit provides a basic introduction to the social sciences, touching on as many important issues as possible in the short number of pages available. It is hoped that these selections will provide much food for thought and some lively discussion.

KEY TERMS

- Genocide
- Ethnic cleansing
- Selfless behaviour
- Social sciences
- Society
- "Nature" versus "nurture"
- Women's movement
- Multiculturalism
- Bias

The task of social science is to make sense of society, which is easier said than done.

The Debate Goes On: Nature or Nurture?

How Much Depends on Genes?

JAMES TREFIL

Freedom or determinism? In terms of molecular genetics, this age-old debate is no longer centred exclusively on the question of whether our genes influence our behaviour, but on which genes influence what behaviour.

PREVIEW

Although social scientists traditionally look to the "social environment" to explain bad behaviour, studies in genetics have convinced many behavioural scientists that genes also play a part. Science writer James Trefil explains the complications of the "one-gene, one behaviour" model. He stresses the importance of more precise mapping of the human genome and urges us to regard human behaviour as a complex blend of social environment and genetic factors.

This question just doesn't seem to go away. And no wonder—in essence, it asks whether human beings are free to behave as they wish or whether their actions are determined in advance. In its modern incarnation, this venerable debate is couched in terms of molecular genetics. Is our behaviour determined by our **genes**, or is every human being shaped exclusively by his or her **environment**?

For most of the middle part of this century, Americans had an almost religious faith in the second of these choices. Human beings, we believed, were infinitely perfectible, and if people behaved badly, they did so because their environment was bad. Fix the environment, we believed, and you could produce perfect human beings. Evidence to the contrary was considered misguided at best, heretical at worst.

But times have changed. Just as we have come to understand that many diseases have their origins in our DNA, so too have we come to realize that genes play an important (but by no means exclusive) role in determining our behaviour. The evidence that changed the view of the **behavioural science** community came in many forms. Extensive studies of animals, from fruit flies to rats, showed clear genetic influences on behaviours such as learning and mating. More directly, the large literature of sophisticated studies of twins clearly demonstrate the importance of genetic factors in mental disease and range of behavioural traits from the vocational interests of adolescents to general cognitive ability. Such studies generally look at either identical twins, who have identical DNA—particularly identical twins raised in different environments—or at fraternal twins, who have different DNA but very similar environments. The general conclusion, based on hundreds of studies, is that genetic factors account for anything from 30 to 70 percent of many human behavioural traits. In many cases the percentages are higher than those for genetic causation of physical ailments.

In fact, over the past few years the debate has shifted from "Do genes have an influence on behaviour?" to "Which gene or genes influence which kind of behaviour?" And here there is a great deal of ferment and debate, because the picture isn't as simple as people thought it would be.

For physical diseases (cystic fibrosis, for example) it is often possible to identify a single gene on a single **chromosome** as the cause of the disease. The original expectation was that behavioural traits would follow the same pattern—that there would be an "alcoholism gene" or an "aggressive behaviour gene." In fact, a number of highly publicized claims for these sorts of results were made, but they now are clouded in controversy.

In general, the one gene-one behaviour model seems to hold for behaviours for which we can make a clean distinction between members of the population who display it and those who do not. Profound mental retardation and autism, for example, seem to fall into this class. But with behaviours that are less clear-cut, like alcoholism and manic-depressive (bipolar) disorders, initial claims for finding a single responsible gene have been questioned. It may be that more than one gene is involved, or it may be that a complex interaction takes place between genes and the environment. In the case of alcoholism, the complexity may arise because different forms of the disease have different genetic bases. New techniques developed in studies of inbred rats give us hope that before too long we will be able to sort out genetic and environmental influences in these more complex situations.

This area has been and will continue to be enormously influenced by the rapid advances in molecular biology. With the **human genome** being mapped with greater and greater precision, it has become possible for researchers to scan all twenty-three chromosomes in every subject. Instead of looking for single genes, as in the past, researchers in the future will be casting a much wider net, sorting through huge amounts of data to find families of genes that differ, in people who exhibit a particular behaviour, from those of the general population.

As these sorts of data accumulate, we will have a better understanding of the role that **inheritance** plays in human behaviour. I don't expect, however, that we'll ever get to the point of thinking that a person's future is determined entirely by his or her genes. Instead, we'll have a more realistic view of why human beings behave the way they do, a view that will mix environment and genetics in complex and unexpected ways. And I am enough of an optimist to believe that when we are able to discard the outworn "either-or" notions of the past, we'll be well on our way to helping people whose behaviour we simply don't understand today.

KEY TERMS

- "Nature" vs. "Nurture"
- Genes
- Social environment
- Behavioural science
- Chromosome
- Human genome
- Inheritance

REVIEW

1. What convinced scientists that genes play an important role in determining human behaviour?

2. How does the identification of genes responsible for behavioural traits differ from that of genes responsible for disease?

3. What "model" or explanation does Trefil think is more likely to emerge as a better explanation of human behaviour?

Are human actions shaped mainly by the social environment or by our biological make-up?

Following Orders

If Hitler Asked You to Electrocute a Stranger, Would You? Probably.

PHILIP MEYER

In the beginning, Stanley Milgram was worried about the Nazi problem. He doesn't worry much about the Nazis anymore. He worries about you and me, and, perhaps, himself a little bit too.

PREVIEW

One of the most famous social psychological studies ever carried out was Stanley Milgram's "obedience experiments" in the 1960s. Anyone puzzled by how normal, decent human beings can commit the most heinous of atrocities against other humans should ponder on his results. Milgram suggests that there may be a human predilection to follow orders mindlessly. In this article, Philip Meyer, a professor of journalism, reviews Milgram's research and ponders the implications.

Stanley Milgram is a social psychologist, and when he began his career at Yale University in 1960 he had a plan to prove, scientifically, that Germans are different. The Germans-are-different hypothesis has been used by historians, such as William L. Shirer, to explain the systematic destruction of the Jews by the Third Reich. One madman could decide to destroy the Jews and even create a master plan for getting it done. But to implement it on the scale that Hitler did meant that thousands of other people had to go along with the scheme and help to do the work. The Shirer thesis, which Milgram set out to test, is that Germans have a basic character flaw which explains the whole thing, and this flaw is a readiness to obey authority without question, no matter what outrageous acts the authority commands.

The appealing thing about this theory is that it makes those of us who are not Germans feel better about the whole business. Obviously, you and I are not Hitler, and it seems equally obvious that we would never do Hitler's dirty work for him. But now, because of Stanley Milgram, we are compelled to wonder. Milgram developed a laboratory experiment which provided a systematic way to measure obedience. His plan was to try it out in New Haven on Americans and then go to Germany and try it out on Germans. He was strongly motivated by scientific curiosity, but there was also some moral content in his decision to pursue this line of research, which was, in turn, coloured by his own Jewish background. If he could show that Germans are more obedient than Americans, he could then vary the conditions of the experiment and try to find out just what it is that makes some people more obedient than others. With this understanding, the world might, conceivably, be just a little bit better.

But he never took his experiment to Germany. He never took it any farther than Bridgeport. The first finding, also the most unexpected and disturbing finding, was that we Americans are an obedient people: not blindly obedient, and not blissfully obedient, just obedient. "I found so much obedience," says

Milgram softly, a little sadly, "I hardly saw the need for taking the experiment to Germany."

There is something of the theatre director in Milgram, and his technique, which he learned from one of the old masters in **experimental psychology**, Solomon Asch, is to stage a play with every line rehearsed, every prop carefully selected and everybody an actor except one person. That one person is the subject of the experiment. The subject, of course, does not know he is in a play. He thinks he is in real life. The value of this technique is that the experimenter, as though he were God, can change a prop here, vary a line there, and see how the subject responds. Milgram eventually had to change a lot of the script just to get people to stop obeying. They were obeying so much, the experiment just wasn't working—it was like trying to measure oven temperature with a freezer thermometer.

The experiment worked like this: If you were an innocent subject in Milgram's melodrama, you read an ad in the newspaper or received one in the mail asking for volunteers for an educational experiment. The job would take about an hour and pay $4.50. So you make an appointment and go to an old Romanesque stone structure on High Street with the imposing name of The Yale Interaction Laboratory. It looks something like a broadcasting studio. Inside, you meet a young, crew-cut man in a laboratory coat who says he is Jack Williams, the experimenter. There is another citizen, fiftyish, with an Irish face, an accountant, a little overweight, and very mild and harmless-looking. This other citizen seems nervous and plays with his hat while the two of you sit in chairs side by side and are told that the $4.50 checks are yours no matter what happens. Then you listen to Jack Williams explain the experiment.

It is about learning, says Jack Williams in a quiet, knowledgeable way. Science does not know much about the conditions under which people learn and this experiment is to find out about negative reinforcement. **Negative reinforcement** is getting punished when you do something wrong, as opposed to positive reinforcement, which is getting rewarded when you do something right. The negative reinforcement in this case is electric shock. You notice a book on the table, titled *The Teaching-Learning Process*, and you assume that this has something to do with the experiment.

Then Jack Williams takes two pieces of paper, puts them in a hat, and shakes them up. One piece of paper is supposed to say, "Teacher" and the other, "Learner." Draw one and you will see which you will be. The mild-looking accountant draws one, holds it close to his vest like a poker player, looks at it, and says, "Learner." You look at yours. It says, "Teacher." You do not know that the drawing is rigged, and both slips say "Teacher." The experimenter beckons to the mild-mannered "learner."

"Want to step right in here and have a seat, please?" he says. "You can leave your coat on the back of that chair … roll up your right sleeve, please. Now what I want to do is strap down your arms to avoid excessive movement on your part during the experiment. This electrode is connected to the shock generator in the next room.

> It is ironic that virtues of loyalty, discipline, and self-sacrifice that we value so highly in the individual are the very properties that create destructive organizational engines of war and bind men to malevolent systems of authority.
>
> Stanley Milgram, social psychologist

Social psychologist Stanley Milgram asked why people follow orders unthinkingly.

"And this electrode paste," he says, squeezing some stuff out of a plastic bottle and putting it on the man's arm, "is to provide a good contact and to avoid a blister or burn. Are there any questions now before we go into the next room?" You don't have any, but the strapped-in "learner" does.

"I do think I should say this," says the learner. "About two years ago, I was at the veterans' hospital … they detected a heart condition. Nothing serious, but as long as I'm having these shocks, how strong are they—how dangerous are they?" Williams, the experimenter, shakes his head casually. "Oh, no," he says, "Although they may be painful, they're not dangerous. Anything else?"

Nothing else. And so you play the game. The game is for you to read a series of word pairs: for example, blue-girl, nice-day, fat-neck. When you finish the list, you read just the first word in each pair and then a multiple-choice list of four other words, including the second word of the pair. The learner, from his remote, strapped-in position, pushes one of four switches to indicate which of the four answers he thinks is the right one. If he gets it right, nothing happens and you go on to the next one. If he gets it wrong, you push a switch that buzzes and gives him an electric shock. And then you go to the next word. You start with 15 volts and increase the number of volts by 15 for each wrong answer. The control board goes from 15 volts on the one end to 450 volts on the other. So that you know what you are doing, you get a test shock yourself, at 45 volts. It hurts. To further keep you aware of what you are doing to that man in there, the board has verbal descriptions of the shock levels, ranging from "Slight Shock" at the left-hand side, through "Intense Shock" in the middle, to "Danger: Severe Shock" towards the far right. Finally, at the very end, under 435- and 450-volt switches, there are three ambiguous X's. If, at any point, you hesitate, Mr. Williams calmly tells you to go on. If you still hesitate, he tells you again.

Except for some terrifying details, which will be explained in a moment, this is the experiment. The object is to find the shock level at which you disobey the experimenter and refuse to pull the switch.

When Stanley Milgram first wrote this script, he took it to fourteen Yale psychology majors and asked them what they thought would happen. He put it this way: Out of one hundred persons in the teacher's predicament, how would their break-off points be distributed along the 15-to-450-volt scale? They thought a few would break off very early, most would quit someplace in the middle and a few would go all the way to the end. The highest estimate of the number out of one hundred who would go all the way to the end was three. Milgram then informally polled some of his fellow scholars in the psychology department. They agreed that very few would go to the end. Milgram thought so too.

"I'll tell you quite frankly," he says, "before I began this experiment, before any shock generator was built, I thought that most people would break off at 'Strong Shock' or 'Very Strong Shock.' You would get only a very, very small proportion of people going out to the end of the shock generator and they would constitute a pathological fringe."

In his pilot experiments, Milgram used Yale students as subjects. Each of them pushed the shock switches, one by one, all the way to the end of the board. So he rewrote the script to include some protests from the learner. At first, they were mild, gentlemanly, Yalie protests, but, "it didn't seem to have as much effect as I thought it would or should," Milgram recalls. "So we had more violent protestation on the part of the person getting the shock. All of the time, of course, what we were trying to do was not to create a macabre situation, but simply to generate disobedience. And that was one of the first findings. This was not only a technical deficiency of the experiment, that we didn't get disobedience. It really was the first finding, that obedience would be much greater than we had assumed it would be and that disobedience would be much more difficult than we had assumed."

As it turned out, the situation did become rather macabre. The only meaningful way to generate disobedience was to have the victim protest with great anguish, noise, and vehemence. The protests were tape-recorded so that all the teachers ordinarily would hear the same sounds, and they started with a grunt at 75 volts, proceeded through a "Hey, that really hurts," at 125 volts, got desperate with, "I can't stand the pain, don't do that," at 180 volts, reached complaints of heart trouble at 195 volts, an agonized scream at 285 volts, a refusal to answer at 315 volts, and only heart-rending, ominous silence after that. Still, 65 percent of the subjects, twenty- to fifty-year-old American males, obediently kept pushing those levers in the belief that they were shocking the mild-mannered learner, whose name was Mr. Wallace, and who was chosen for the role because of his innocent appearance, all the way up to 450 volts.

Milgram was now getting enough disobedience so that he had something he could measure. The next step was to vary the circumstances to see what would encourage or discourage obedience. There seemed very little left in the way of discouragement. The victim was already screaming at the top of his lungs and feigning a heart attack. So whatever new impediment to obedience reached the brain of the subject had to travel by some route other than the ear. Milgram thought of one.

He put the learner in the same room with the teacher. He stopped strapping the learner's hand down. He rewrote the script so that at 150 volts the learner took his hand off the shock plate and declared that he wanted out of the experiment. He rewrote the script some more so that the experimenter then told the teacher to grasp the learner's hand and physically force it down on the plate to give Mr. Wallace his unwanted electric shock.

"I had the feeling that very few people would go on at that point, if any," Milgram says. "I thought that would be the limit of obedience that you would find in the laboratory."

It wasn't. Although seven years have now gone by, Milgram still remembers the first person to walk into the laboratory in the newly rewritten script. He was a short man, "so small," says Milgram, "that when he sat on the chair in front of the shock generator, his feet didn't reach the floor. When the experimenter told him to push the victim's hand down and give the shock, he turned to the experimenter, and he turned to the victim, his elbow went up, he fell

The doctrine of blind obedience and unqualified submission to any human power, whether civil or ecclesiastical, is the doctrine of despotism, and ought to have no place among Republicans and Christians.

Angelina Grimké, U.S. abolitionist

Adolph Hitler. "Following orders" was an unsuccessful defence at the Nuremberg war crimes trials.

REVIEW

1. What is the Shirer thesis, and what is its appeal?

2. How are Milgram's actions in conducting his experiment similar to those attributed to the Third Reich?

3. How do the results of Milgram's experiment impact on your opinion of the Germans who executed atrocities? What do these results tell us about ourselves?

down on the hand of the victim, his feet kind of tugged to the side, and he said, 'Like this, boss?' ZZUMPH!"

The experiment was played out to its bitter end. Milgram tried it with forty different subjects. And 30 percent of them obeyed the experimenter and kept on obeying.

"The protests of the victim were strong and vehement, he was screaming his guts out, he refused to participate, and you had to physically struggle with him in order to get his hand down on the shock generator," Milgram remembers. But twelve out of forty did it.

Stanley Milgram believes that in the laboratory situation, he would not have shocked Mr. Wallace. His professional critics reply that in his real-life situation he has done the equivalent. He has placed innocent and naïve subjects under great emotional strain and pressure in selfish obedience to his quest for knowledge. When you raise this issue with Milgram, he has an answer ready. There is, he explained patiently, a critical difference between his naïve subjects and the man in the electric chair. The man in the electric chair (in the mind of the naïve subject) is helpless, strapped in. But the naïve subject is free to go at any time.

Immediately after he offers this distinction, Milgram anticipates the objection. "It's quite true," he says, "that this is almost a philosophic position, because we have learned that some people are psychologically incapable of disengaging themselves. But that doesn't relieve them of the **moral responsibility**."

The parallel is exquisite. "The tension problem was unexpected," says Milgram in his defense. But he went on anyway. The naïve subjects didn't expect the screaming protests from the strapped-in learner. But they went on.

"I had to make a judgement," says Milgram. "I had to ask myself, was this harming the person or not? My judgement is that it was not. Even in the extreme cases, I wouldn't say that permanent damage results."

Sound familiar? "The shocks may be painful," the experimenter says, "but they're not dangerous."

Kurt Vonnegut put one paragraph in the preface to *Mother Night*, in 1966, which pretty much says it for the people with their fingers on the shock-generator switches, for you and me, and maybe even for Milgram. "If I'd been born in Germany," Vonnegut said, "I suppose I would have been a Nazi, bopping Jews and gypsies and Poles around, leaving boots sticking out of snowbanks, warming myself with my sweetly virtuous insides. So it goes."

Just so. One thing that happened to Milgram back in New Haven during the days of the experiment was that he kept running into people he'd watched from behind the one-way glass. It gave him a funny feeling, seeing those people going about their everyday business in New Haven and knowing what they would do to Mr. Wallace if ordered to. Now that his **research results** are in and you've thought about it, you can get this funny feeling too. You don't need one-way glass. A glance in your own mirror may serve just as well.

TALKING CURES

FREUD IN BRIEFS

BRIAN BURNIE

The foundation of psychoanalytic theory was laid by Austrian physician and neurologist Sigmund Freud (1856-1939). The commonplace adage "a Freudian slip" (e.g., "Freud in Briefs," above) derives from the extraordinary emphasis Freud gave in his theory to the importance of repressed sexual fantasies in shaping human behaviour. Nowadays, the so-called "talk therapies" (psychoanalysis) are under attack from less costly "short therapies" involving behaviour modification and even drugs.

The central tenet of Freudian **psychoanalysis** is the idea that instinctual drives originating in childhood influence human behaviour. According to Freud, during the course of a person's development unacceptable sexual and aggressive drives are forced out of consciousness. These repressed urges, constantly striving for release, are sometimes expressed as neurotic symptoms.

Freud believed that such symptoms could be eliminated by bringing these repressed fantasies and emotions into consciousness. **Free association** (whereby patients report whatever thoughts come to their minds about dreams, fantasies and memories) and **transference** (the patients' emotional response to therapists) are the central features of Freudian psychoanalysis. The main concepts of Freudian theory are described below.

LEVELS OF AWARENESS

Freud argued that there are three **levels of awareness**:

- **Conscious**: those things that we are aware of currently, for example, the words on this page, your name and so on.

- **Preconscious**: those things that we are not currently aware of but which we can easily bring to mind, for example, your telephone number, your Grade 2 teacher's name (or, your current teacher's name) and so on.

- **Unconscious**: underneath the conscious and preconscious, are thoughts, memories and traumatic events of which we are unaware, but which exert powerful forces on our personality and behaviour.

Freud further developed a tripartite division of the mind in which he held that the different functions of the mind operated at different levels.

PREVIEW

Psychoanalysis is the name generally given to the investigation of unconscious mental processes. Psychotherapy is the name given to the treatment of mental illness using techniques that rely heavily on verbal and emotional communication. Because communication is the primary means of healing, the relationship between the therapist and the patient is more important than in other forms of medical treatment. Although never accorded full recognition during his lifetime (and dismissed by many, especially some feminist groups), Sigmund Freud is generally acknowledged as the founder of psychoanalysis and one of the great creative minds of modern times.

These he identified as the **id**, **ego** and **superego**. The interaction of these three "systems" constitute the building blocks of Freudian theory.

- **Id:** when a baby is born, she or he wants only to eat, drink, urinate, be warm and be held. As a result of these desires, the baby craves immediate gratification; the baby is ruled by what Freud called the "pleasure principle," which translates into "Give it to me NOW!"

- **Ego:** as the baby learns that immediate gratification is usually impossible, the ego begins to form; Freud saw that the ego was ruled by what he called the "reality principle." The ego acts as a go-between in the id's relations with reality, often suppressing the id's urges until an appropriate situation arises.

- **Superego:** while the ego may temporarily repress certain urges of the id in fear of punishment, the superego uses guilt and self-reproach as a means of enforcing rules. (See the Oedipal stage to understand the development of the superego.)

DEFENCE MECHANISMS

The cornerstone of modern psychoanalytic theory and treatment is the concept of **anxiety** from which develop appropriate **defence mechanisms**. In the never-ending battle between the id, ego and superego, the mind must constantly repress anxiety-causing impulses or memories. According to Freud, defence mechanisms help us to maintain our stability and sanity. These mechanisms are:

- **Repression**: Freud saw this as the most important defence mechanism. When we have experienced painful or traumatic events in our life, we tend to forget (repress) these events even though they still have impact on our behaviour. For example, a young woman, who may have been accosted by a male relative in her youth, represses this memory and can't understand why she can't have a successful relationship with a man.

- **Projection**: unacceptable urges are attributed to others. A young man who has been taught that anger is wrong projects his anger onto a friend and says, "Why are you angry with me?"

- **Reaction Formation**: to avoid anxiety-causing impulses, one may do or say the opposite of what one really wants to do. For example, a girl who is jealous of her sister's popularity at school (and almost hates her for it) continually compliments her on her accomplishments.

- **Displacement**: when a person feels angry at someone whom is perceived to be more powerful, he or she may take this anger out on someone perceived to be less powerful. For example, a man is yelled at by his boss at work, and instead of responding in kind, he comes home and yells at his wife.

- **Rationalization**: we make up reasons for what may be seen as unacceptable behaviour. For example, a student who has spent the night before a test in a bar fails the test and says, "Boy, is he a rotten teacher!"

FREUD'S PSYCHOSEXUAL STAGES OF PERSONALITY DEVELOPMENT

Freud also elaborated a theory of personality development. His theory asserted that the effects of sexual pleasure (entering on the erogenous parts of the body–the mouth, anus and genitals) created conflicts that must be resolved before one moves on to a subsequent developmental stage. He elaborated the concept of sexual energy, which he called "libido." Freud's stages of personality development were:

- **The Oral Stage** (birth to 1-1/2 years): The oral stage begins at birth when the mouth is the focus of the libido; the child is centred on the pleasures derived from sucking and being fed. Freud saw that different characters develop as a result of how this stage is handled by caregivers. The oral character who is frustrated at this stage by very inconsistent feeding is characterized by pessimism, suspicion, envy and sarcasm. The overindulged oral character, one who is excessively satisfied, may be gullible, optimistic and full of admiration for others (some suggest that smoking and alcoholism may have their roots here).

- **The Anal Stage** (1-1/2 to 2-(½) years): As the child enters the toilet training years, she or he becomes obsessed with the erogenous zone of the anus and with the retention and expulsion of feces. It is in this stage that children develop the concept of shame. The anal character develops as a result of the methods used to toilet train, and the child's reactions to this training. Children react to toilet training in two ways: she or he either puts up a fight or gives in to parental demands. If parents are too lenient and the child derives pleasure and success from the expulsion of feces, the child takes on elements of the anal expulsive character, who, later in life, may develop into a disorganized, messy, careless, reckless and defiant character. On the other hand, the child may opt to retain feces, thereby upsetting the parents who just want the job to be done. If this tactic is successful and the child is overindulged, the child will develop into an anal retentive character who will eventually be neat, orderly, selfish and obstinate. It is at this stage that the child develops its attitude towards authority.

- **The Phallic (Oedipal/Electra) Stage** (2-1/2 to 6 or 7 years): Freud sees this as the stage that creates the most conflict in children, as the child becomes interested in the genital region of his or her body. In this stage, the boy feels a natural love for his mother, becomes jealous

Sigmund Freud believed that human behaviour is often rooted in unconscious motives.

of the father's relationship with her and fantasizes about killing the father so he can have the mother to himself. He notices that mother doesn't have a penis and thinks father might cut his off (castration anxiety/complex), and he represses his desire for mother and starts trying to become like father. Girls, noticing that they don't have a penis, blame the mother and develop what Freud called penis envy; when she realizes that she never will have a penis, she then attempts to become like mother. It is in this stage that the child acquires the concept of guilt and both boys and girls prepare to accept the sex roles dictated by society. (Freud thought that the faulty resolution of the Oedipal conflict might be one explanation for homosexuality.)

- **The Latency Stage** (7 to 11 or 12 years): In the latency stage, sexual energy becomes dormant and children go about their job of becoming sex-role-appropriate little human beings; boys play with boys, girls with girls, and they practice those roles that will help them to be successful adults.

- **The Genital Stage**: In the genital stage, sexual energy once again returns to the genital area and (most) children's interest turns to heterosexual relationships. The child who has successfully resolved conflicts from earlier stages will now be able to develop normal relationships with the opposite sex.

FREUD'S HEIRS

While Freud is acknowledged as the founder of psychoanalysis, some of his followers developed variations on his theories and went on to found entire schools of psychoanalytic thought.

Immediate descendants. The two immediate descendants of Freud were Carl Jung and Alfred Adler. Both students broke with Freud and established their own schools of thought. Carl Gustav Jung, a Swiss psychiatrist, believed that Freud overemphasized sexual instincts as a source of behaviour. Jung believed that nonsexual potentials should be recognized, and Jungian therapists emphasize their patients' own inner resources for growth and for dealing with conflict. Alfred Adler, an Austrian psychologist and former student of Freud, also minimized the importance of sexual drives in human behaviour. He believed that the smallness and helplessness of children led to feelings of inferiority. A key concept for Adler was that of social interest (empathy and identification with other people) and that psychological disorders result from an underdeveloped social interest. Adler emphasized the importance of re-educating patients, convincing them of their errors and encouraging them to develop more social interest.

The Neo-Freudians. Erich Fromm, Karen Horney and Erik Erikson, three so-called neo-Freudians, immigrated from Germany to the U.S. in the 1930s. All three elaborated theories of neuroses that emphasized the role of social and cultural influences in the formation of personality.

Humanistic psychotherapy. Begun as a reaction against psychoanalytic psychotherapy, humanistic therapies emphasize the human potential for goodness. Proponents include Carl Rogers, an American psychologist, who emphasized the individual's capacity for self-understanding and constructive change; and Frederick S. (Fritz) Perls, a German-born immigrant to the U.S. Perls developed *Gestalt therapy*, which was based on exercises designed to enhance the patient's awareness of his or her emotions, physical state and repressed needs.

Other forms of psychotherapy have emerged in more recent years. These include *group therapy*, *family therapy*, *child therapy* and a number of new psychotherapies—*primal therapy* (reliving early experiences with an intensity that was repressed at the time), *transactional analysis* (involving the notion that when interacting with others, a person functions as either a parent, adult or child), and *"brief" psychotherapy* (involving intervention at critical times such as the death of a loved one).

A major distinction is between those "Freudians" who base their work on **theories of neuroses** (hidden psychological conflicts of some kind or other) and those who focus on correcting behaviour that they believe is basically **learned behaviour** (and therefore unlearnable).

ENTER THE "SHORT THERAPIES"

More recently, traditional talk therapy (psychoanalysis) has come under criticism not only in terms of the validity of its central concepts but also because of the length of time psychotherapy treatment typically takes. There is pressure to move away from the costly services of traditional psychotherapy, involving many one-on-one sessions between therapist and patient, towards less expensive "behaviour therapy" and the prescribing of drugs to treat mental distress of various kinds.

In contrast to most other forms of treatment, **behaviour therapy** is not based on a theory of neurosis, but rather involves the application of research findings in experimental psychology. Behaviour therapists are usually trained as psychologists. They believe that basic learning principles—for example, those developed by Ivan Pavlov (Pavlov's "salivating dog") and B.F. Skinner (the "Skinner box")—can be used to correct troublesome behaviour. They do not look for "hidden psychological meanings" but instead concentrate on observable and measurable phenomena. Their techniques, which can be very effective, include *desensitization* (helping the patient to relax and then gradually to approach situations or objects that are feared) and *cognitive therapy* (changing beliefs and habits of thought that appear to cause distress). A powerful addition to this arsenal of new **short-term therapies** has been a crop of highly effective drugs, many of which are now household names.

The move towards behaviour therapy and the pressure on traditional psychotherapy is the subject of the following selection.

KEY TERMS

- Psychoanalysis
- Free association and transference
- Freud's "levels of awareness"
- Id, ego and superego
- Anxiety
- Defense mechanisms
- Personality development (Freudian)
- Theories of neuroses
- Learned behaviour
- Behavioural therapy
- Short-term therapies

REVIEW

1. Which of Freud's students broke away from him and developed their own separate schools of thought? How do their theories differ from Freud's?

2. On what is behaviour therapy based? What beliefs underlie this therapy?

3. Comment on why feminists might dismiss the theories of Freud.

Freud's Falling Market Share

The Unbalanced State of Our Mental Health

KRISTA FOSS

Why is psychotherapy being squeezed out? Critics say the couch is too slow, too ineffective and costs "too much money."

PREVIEW

Traditional long-term psychotherapy is being phased out by shorter and less expensive types of therapies, a trend that will soon affect mental health care policy. Canadian journalist Krista Foss examines the issues of effectiveness and mental health needs raised by the recent increase of quick, solution-based treatments, and reports on the unequal distribution of psychiatrists throughout Canada.

Gordon Warme is looking for Hamlet. The Toronto-based psychiatrist specializes in long-term depression, and he is helping a patient find the part of himself that, as with the Danish prince, is inward looking, wistful and aware of his foibles.

It won't be a short treatment. Finding Hamlet in the fractured lives on his client roster, parsing out the meaning of past experiences and the purpose of finding new ones, takes time. So Dr. Warme's patient will return next week and the next and the next, likely for more than two years, chalking up at least 200 hours of treatment and $20,000 worth of billings to the provincial government, not including the prescriptions for antidepressants.

But when the crunch on mental health resources is severe, can the **health care system** afford Dr. Warme's treatment? Many of his colleagues across Canada, and a growing number around the world, don't think so. And what's even more damning is that they question whether this traditional talk therapy even works.

Dr. Gavin Andrews, a professor of psychiatry at the University of New South Wales in Darlinghurst, Australia, is like the messiah of mental health's new order, and, as with any saviour-like figure, he is a pariah among his profession's old guard. Dr. Andrews is a researcher and practitioner of short-term, solution-based therapies, the antithesis to looking for Hamlet.

"The day of long-term **psychotherapy** is dead," he said. "It's too expensive, it doesn't work and it's associated with three times the risk of having sex with your therapist." It seems that Sigmund Freud's legacy to psychiatry, whether in the form of psychoanalysis, dynamic psychotherapy and its various hybrids, is being eclipsed by something decidedly less chatty.

Unlike Dr. Warme's preferred treatment, the new therapies don't allow patients to wallow in the muck of their own past, interpret dreams, play-act their anger against domineering mothers or grieve old wounds. Instead, these treatments, which are proliferating as fast as guppies, are staunchly here-and-now. They address the patients' problematic behaviour with step-by-step solutions laid out in breezily written manuals—as opposed to why they have the problems in the first place. And they are quick. Therapists expect to see results in 30 days (or four weeks of treatment) and most treatments don't last beyond 10 to 12 one-hour sessions.

They are being used for such things as chronic fatigue syndrome, eating disorders, panic attacks and even psychotic disorders that don't respond to medicine. Pre-eminent among the methods is cognitive behavioural therapy, which helps teach patients how to control moodiness and disturbing thoughts and actions through relaxation techniques, replacing negative thoughts with more positive ones and what's called graded exposure, gradually introducing a feared thing or anxiety-producing situation into a person's life.

A powerful ally to the new shorter therapies have been the crop of highly effective drugs developed in the past 15 years for mental health problems, including Paxil, a powerful antidepressant, and Clozapine, one of the newest tranquillizing drugs. The evidence is piling up that short therapies work, often with the suggestion that they work better than talk therapy. "The detractors say you can't subject long-term therapy to the same test. But you better design a test that does measure efficiency," said Dr. Russell Joffe, dean of the faculty of health sciences at McMaster University in Hamilton and an eminent authority on depression.

But advocates of long-term talk therapy are not going gently into the good night of obscurity; in fact, they are politely raging. "Just use common sense," said Dr. Norman Doidge, head of the University of Toronto's long-term psychotherapy program. "You know how difficult it is to quit smoking—and that's just a single behaviour—so imagine how complex and difficult it is to change aspects of character that have been 30 years in the making.... Some short therapies last as long as it takes to watch two Super Bowl games."

Dr. Warme is less subtle. He calls the swooning over short-term therapies dogmatic and cultish, a kind of cosmetic psychiatry that depends on the strength of its drugs. But even he acknowledges that there is a big problem with psychiatric resources and that long-term talk therapy might be a luxury the system can no longer afford.

"It is a grotesque distortion of help to allow people to see someone for 600 to 800 hours at a $100 a crack," he said. "It's too much money. Psychoanalysts are very aware of their own asses right now—they're afraid they'll get kicked out of OHIP [the Ontario Health Insurance Plan]."

Aye, there's the rub. The squeeze on psychiatric services is getting uncomfortable. Across Canada, psychiatric hospitals and wards have been closed or amalgamated as the three Rs of health care—re-engineering, restructuring and restraint—have hit each province in successive waves.

Doing more with less has simply meant that fewer psychiatrists with less support staff, such as mental health nurses, have been put in charge of more

Nothing defines the quality of life in a community more clearly than people who regard themselves, or whom the consensus chooses to regard, as mentally unwell.

Renata Adler, U.S. author

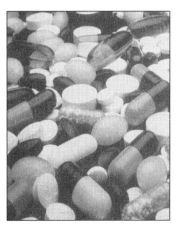

Quick cures? Treatments involving less costly drugs is undermining traditional "talk therapies."

patients. As a result of the pressures on psychiatry, a lot of mental illness goes untreated. According to the largest and most comprehensive study available on the prevalence of mental disorders, the U.S. Epidemiological Catchment Area Study of 1993, about 30 percent of the population meets the criteria for a mental disorder in a year, but only 4 percent ever gets treatment.

In the context of unmet need, a therapy that takes less time and can reach more people makes sense. Certainly, some Canadian psychiatrists think so. "I have people with anorexia nervosa who weigh 60 pounds and they are on waiting lists for treatment. Anything that can speed up the time they get treatment and treat them effectively is better for them," said Dr. Blake Woodside, a psychiatrist and director of the Toronto Hospital's In-patient Eating Disorders Clinic. "There aren't enough of me to go around."

So Dr. Woodside uses a lot of short therapies: He deploys **structured problem solving** to help couples in marriage counselling deal with a specific issue such as communication. He sends his patients with bulimia to six sessions of **psycho-education** in which the patients learn to recognize the triggers of their disorder (results show they stay symptom-free for a year afterward) and he uses **cognitive behavioural therapy** to help severe anorexics kick their laxative habit.

"My belief is that, while everybody is conscious of resources, what drives the system is good outcomes," Dr. Woodside said. So far, the short therapies don't fall short by that yardstick. New South Wales University's Dr. Andrews investigated how psychiatric therapies would fare if they had to go through the same rigorous screening as a new drug would to get by regulatory agencies. He found that half a dozen of the cognitive behavioural therapy programs in use met the criteria, which includes demonstrating safety, having results that are better than a placebo effect and doing at least four clinical trials showing the same result in addition to proof of harmlessness. "There was insufficient evidence for long-term psychotherapy," Dr. Andrews said.

Dr. Doidge said one reason long-term therapy doesn't have the same critical mass of studies is that it is unethical to withhold treatment to a control group of people for a long time. Additionally, he noted that one major study that followed patients with depression who had been treated with short-term therapies found that the majority of those in the sample relapsed by 18 months. Even so, the ears of the policy analysts are pricking up. The B.C. Health Ministry is preparing to launch a pilot project to train older general practitioners, who want to work part time, to deliver cognitive behavioural therapy to patients at community health services.

In Australia, Dr. Andrews is also training family doctors to deliver shorter therapies because that is where most people first report a mental health problem—and often where they stop pursuing help.

For some psychiatrists, it's the decline and fall of the **Freudian empire** and further evidence of U.S.-style health care, which has largely de-insured coverage of any long-term mental health treatment, creeping quietly into Canada. But for Dr. Warme, the worse insult is to his clients. He feels that short-term behavioural therapies reduce the complexity of the human psyche to a machine that only needs tweaking with little "mind control" exercises.

Dr. Andrews is unapologetic. "Oh, the conceit of the middle class," he said. " 'Oh, I am so special only five years of analysis will help me.'… We just want people to get better."

YOUR MENTAL HEALTH—IT MATTERS WHERE YOU LIVE

When it comes to finding a psychiatrist in Canada, success can be boiled down to the old real-estate maxim: location, location, location. In 1988, the Royal College of Physicians and Surgeons of Canada recommended that the national standard should be one psychiatrist available to serve every 8,400 people. Ten years later, many urban areas struggle to achieve that standard, and the shortage of psychiatrists is increasingly worse for those who live outside cities.

The Ontario Medical Association says that in the OMA district of Toronto and the surrounding regions, there is one psychiatrist for every 5,428 people, but in the northeastern area of the province there is one psychiatrist for every 20,132 people. Ditto for the rest of Canada. While the Vancouver-Richmond area is knee-deep in psychiatrists—one for every 1,730 people—the Cariboo region of the province has one for every 100,000 people.

"The absolute insanity of letting the market determine the distribution of high-cost specialists is best exemplified in the distribution of B.C.'s psychiatrists," said Dr. Rick Hudson, a health-policy analyst with the province's Health Ministry.

One doesn't have to travel to remote parts of Canadian provinces to find shortages, however. Burnaby, just outside of Vancouver, has one psychiatrist for every 13,700 people. Meanwhile in Newfoundland, where one disgruntled medical association official said there is a shortage of everything, the province's second-largest city of Corner Brook (population 23,000) doesn't have a single psychiatrist with a permanent practice. In the Welland-St. Catharines area, just an hour's drive from Toronto, there are nine psychiatrists for a population of 450,000.

Dr. Thoppil Abraham, chief of psychiatry at Welland Country General Hospital in Welland, is one of those overburdened nine. He and a colleague are responsible for addressing the mental health needs of 100,000 people in their hospital's catchment area. That means that Dr. Abraham is on call every other day of the week. It also means that only the sickest people get treated—and not very well at that.

"Ideally, we would see people who are discharged about once a week," Dr. Abraham said. "But now we see them only about once every two months. We're not providing a quality service."

KEY TERMS

- Health care system
- Psychotherapy
- Behavioural therapy
- Short-term therapies
- Long-term therapies
- Structured problem solving
- Psycho-education
- Cognitive behavioural therapy
- Freudian empire

REVIEW

1. How does the Canadian trend towards short-term therapies mirror "U.S.-style" health care?

2. What are the merits of short-term therapies? Comment on Dr. Warme's assertion that "short-term behavioural therapies reduce the complexity of the human psyche to a machine."

3. A major study of patients of depression who had been treated with short-term therapies revealed that the majority had relapsed in 18 months. Does this finding have serious implications for the long-term status of our mental health?

A Nation without Memory?

Who Killed Canadian History?

MARK STAROWICZ

Deserted by their own broadcast system, bombarded by American television, Canadians are so cut off from each other and the country's past that they seem to have suffered a catastrophic stroke.

PREVIEW

The failure of the Canadian "body politic" to provide a Canadian counterpart to American telecasts and the aversion of teachers to the volatile political issues of Canadian history have created a void in our knowledge of ourselves and each other. In this article, historian and journalist Mark Starowicz shares his enthusiasm for the past in a television documentary, offering a vital and heretofore untold version of our history.

There is a profound crisis in the teaching of history in Canada. We all know the desolate statistics and surveys. But it goes much further: There is a crisis in the transmission of our society's memory. In fact, there is no real memory. Canadian society has had a stroke that has virtually eliminated long-term memory, leaving us with flickering short-term memory, our emotions buffeted by a sound bite, bewildered by a film clip, stampeded by a phone-in show or a pundit's column.

We in Canada have not only impaired the links to the past, we have impaired and severed the arteries that connect us in the present.

We obviously live within our **linguistic cultures**, but also within hundreds of particularities of regions, ages, beliefs or tastes—that is the nature of any human population. But unlike most European countries and the United States, Canada has few highways linking those particularities. The communication arteries of discourse and exchange are decaying, like roads that haven't been maintained for 20 years. The dots don't connect in this puzzle.

Ten years ago, when I went around the country speaking to a lot of high school assemblies about television, I developed a little interlude in each presentation.

I'd say: Have you ever realized that, on English television, French Canadians exist only in three kinds of programs: newscasts, public affairs shows and hockey games?

Then I'd pull out a stopwatch and say: Tell me the last French Canadian you saw on English television, public or private, network or local—a character in a drama or a sitcom, a teenager, a child, an adult, anyone—outside of a newscast, public affairs show or hockey game. At some of the best high schools in English Canada, with the brightest students of all races, I never got an answer in less than 90 seconds, and I usually logged three to four minutes of aching silence in the room.

In two schools in Montreal, I got the same result when I asked students to name an Anglo-Canadian they'd seen on TV outside of an information or sports program. Anyone they identified turned out to be American.

I suggested to each group that we had constructed in Canada a **cultural apartheid** in the very middle of the satellite and digital age.

A teenager in Calgary will almost certainly never see a teenager in Trois Rivières in the televisual or cinematic universe. There will be no communality of experience. She'll see *Dawson's Creek* or *Clueless*, and ascertain that her preoccupations are shared by others–but those "others" are never in her country. They are forged in the American experience. As Peter Herrndorf, one of the finest minds in Canadian television, warns, English Canadians are becoming "citizens of Video-America."

A lot of academics, historians in particular, don't like television and tend to dismiss it. This is a mistake. The average Canadian watches TV for more than three hours a day, or more than 21 hours a week. In an average lifespan, that means nine years in front of a TV set.

A Canadian child, by the age of 12, will have spent more of her life in front of a television set than in a Canadian school. In English Canada, it's worse. Since most of English-Canadian television is still American, this 12-year-old will have logged more hours watching American programs than she will have spent in a Canadian school.

Maybe they shouldn't watch that much TV. But they do. This is the marketplace of fiction, discourse and entertainment. To dismiss it is to dismiss our own people. I think television is the most powerful stage in human history, and anyone who holds precious any idea, cause or sensibility has the moral obligation to bring those ideas to where the people are.

The problem is not American television. It's the relative absence of Canadian equivalents. This is not a problem of **cultural invasion**. This is a problem of the failure of the Canadian **body politic** to give us choices....

The answer to the question "Why isn't history getting through?" is: Because hardly anything else is getting through, except news. People can't name the capital of New Brunswick, the surveys repeat. One of the reasons is that they hardly see New Brunswick in their media unless a snowstorm hits it.

I am suggesting that, as keepers of our constituent pasts and current identities, the historical community should actively participate in the shaping of the communications policies this country will have to develop in the years ahead. The arena goes beyond the classroom, to the regulatory authorities and the political committee rooms....

The antidote to an ever fragmenting information spectrum is context and history, we believed. We have to situate our present in the time spectrum. We are the children of our pasts. The country, whatever becomes of it, is a constant living negotiation among the people in the northern half of this continent. The answer to the frustrated question "When are we finally going to settle this mess?" is never. That's the point.

But what experience and history teach is this—that peoples and governments have never learned anything from history, or acted on principles deduced from it.

Georg Hegel, German philosopher

Is the RCMP's deal with Disney to market the RCMP name worldwide a wise precedent?

And it's a point you only get if you feel the past breathe, and realize that we are merely the expression of our own time–that ours is not the only time we have known, or will know. We are boats on a large ocean. So, in an effort to bring this past to a modern audience, we decided to produce a 30-hour documentary history of Canada, co-produced by **CBC and Radio Canada**. It will appear on both networks starting in 2000....

So whose history *are* we telling? There are at least two perfectly valid and distinct views of **Canadian history**: English and French. I would add a third, the aboriginal view, and a fourth, the 20th century immigrant view, and one can go on with the perspective of women, the perspective of labour and class. There are those who believe it is wrong to attempt to create a French-English mixed linguistic team, with historians from all those perspectives, because we will drown the particularity of each....

That's why we're paralyzed about teaching or portraying Canadian history. Not because it's boring: Because it's alive! Because it's alive, we'd better not go into those dark woods. Everything is still in play.

But that's the very reason to do it. It has been in play for 400 years, for 20,000 years. It will always be in play. The same themes and forces recur. Wilfully refusing to see the evolution of those themes and forces in their **temporal context** is paralysis.

There is no contradiction in embracing the particular perspectives of people in their times and showing that complex tapestry to everyone. They shared their time. They interacted with each other. In the siege of Quebec in 1759, Marie de la Visitation lived it, Abbé Recher lived it, Lieutenant John Knox lived it–their diaries bring each day to life. They shared a historical frame, as invaders and invaded, and it is well within the capacities of our craft to bring those times and perspectives alive, with all their contradictions. Cabot or Cartier: Which story will you tell? we're often asked, as if you had to choose one and omit the other.

The ultimate resolution to the question "Can you teach the same history in Toronto and Montreal?" seems to be: Why don't we teach as little history as possible? After all, a poor high school history teacher might bump into something controversial and alive.

I think I know more history than the average Canadian. I have a BA in history, and I have spent 35 years covering evolving history.

I thought I knew it pretty well. Then I began to read the books, the monographs, the diaries, the unpublished works, the works long out of print, and I had to admit, with some shame, that I hadn't grasped or felt 99 percent of the past's life and drama. I have never seen a more vibrant, living, extraordinary thing in all my years as a journalist: Shakespearean human drama, collisions of empire, land, legacy and identity, explorations that dwarf any other on the planet, survival of individuals and communities pitted against a fearful and beautiful geography. Every theme was there. And everything was alive and meaningful today.

I didn't know that a quarter of the British navy came up the St. Lawrence River more than 200 years ago in a line stretching 60 miles. I never knew

Insensitive to Canadian history? A statue of Edward, King of England, in downtown Montreal.

that almost a hundred French ships and rafts loaded with mountains of powder and combustibles were released in a necklace of fireships a mile wide to attack the British fleet. I hadn't read Catharine Parr Traill's diary of the cholera in Montreal, I hadn't heard of Hannah Ingraham, an 11-year-old girl who kept a diary of the Loyalists' flight.

All of us on the project feel the thrill of piecing together the fragments of lives, and seeing their words, their fears and hopes take shape before us. We run into each other's offices and say: I didn't know this! Nobody in the public knows this. We're going to succeed on the sheer strength of people saying: I can't believe that, did that happen here? Is that our history?

Canada: A Peoples' History is going to evoke and illustrate Canadian history by using the personal testimony of those who lived it. We will be informed by the present, but move into the frame of the past. We shall see the past unfold the way people see their world—their history—unfold today, with all its passions and uncertainties.

We will not attempt to act as a Supreme Court on history. Our task is to evoke and bring to life the full complexity of the First World War conscription crisis, not to pronounce on it. We will consult profoundly with all historians in the particular field, to help us understand the time and the issues, but we will not have modern-day observers passing judgement. We will use the material of the past.

This is a documentary history, and a narrative history. We are journalists and documentary filmmakers whose craft is to illustrate and evoke according to established rules of testimony and criteria of fact.

We're not naive. All documentary involves selection and exclusion, and thereby judgement and unconscious cultural bias. That's why we call it a history, not *the* history.

Somewhere in our audience there will be 14- or 15-year-olds who will watch this series again in 15 or 20 years, smile at the peculiar obsessions of the generation that made it, see it as a contribution, but also see its flaws. Then, informed by their own needs, and by the historical work of the future, they will determine this history project must be done again. And they will do the next one. That's as it should be.

KEY TERMS

- Linguistic cultures
- Cultural apartheid
- Cultural invasion
- Body politic
- CBC and Radio Canada
- Canadian history, views of
- Temporal context
- Personal testimony
- Documentary history

REVIEW

1. What role does Starowicz believe the historical community should play in addressing the crisis in "our society's memory"?

2. What led Starowicz to conclude that he had not grasped the "life and drama" of the past, despite his many years of studying history?

3. "Canada: A People's History" is a documentary history. How will the history revealed in this format differ from the one put forth by historians?

The Problem That Has No Name

Women Ask, "Is This All?"

BETTY FRIEDAN

The feminist movement in North America began with the realization by women that there had to be more to life than looking after husband and home.

PREVIEW

Betty Friedan (1921-) has been the senior spokesperson for women's rights in the United States over the past quarter of a century. Her book **The Feminine Mystique** (1963), from which this selection was taken, was responsible for starting a nationwide feminist movement. She was a founder and the first president (1966-70) of the National Organization for Women (NOW).

The problem lay buried, unspoken, for many years in the minds of American women. It was a strange stirring, a sense of dissatisfaction, a yearning that women suffered in the middle of the twentieth century in the United States. Each suburban wife struggled with it alone. As she made the beds, shopped for groceries, matched slipcover material, ate peanut butter sandwiches with her children, chauffeured Cub Scouts and Brownies, lay beside her husband at night–she was afraid to ask even of herself the silent question–"Is this all?"

For over fifteen years there was no word of this yearning in the millions of words written about women, for women, in all the columns, books and articles by experts telling women their role was to seek fulfilment as wives and mothers. Over and over women heard in voices of tradition and of Freudian sophistication that they could desire no greater destiny than to glory in their own femininity. Experts told them how to catch a man and keep him, how to breastfeed children and handle their toilet training, how to cope with sibling rivalry and adolescent rebellion; how to buy a dishwasher, bake bread, cook gourmet snails, and build a swimming pool with their own hands; how to dress, look, and act more feminine and make marriage more exciting; how to keep their husbands from dying young and their sons from growing into delinquents. They were taught to pity the neurotic, unfeminine, unhappy women who wanted to be poets or physicists or presidents. They learned that **truly feminine women** do not want careers, higher education, political rights–the independence and the opportunities that the old-fashioned **feminists** fought for. Some women, in their forties and fifties, still remembered painfully giving up those dreams, but most of the younger women no longer even thought about them. A thousand expert voices applauded their femininity, their adjustment, their new maturity. All they had to do was devote their lives from earliest girlhood to finding a husband and bearing children....

In the fifteen years after World War II, this **mystique of feminine fulfilment** became the cherished and self-perpetuating core of contemporary American culture. Millions of women lived their lives in the image of those pretty pictures of the American suburban housewife, kissing their husbands goodbye in front of the picture window, depositing their stationwagonsfull of children at school, and smiling as they ran the new electric waxer over the spotless kitchen floor. They baked their own bread, sewed their own and their children's clothes, kept their new washing machines and dryers running all day. They changed the sheets on the beds twice a week instead of once, took the rug-hooking class in adult education, and pitied their poor frustrated mothers, who had dreamed of having a career. Their only dream was to be perfect wives and mothers; their highest ambition to have five children and a beautiful house, their only fight to get and keep their husbands. They had no thought for the unfeminine problems of the world outside the home; they wanted the men to make the major decisions. They gloried in their role as women, and wrote proudly on the census blank: **"Occupation: housewife...."**

If a woman had a problem in the 1950s and 1960s, she knew that something must be wrong with her marriage, or with herself. Other women were satisfied with their lives, she thought. What kind of a woman was she if she did not feel this mysterious fulfilment waxing the kitchen floor? She was so ashamed to admit her dissatisfaction that she never knew how many other women shared it. If she tried to tell her husband, he didn't understand what she was talking about. She did not really understand it herself. For over fifteen years women in America found it harder to talk about this problem than about sex. Even the psychoanalysts had no name for it. When a woman went to psychiatrist for help, as many women did, she would say, "I'm so ashamed," or "I must be hopelessly neurotic." "I don't know what's wrong with women today," a suburban psychiatrist said uneasily. "I only know something is wrong because most of my patients happen to be women. And their problem isn't sexual." Most women with this problem did not go to see a psychoanalyst, however. "There's nothing wrong really," they kept telling themselves. "There isn't any problem."

But on an April morning in 1959, I heard a mother of four, having coffee with four other mothers in a suburban development fifteen miles from New York, say in a tone of quiet desperation, "the problem." And the others knew, without words, that she was not talking about a problem with her husband, or her children, or her home. Suddenly they realized they all shared the same problem, the problem that has no name. They began, hesitantly, to talk about it. Later, after they had picked up their children at nursery school and taken them home to nap, two of the women cried, in sheer relief, just to know they were not alone.

Gradually I came to realize that the **problem that has no name** was shared by countless women in America....

KEY TERMS

- Feminist movement
- "Truly feminine women"
- Mystique of feminine fulfilment
- "Occupation housewife"
- .Problem that has no name

REVIEW

1. What is the underlying "problem" that Friedan is referring to? Does it now have a name?

2. Has the situation in which women find themselves in our society changed since Friedan wrote her book in the early 1960s? In what way?

3. One of the biggest changes in our society since the 1950s has been the extent to which women have become part of the employed labour force. What has been the effect of this change on the status of women in our society? To what extent do you think this has placed a "double burden" on women?

Poverty Is Single and She Has a Child

Women, Children and Poverty

BRUCE LITTLE

A concerted political effort has improved life for the elderly (e.g., old-age pensions). However, the new face of poverty is single-parent families headed by women. Something needs to be done, and fast.

PREVIEW

Journalist Bruce Little reports on the enormous changes in the nature of Canadian families in recent years—particularly the replacement of the elderly, as the segment of our population most affected by extreme poverty, with single mothers. Little urges us towards concerted action in addressing this issue of women and families in poverty.

The headlines for the latest study of **family incomes** from Statistics Canada were predictable: The rich get richer and the poor get poorer. There was some truth to that wild simplification, but it utterly missed the most fascinating material to come out of the report.

There's no question that the last two **recessions**—in the early 1980s and early 1990s—were tougher on low- and middle-income families than on upper-income families. Between 1970 and 1995, the top 30 percent saw their share of all income increase 1.9 percent (to 55.5 percent from 53.6), while the bottom 70 percent saw their share fall 1.9 points (to 44.5 percent from 46.4). Most of the shift occurred in the wake of the two recessions. But when you look at how the income pie is shared, there's a big difference between individuals and families. Families come in all shapes and sizes, and they have more opportunities to gather income than individuals do.

What is most striking from the Statistics Canada study are the huge changes in the nature of families, and their income, over a quarter-century. Analyst Abdul Rashid's report appears in the agency's quarterly publication Perspectives on Labour and Income.

Using census data, Mr. Rashid took the total number of families, split them into 10 equal groups (called deciles) and ranked them according to income. In effect, he provides answers to the questions: Who's rich? Who's poor? And were these the same kinds of people in 1995 as in 1970?

Because the changes are most evident at the extremes of the income scale, we'll focus on the bottom and top deciles, and only occasionally stray into the others. Those at the bottom had income under $15,158 in 1995, compared with more than $98,253 for those at the top.

Begin with age. In 1970, fewer than 12 percent of Canadians were 65 or older, yet they accounted for more than 26 percent of the families in the bottom decile. To a considerable degree, **extreme poverty** was a problem of the old, which is why politicians of the day worked so hard to improve old-age security and launched the Canada Pension Plan.

The politicians succeeded. By 1995, more than 15 percent of all families were headed by someone 65 or older, but they constituted a mere 6 per cent of the bottom income group. The old had not grown rich by any stretch, but many had moved up the income scale; they accounted for 30 percent of those in the third income decile, double their share in 1970. In 1995, the bottom 10 percent were still receiving about 1.5 percent of all income, just as they had in 1970. But if the old have moved up the income ladder, who are today's poor?

Largely, they are **single mothers**. In 1970, they headed just over 7 per cent of all families; by 1995, the figure topped 12 percent. That's a huge jump—nearly double—and it was reflected in the figures for the very poor. Single mothers accounted for 24 percent of those in the bottom decile in 1970 and a staggering 40 percent in 1995.

What about the top end of the income scale, the best-off 10 percent? Again, the group's composition has changed dramatically. In 1970, both the husband and wife had jobs in 50 percent of the families. In 45 percent, only the husband worked.

So even then, it seems, and even in the highest-income families, the *Leave It to Beaver* stereotype of the stay-at-home mom was outdated. (Single parents and families in which the husband did not work made up the other 5 percent.) By 1995, both the husbands and wives were working in 81 per cent of those upper-income homes. Just below them, in the ninth decile, the figure was 79 percent, up from 58 percent in 1970. The trend toward **two-income families** is evident across all income groups, but it's most intense at the upper end.

Over the 25-year period Mr. Rashid studied, it's likely that many fami lies moved around from decile to decile. A young married couple, both working, might give up an income for several years when one (almost always the wife) stays home to raise the children. As the kids reach school age, her return to work would restore the second income. Clearly, as Mr. Rashid says, changes in family structure and the work patterns of spouses can affect income, both up and down. More single moms depressed overall family income, but more dual earners enhanced it.

It's more important to understand changes among the bottom 10 percent because most governments try to do something about poverty. If they don't understand that young mothers and their kids moved into the poverty neighbourhood as the old moved out, they're likely to come up with wrongheaded **policies**.

It would be easy to blame recessions (and rant at the Bank of Canada for causing them) for the slightly wider overall gap between high- and low-income families. But just as it took very focused action a generation ago to alleviate poverty among the old, it would take far more than inter est-rate cuts today to ease the poverty of single mothers and their children.

KEY TERMS

- Family incomes
- Economic recessions
- Extreme poverty
- Single mothers
- Two-income families
- Social policy

REVIEW

1. How did the last two recessions affect the income of families?

2. What changes took place in the nature of families in the bottom and top deciles over the 25-year period?

3. What political policies might be put in place to address the poverty of single mothers?

Modern Times. The experience of women in poverty is captured by Canadian painter Nathan Petroff.

Women Invade Mars

The Longest Revolution

THE ECONOMIST

In their struggle for equality with men, women made great progress by the end of the twentieth century, especially in the economically developed countries. But even here progress has been slow and equality of the sexes must still be a number one goal in the twenty-first century. A place to start may be in the home ...

PREVIEW

The large strides made by women in their march towards equality have discomforted some men. Though applauding the progress of women, this editorial, taken from "The Economist" (a weekly newsmagazine from Britain), points out the lack of a factual basis for such discomfort, and suggests that steps towards full equal rights for both sexes remain to be taken in many fields, such as the domestic one.

Poster by the Ontario Women's Directorate encouraging women to enter traditional male professions.

"WHY can't a woman be more like a man?" mused Henry Higgins in *My Fair Lady*. His wish is coming true. Over the past couple of decades, women have gained much ground in the battle between the sexes. In principle, many have the right to **equal pay**; at school, girls are now getting better grades than boys; and in most rich economies women are taking the lion's share of the new jobs, while traditional jobs for the boys in heavy industries disappear. Finance used to be a man's world, about which women were told not to worry their pretty little heads. But according to a study by two American economists, women are better investors than men, earning a higher average return on their money. Even male sports are no longer safe, with ladies' football teams and female boxers. And experts predict that women could soon outperform men in long-distance swimming and the marathon. Where will it end?

With a further indignity, that's where (though for whom is less clear). One area where men have always had a huge advantage over women is in the call of nature: women, unlike men, have to endure long queues outside the "ladies room." But equality is emerging here, too. Thanks to a Dutch invention, a women's urinal is now on sale. The so-called "Lady P" is designed to speed the flow and cut those queues.

Men will surely not take this sitting down. Understandably, the poor things feel threatened. In recent years, Britain's Equal Opportunities Commission has received more complaints from men than women. And as male executives supposedly feel downtrodden by female rivals, several British firms are setting up male-only self-help groups to give men the confidence to assert themselves in the office. Another study published this week suggests that the more a woman earns relative to her partner, the greater the risk of a family breaking up, whereas higher male earnings increase the chances of its survival. If so, an economist might conclude that equality for women has gone too far, creating "**negative externalities**." But then most economists are men.

In fact, things haven't proceeded quite as far as these anecdotes suggest: women still earn less than men in comparable work and have a small share of top jobs. In America, only two of the chief executives of Fortune 500 companies are women, and only 11 percent of company directors. Nevertheless, men (your female leader-writer feels obliged to point out) do seem worried. It is a puzzle. But men are essentially irrational.

The rational answer would surely be for men to seek new, equal rights themselves. For example, in many countries conscription applies only to men, and maternity leave mainly to women. Many women have to make the agonizing choice between **work and children**: men would love to face such a dilemma. Men are also discriminated against in pension schemes: they face the same contribution rates as women even though they die earlier. And the next time someone shouts "women and children first," ask why.

There are plenty of solutions. Women take time off with the excuse of "women's problems," so men must be allowed to recover from hangovers and other "men's problems." Nightclubs often have free ladies' nights, so men should have free lads' nights. And once inside they should demand that women buy their fair share of drinks. But most important of all, men should immediately claim **equal rights** to do the cleaning, the ironing, the cooking and the nappy changing. It's simply not fair that women monopolize all those jobs.

KEY TERMS

- The longest revolution
- Equality of the sexes
- Equal pay
- Negative externalities
- Choice between work and children
- Equal rights

REVIEW

1. In which areas of endeavour have women gained ground in the battle of the sexes?

2. How have men responded to the economic progress of women? What facts support the author's assertion, in light of their response, that "men are essentially irrational"?

3. The author suggests that the domestic arena is still host to the ongoing struggle for equality. What is she implying by deeming this "most important of all" in her list of proposed solutions?

Sexual Harassment

Fighting Back

VANCOUVER RAPE RELIEF AND WOMEN'S SHELTER

Sexual harassment continues to poison our workplace and living environments. Despite prohibitive laws and the work of human rights' agencies, women are victimized, not only by this abusive behaviour, but in their attempts to take action.

PREVIEW

Sexual harassment and other forms of harassment based on gender are sometimes difficult to recognize and often hard to address. Victims of such harassment frequently feel powerless and at fault. In this brief article, a Vancouver women's shelter outlines the causes and consequences of this abuse of power, and concludes that the solution is social, economic and political equality for women.

Sexual harassment is sexual behaviour that is unwanted. Often the harasser is someone in a position of formal authority, but harassment occurs between co-workers or peers as well. Men are sometimes harassed, but most of the victims of harassment are women. The harasser is almost always male.

Sometimes the harassment is directed at a particular woman. It could be in the form of suggestive comments, pressure for sexual contact or demands for sex in return for a job or other benefit. It can involve unwanted sexual touching or rape (both are sexual assault). Sexual harassment also happens when sexual jokes, sexist remarks or pin-ups create a hostile and intimidating environment for women. Sometimes the harassment is also directed at a woman's racial or cultural background, sexual orientation, disability or other personal characteristics. In these cases, the woman is multiply victimized. For example, racial minority women face prejudice and discrimination on two grounds; often, their harassment involves both racism and sexism.

It is an **abuse of power**, the social and economic power that men hold over women. When men use their power to treat women sexually in a non-sexual context, they interfere with women's right to work, to learn, to walk on the street without fear and to be treated as equal and respected participants in public life. Like other kinds of woman abuse, sexual harassment both reflects and reinforces women's unequal position in our society.

Workplace harassment reflects women's **economic inequality**. Despite laws against discrimination in the workplace, women generally remain in poorly paid, lower status and less secure jobs. More than twice as many women as men work in clerical, sales and service occupations. Women continue to be underrepresented in managerial and leadership positions in our economy. When women do enter nontraditional fields–whether blue-collar or professional–they may face harassment from hostile male co-workers. Over 90 percent of women who responded to a "Women in

Trades" survey said that they had been sexually harassed. A study of large U.S. corporations found that the highest rates of sexual harassment complaints are at companies with the lowest percentage of women workers.

Poverty, race, language and other barriers also put women at risk. Being at risk economically can be aggravated by other social differences. In a Montreal study of sexual discrimination against women tenants by landlords and neighbours, single mothers and women on welfare reported the highest levels of sexual harassment. Immigrant women, who often occupy the most low-paying and least secure positions in the work force, may lack the support groups and language skills that are necessary to confront harassment.

Sexual harassment can have serious consequences. Not all women react the same way, but many women feel degraded and humiliated by sexual harassment. Some women feel confused. They question their own feelings and reactions, before they realize that the harasser is responsible for the problem. They are angry, anxious and, if the harassment persists, may become depressed and demoralized. The emotional strain can cause physical illnesses such as nausea, headaches and fatigue. It can affect a woman's personal life, and the quality of her work. She may be fired, or forced to leave her job or school program to avoid the harasser. Loss of self-confidence, health problems, unfair evaluations, poor references and a disrupted work record can have a long-term economic impact, such as not being able to find another job.

Sexual harassment is against the law. Canadian law prohibits sexual harassment. Federal, provincial and territorial human rights commissions are responsible for investigating and resolving harassment complaints. Employers have been held accountable for sexual harassment in the workplace. As a result, many large companies, unions, universities, professional bodies and other institutions have adopted their own policies against sexual harassment.

Yet many women still feel they have few options. Only 4 of every 10 Canadian women who suffer sexual harassment at work take any formal action. Only one out of every two women believe that a complaint would be taken seriously in their workplace.

Often, women who report harassment are not believed, are discredited or are even blamed for the problem by their colleagues. As well, the harasser may retaliate. Legal action is slow, stressful and expensive, and awards are usually small. Publicity surrounding a complaint may hurt a woman's job prospects and personal life. Few women can afford to take these risks.

• The real solution is equality for women

Human rights agencies should be made more effective and accessible, and should provide better compensation to women who are sexually harassed. But human rights law by itself cannot end sexual harassment. The fundamental solution to sexual harassment is social, economic and political equality for women.

KEY TERMS

- Sexual harassment
- Abuse of power
- Workplace harassment
- Economic inequality
- Sexual discrimination
- Harassment complaint
- Human rights agencies
- Equality for women

REVIEW

1. How is sexual harassment an abuse of the power men hold over women?

2. What are the consequences for women of sexual harassment?

3. Colleagues of women who report incidents of sexual harassment often respond with disbelief and even blame them for the problem. Why do you think this is so?

Aboriginal Peoples in Change

A Painful Legacy

WSEVOLOD W. ISAJIW

The story of Canada's Aboriginal peoples remains to be told. From reserves to residential schools, their relationship with the rest of Canada is now evolving into one of equality as Canada's First Nations fight for self-government and sovereignty.

PREVIEW

Wsevolod Isajiw journeys through the dark stages of the evolution of the relationship of Canada's First Nations with non-Aboriginal society, from one of treaties to one of struggle for self-governance. He explores the attempts to effectively assimilate Aboriginal peoples into Canadian society with the implementation of the Indian Act of 1876, outlines the resultant social problems and issues now confronting us, and informs us that Aboriginal peoples seek to solve these issues for themselves. Wsevolod Isajiw is Robert F. Harney Professor of Ethnic, Immigration and Pluralism Studies at the University of Toronto.

The early history of the Aboriginal peoples, or as they call themselves today, the **First Nations**, has been a movement from what originally appeared to be a trading and treaty relationship to what became an increasing control by, and dependence on, the Canadian government to what is an evolving process of self-control and self-governance. Most of the issues in the relationship between the Aboriginal peoples and the non-Aboriginal society are related to one or the other of these three stages. The initial contact between the two established a trading relationship that appeared to be beneficial to both the Aboriginal communities and the European settlers. The European desire and market for fur pushed the early settlers ever further into the Canadian forested and open landscape, but it also made the non-Aboriginal settler rely on the Aboriginals' knowledge of this landscape and their collective efficiency in animal trapping. The Native trappers, however, developed an interest in the efficiency of the settlers' firearms, their metal implements, clothing material, alcohol, decorative objects and other goods (Innis, 1930; Trigger, 1985).

If it appeared that such a **trading relationship** would serve as a basis for a balanced social order between the two peoples, it should be remembered that the early numbers of non-Native settlers were small and the contacts between them were often indirect, through the contacts of the *courier du bois* or other intermediaries. As the European population increased and developed a strong demand for land, this kind of social order changed completely. Throughout the eighteenth, the nineteenth and into the twentieth century, the Native peoples were gradually displaced from their lands by the non-Aboriginal settlers. In the period of New France, the French Crown assumed that all the land that was not owned by the settlers was in its jurisdiction, and it could make land grants to French missionary orders so that they in turn would grant sections of it to the Indians for their life and subsistence. This was the origin of the idea of **reserves**. The idea remained after the conquest of New France. The British, however, created most, though not all, reserves by means of **treaties** with the Native peoples....

In all these treaties, the Crown and the Canadian government's purpose was to secure as much land from the Aboriginal peoples as possible for the purpose of settlement and development. As the nineteenth century progressed, the goal pursued by the government became more definite and determined. It was the goal of assimilating the Aboriginal peoples into Canadian society completely. This aim became the centrepiece of the legislation that for years to come would be, as it were, a Sisyphean stone for the Aboriginal people, who tried to change it yet found behind it a protection of their basic right to land, i.e., the Indian Act of 1876. The Act reinforced the right to land principle set out in the Royal Proclamation of 1763, but it defined a formal land-surrender process, according to which the Aboriginal land could not be simply appropriated but must be purchased on a tribe to tribe basis. Further, the Act regulated almost every important aspect of Indian people's daily life. Finally, it defined who was not an Indian. It created the category of "status Indians," referring to male persons of Indian blood who belong to one or another Indian band, children of such persons and women who were lawfully married to such persons. A highly controversial part of the Act was the regulation of marriage outside of the reserve. According to it, a woman who married a non-Indian man would be completely deprived of her Indian status, could not inherit any property left to her by her parents, was barred from any formal participation in the affairs of her band, was prevented from returning to live with her family on the reserve and could not even be buried on the reserve. The same applied to all her children (Royal Commission on Aboriginal Peoples, 1996: 1:281-319). There were many attempts to modify or change the Indian Act and a number of changes have been made. Among them was an amendment in 1985, known as Bill C-31, which reinstated women who married outside the reserve to their Indian status.

• A Painful Legacy

The process through which Aboriginal peoples were dispossessed of their land and livelihood and through which their culture and institutions were being lost and the fact of discrimination and racism against them left, as a consequence, a legacy that is only now being confronted. The policies towards the Aboriginal peoples were based on the assumption that Aboriginal ways of life were at a primitive level of evolutionary development and that cultural and social development could be achieved only by adopting the culture of the European societies (Royal Commission on Aboriginal Peoples, 1996: 3:2). The purpose of the Indian Act and of all the measures used for its implementation was to **inculturate and incorporate** the Aboriginal peoples into Canadian culture and society. However, the effect of all these efforts was far from incorporation. The Aboriginal people were effectively trapped between their Native community and Canadian society. Economically, while the rest of Canada was rapidly industrializing and

First Nations' peoples in Canada are pressing their demands for self-government and sovereignty.

References

• Frideres, James S. 1993. *Native Peoples in Canada: Contemporary Conflicts.* Scarborough, Ont.: Prentice Hall Canada Inc.

• Innis, Harold A. 1930. *The Fur Trade in Canada: An Introduction to Canadian Economic History.* New Haven: Yale University Press.

• Royal Commission on Aboriginal Peoples. 1993. *Path to Healing.* Report of the National Round Table on Aboriginal Health and Social Issues. Vancouver: Canada Communication Group Publishing.

• Royal Commission on Aboriginal Peoples. 1996. *Looking Forward, Looking Back*, Report of the Royal Commission on Aboriginal Peoples. Ottawa: Canada Communication Group Publishing.

• Satzewich, Vic, and Terry Wotherspoon. 1993. *First Nations: Race, Class, and Gender Relations.* Scarborough, Ont.: Nelson Canada.

• Smandych, Russell, Robyn Lincoln, and Paul Wilson. 1993. "Toward a Cross-Cultural Theory of Aboriginal Crime: A Comparative Study of the Problem of Aboriginal Overrepresentation in the Criminal Justice System of Canada and Australia." *International Criminal Justice Review* 3: 1-24.

• Statistics Canada. 1993. *1991 Aboriginal Peoples Survey.* Catalogue 89-533. Ottawa: Ministry of Industry, Science and Technology.

• Trigger, B. 1985. *Natives and Newcomers: Canada's Heroic Age Reconsidered.* Montreal: McGill-Queen's University Press.

generally changing its occupational structure to secondary and tertiary levels, the reserves remained essentially at the level of primary subsistence. Although a percentage of people from various tribes came to be engaged in industrial work, mostly as labourers, fishing, hunting, trapping and agriculture remained the main type of economic activity. Dependence on the government became part of the Aboriginal economy of both the Indians and the Inuit and both on and off the reserves. While there have been variations in the economic level and living conditions among the reserves, in the 1980s, for around 30 percent of the Aboriginal persons and families, government transfer payments were the major source of income. Employment was the major source of income, on the average, for only 30 percent of individuals and families, and about 25 percent received no income at all (Frideres, 1993: 160-62; Satzewich and Wotherspoon, 1993: 95).

The justice system also involves Aboriginal people proportionally more than it involves the general population. Aboriginal people, both Indian and Inuit, make up about 10 percent of the inmate population in federal penitentiaries, while they are only about 2 percent of the total Canadian population. In the Western provinces of Canada, where Aboriginal people make up about 10 percent of the total population, the Aboriginal inmate population of federal penitentiaries reaches 40 percent, while the Aboriginal population of provincial jails exceeds 50 percent. Aboriginal people are more likely to be involved with the justice system at a younger age than non-Aboriginal people. They are apprehended in much higher rates than are non-Aboriginal people by both the child welfare authorities and by the youth justice system (Royal Commission on Aboriginal Peoples, 1993: 86).

The **Royal Commission on Aboriginal Peoples** (1993: 86-87) concludes that the justice system discriminates against the Aboriginal people. The people feel discriminated against by the police, lawyers, Crown attorneys, judges and probation officers because of their different culture, their different languages and because of their low social standing, low educational levels and high unemployment. As a result, justice officials too often choose apprehension and punishment instead of discretion and alternatives to incarceration. Comparative research on Aboriginal peoples in other countries confirms a number of these conclusions (Smandych, Lincoln and Wilson, 1993).

Yet, the process of movement of younger people out of the reserves into urban centres has begun and is changing the character of the Aboriginal community. By 1990, 40 percent of all Aboriginal population lived off reserves (Satzewich and Wotherspoon, 1993: 95). The move off reserves has had an ambiguous consequence on the Aboriginal identity. On the one hand, it has added to the many social problems already emerging on the reserves. One such problem has been child welfare. In all Canadian provinces and territories, Native children are overrepresented in the proportion of children in foster homes, adoptions or in care of agencies. Studies have shown that Native children are in the care of provincial and federal child welfare agencies more than three times the rate of all Canadian children. In some provinces, like British Columbia, Alberta, Saskatchewan and Manitoba, they make up 40 to 60 percent of all children in care, and their rate of discharge is below that of non-Aboriginal children (Satzewich and Wotherspoon, 1993: 89).

Child problems often derive from problems in the family. Many families in the Aboriginal community are dysfunctional, due to poverty, high unemployment, alcoholism, poor housing and community turmoil. A survey by Statistics Canada (1991) indicated that over 39 percent of all the Aboriginal respondents surveyed (including on- and off-reserve Indians, Métis and Inuit, but over 44 percent of the on-reserve Indian and over 43 percent of the Inuit respondents) saw family violence as one of the most important issues in their communities. Along with unemployment, alcohol and drug abuse, other burning issues related to family life were: suicide (indicated by over 25 percent of all the respondents, but by over 34 percent of the on-reserve Indian, and over 41 percent of the Inuit respondents), sexual abuse (over 24 percent of all respondents, 29 percent of the on-reserve Indian, and over 35 percent of the Inuit respondents) and rape (15 percent of all respondents, over 16 percent of the on-reserve Indian, and 25 percent of the Inuit respondents) (Royal Commission on Aboriginal Peoples, 1996: 3:58).

A factor in the Aboriginal family dysfunctionality is the generational effect of the former **residential schools**. Many children in care of welfare agencies are children of parents who were raised in residential schools when they were young or were themselves children of parents who were raised in residential schools. The intent of the residential school policy was to erase Aboriginal identity by separating generations of children from their families and socializing them, not in the culture of their ancestors, but in the culture of the Canadian mainstream. This process, however, was often done virtually by force with damaging effects to the personality of students. The Royal Commission on Aboriginal Peoples (1996: 3:34-36) has collected a number of testimonials from persons who were raised in residential schools. Among them are such statements as the following, from three different persons:

> I stayed in that residential school for ten years. I hurt there. There was no love there. There was no caring there, nobody to hug you when you cried; all they did was slap you over: "Don't you cry! You are not supposed to cry." Whipped me when I talked to my younger brother. That's my brother, for God's sake. We were not supposed to talk to these people.

> I was one of the fortunate ones in the residential school, but the boy who slept next to me wasn't very fortunate. I saw him being sexually abused. As a result, he died violently. He couldn't handle it when he became of age.

> I have heard people who have said, "I left that residential school, and I have been like a ship without a rudder." I have heard people say, "I have left that place, and I left there just like a robot, with no feelings, with no emotions."

For Aboriginal persons, leaving the reserve for residential schools or to move into urban areas has often meant a loss of self-esteem and a loss of identity. In urban areas, often living in a condition of poverty and barred

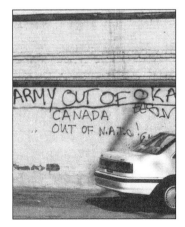

The "Oka Crisis" in the summer of 1990 brought Native issues to the forefront of Canadian politics.

REVIEW

1. What are the three stages in the relationship between the First Nations and non-Aboriginal society?

2. What measures did the Canadian government use to "inculturate and incorporate" the Aboriginal peoples into Canadian society? What were the results of these measures?

3. How did the Aboriginal peoples respond to the recommendations of the federal government's 1969 White Paper? What is the current focus of their demands?

by prejudice and discrimination from acceptance into the society around them, young Aboriginal persons have tended to feel trapped between their Native identity and the identity of the larger society, neither of which they fully possess. Unlike a number of other minority groups, the Aboriginal groups in urban areas generally have not formed effective social service agencies of their own that could extend assistance and counselling to their own people, particularly to their own young people. The publicly available services have rarely included appropriately trained personnel who understood the background and the identity problems of persons caught between two cultures. The work of public service agencies has been based on a non-Aboriginal value system and worldview. All the initiatives undertaken to remedy this are rather recent (Royal Commission on Aboriginal Peoples, 1996: 3:34, 668-669)....

Although there have been some Aboriginal politically oriented organizations since the turn of the century, the big quantum jump in Aboriginal organizing came at the end of the 1960s. A precipitating factor was the federal government's White Paper of 1969, which recommended that the Indian special citizenship rights be terminated and that Indians should be given the same citizenship rights and obligations as all non-Indians. It further recommended that the Indian Act be repealed, that the Indian Affairs Branch of the Department of Indian and Northern Affairs be phased out and that the responsibility for all matters concerning the Indians be shifted to the provincial governments. The reaction of the Aboriginal leaders to the White Paper was quick and negative. It stimulated an emergence of new organizations and politicization of the old ones (Satzewich and Wotherspoon, 1993: 228-232). According to a study by James Frideres (1993: 288), while prior to 1970 there had been a total of 119 Aboriginal organizations on national, provincial and regional levels, by 1991 there were 239 such organizations. The focus of their work became the question of citizenship, in particular the elimination of certain restrictions on their citizenship rights, but at the same time retention of other rights that would recognize their status as First Nations (Satzewich and Wotherspoon, 1993: 220).

By the 1990s, the focus of the Aboriginal demands has become **entrenchment of Aboriginal rights** in the Canadian constitution and eventual Aboriginal **self-government** and **sovereignty**. The thrust of the demands has been the premise that a satisfactory solution to social, family, welfare, educational and cultural Aboriginal problems can be achieved only through the attainment of self-control over these issues. All recommendations of the 1996 Royal Commission on Aboriginal Peoples advise that this should be the case.

I Am Canadian!

The Meaning of Being Black in Canada

CECIL FOSTER

The feelings of the black community for Canada resemble those of an off-and-on love affair. Cold and hot in turn, they are chilled by instances of discriminatory policing and warmed by the cultural richness of Toronto's colourful Caribana festival.

O n an evening like this, with a hint of spring and a sense of renewal in the air, I was once again in love with Canada. Immigrating to this country in 1979 was one of the best decisions—if not *the* best—I had ever made. Obviously, this place can be heavenly when it wants to be, a place to raise my kids and offer them all those opportunities that I could only have dreamt about for myself. But alas, as we all know, as is so typical of Canada, one pleasant evening does not mean the end to a harsh winter. The unusual warmth can be just a delusion, a passing respite at most, something to lull us into dropping our guard.

I saw flashing lights in my rear-view mirror. The police. *Shit*, I thought, *what's up now?* At the first break in the traffic, which had been pushing me along as part of the flow, I pulled over to the side of the roadway and waited for the policeman to pull up behind me. He approached from the passenger side. I rolled down the window and waited.

"Is this *your* car?" he asked. *So that is why he stopped me*, I thought. *He is on the lookout for a stolen car.*

"Yes," I said.

"Your driver's licence!" he snapped.

Slowly, I opened the front of my overcoat and jacket to let the officer see that I was reaching for my wallet, and not for a weapon. I very deliberately took out my wallet, removed the licence in its plastic folder and handed it to him. He took a quick look at the picture and then at me, matching my face with the picture on the licence.

"Ownership and insurance," he demanded. By now he was leaning into the car, his elbows propped on the window, noisily flicking the end of the licence with his fingers, as if showing his impatience, intolerance and superiority.

Through my rear-view mirror, I watched this representative of Metro's finest get into the car, turn off the flashing lights and merge with the traffic

PREVIEW

The experience of being black in Canada is ambivalent in nature, as members of this community must cope with such contrasting experiences as the grim aftermaths of questionable police action and the "spiritual tonic" offered by the Caribana festival. In this piece, Canadian author Cecil Foster explores the mutual distrust of Blacks and police and shares his joy at the freedom and healing found in mutual celebration with other Blacks and Caribbeans.

The Caribana celebration takes place each summer in Toronto, attracting hundreds of thousands of visitors from all over North America.

zooming by. I still wondered why he was so angry and why he would use that tone for an alleged traffic violation. And I remembered all the stories and anecdotes by Blacks about how they were stopped by the police for driving fancy cars–not that my fairly new Chrysler Intrepid was all that fancy–and how not so long ago police used to hand out DWBBs–Driving While Being Black violations–just for the fun of it. And I reflected on how in the past week I had tried to explain, as a guest on a talk show on CFRB, why so many black people everywhere are distrustful of the police, why they do not like the way some bad apples in the force treat Blacks and how, as I had said, we all have to start breaking down barriers, build bridges of understanding and trust, stop shouting at one another and open a dialogue in the hope of producing a better society.

And while sitting in my car, I remembered something else about February 24, 1996. That was the day the black community buried the black man in Toronto most recently killed by a police bullet–in this case three bullets and all apparently fired from close range. Tommy Barnett, a 22-year-old, was gunned down when police said they were driving by in their cruiser and stopped to deal with a man brandishing a Samurai sword in the middle of the road early one morning. Once again, the black community had questioned the killing and was calling for an independent investigation. Barnett's family had delayed the burial for 46 days so an independent pathologist could come into the city and examine the body. Ironically, the family included an elder sister who, as a respected community activist, had campaigned relentlessly for Blacks to gain a better appreciation of police work. Now, she found that justification for the shooting was lacking, and wondered how she could continue to work to raise the level of respect between the police and black youth.

I remember my first year in Canada, how four months after arriving in a new country and feeling homesick, I went to the Caribana festival in downtown Toronto and instantly felt at home. There, I found the music, the faces, the people, the accents, the food and the excitement of the Caribbean. Over the years, we would joke that Caribana is the best spiritual tonic for the **social and political alienation** so many of us feel in Canada, including so many of us born and raised in this country.

One of the great things about this festival is that you never know who you will meet for the first time, or which old friend or acquaintance you will rediscover in the crowd. Perhaps an actor like Lou Gossett Jr. or Billy Dee Williams will show up and mix, excited as little boys at being in such a festival. The parade with its glamorous costumes is secondary to the joyful camaraderie along the parade route. And for the participants, Caribana is not first and foremost about making money, about their festival being reduced to simple balance sheet issues. Caribana is always a renewing of the spirit–more than just dancing, something spiritual.

And over the years, I have noticed how young black and Caribbean people, especially teenagers, blossom during Caribana. So many of our children seem so lost. They do not know who they are, confused by what they are hearing at school and in their home and church, unsure of their place in a **white-dominated society**.

With Caribana comes a breaking out. Suddenly, these youths appear free, strong and confident. They are proud of discovering their heritage and exult in it by dancing in the streets, just like their elders. Oh, to see the young people liberated! Could this freedom come about through paying an admission fee and sitting passively while watching some pageant? I don't think so; Caribana's spirituality is fed by spontaneous participation, by the celebration of a way of life.

On the Canadian cultural calendar there is simply nothing like Caribana. Nothing so authentically outside the mainstream that makes as big an impact on the cultural landscape of Canada. Nothing is so beneficial to the psyche of black and Caribbean people in this country. Nothing is so capable of causing the colourful political leaders in this community to be so divisive and so viciously attack one another as putting together one of the world's most spectacular and glamorous festivals. Nothing so epitomizes the mountain peaks and deep valleys of being black in Canada. For Caribana has become a symbol of the divergent paths facing Canadians in the area of **race relations**: the harmony that can arise from different ethnic groups working together with the financial help and encouragement of the wider society, or the discord and economic uncertainty that can result from too much distrust and infighting.

Caribana is a two-week festival of rhythmic Caribbean and African music, of humour and brotherly and sisterly love openly displayed, of dancing on the streets and meeting new friends, of enjoying exotic foods and, for many businesses, hearing cash registers ring. Caribana is all pageantry and glamour, when men, women and children abandon themselves to frolicking, to decking out in elaborately designed costumes and parading on a route in downtown Toronto, with the eyes of the world looking on. It is a musical cacophony of different voices and accents; of faces representing the cultures of the world and, in turn, reflecting back a peaceful **multicultural Canada** to the rest of humanity.

KEY TERMS

- Black community
- Community activist
- Caribana festival
- Social and political alienation
- White-dominated society
- Race relations
- Multiculturalism in Canada

REVIEW

1. Foster concludes that the behaviour of the police officer towards him was racist in origin. Does his anecdote provide sufficient evidence to support this conclusion? Could another conclusion be drawn?

2. How does the staging of the Caribana festival mirror the choice facing Canadians in the area of race relations? How does it illustrate the experience of Blacks in Canada?

3. Foster has stressed the worst and the best experiences of Blacks in Canada. Does this provide us with an accurate picture of their experience? What has he left out?

EXPLAINING THE UNACCEPTABLE

THEORIES OF PREJUDICE

WSEVOLOD W. ISAJIW

One major "social problem" that continues to defy understanding is racial and ethnic prejudice and all its horrifying consequences (such as "ethnic cleansing" and genocide). And understanding prejudice is only half the battle—the point is to put an end to it altogether.

PREVIEW

Developing theories about how societies work, or don't work, and then testing these theories to see if they hold up is what social scientists do for a living. In this essay Wsevolod Isajiw updates and expands on the classical typology of racial prejudice by Gordon W. Allport. Isajiw offers five types of theories that address both the emergence and persistence of ethnic and racial prejudice. Wsevolod Isajiw is Robert F. Harney Professor of Ethnic, Immigration and Pluralism Studies at the University of Toronto.

How do we explain **prejudice**? Why do some people become prejudiced against others? Why do some people become very **ethnocentric**? A variety of theories that attempt to answer these questions have been proposed by sociologists and social psychologists. Here we will review and elaborate on five different types of theories. Some of these theories better explain the emergence of prejudice; others, their persistence. However, the two processes, emergence and persistence, different as they are, are nevertheless interrelated and hence for most theories it is difficult to identify them as theories of either one or the other. Furthermore, it should not be assumed that these theories are exclusive of one another. Rather, they are complementary. Each type of theory focuses on a different aspect of the issue....

• Socialization Theory

Socialization theory holds that prejudice is transmitted in the process of a person's socialization from childhood to adulthood. Instrumental in this process are the agencies of socialization, parents, peers, school and the media. The process of socialization is of particular importance because it is during this process that one's personality and identity are formed. When transmitted in the process of socialization, prejudice can become part of one's personality and part of one's identity to the extent that it becomes difficult to change it or eradicate it in adult life.

Parents may transmit prejudice early in their children's life by telling them not to play with children of a different skin colour or a different ethnic group. They may associate the colour black with bad things and white colour with good things and thus indirectly teach stereotypes (Horowitz and Horowitz, 1938; Ehrlich, 1973). They may also point to children of another ethnic group in the neighbourhood as examples of bad behaviour, not to be followed by their own children....

In modern times, however, the influence of the family on children has somewhat diminished and the other agencies of socialization have become more influential. Daycare workers and teachers have become parent surrogates and a child's or an adolescent's significant others. If the teachers themselves are prejudiced, consciously or unconsciously, they will transmit prejudice to their students. Educational research has shown that students can judge a teacher's attitude from verbal and non-verbal behaviour, even when the teacher believes that he or she is concealing an attitude (Babad, 1991; Hansen, 1993)....

In the lives of adolescents, the peer group becomes a powerful agency of socialization. This is particularly so because adolescent peers are in the process of identity formation, and prejudice against selected groups can function as an instrument in this process. Peer groups provide a sense of belonging, ostensibly by choice, which serves as an identity boundary in relation to family belonging, which for a young person symbolizes childhood and dependence. The need to distance oneself from childhood creates a momentum that pushes young persons to develop loyalty, often strong loyalty, to the peer group. But the peer group, made up of a number of persons with the same momentum, can claim loyalty from its members only if it generates its own boundary that will provide it with its own identity. The easiest way in which this boundary is established is in terms of a negative reaction to another group, to society as a whole, or in contradiction of the traditional cultural norms. That is, the peer group readily develops the "we versus them" perspective. Racial categories and ethnic groups provide a ready-made, easily visible, target for the "them" designation. For this reason, in peer group communication, racial and ethnic stereotypes may abound among other stereotypes, such as sexual, regional, religious, political and other (Brake, 1985)....

We have already discussed the media in relation to the transmission of racism. The media, however, has been acquiring a continuously more significant role as an agency of socialization of children and adolescents. This is particularly true of television and video (Liebert, Sprafkin and Davidson, 1989). Until the 1960s or so, some of the most popular films were "Westerns," which often portrayed victorious cowboys and usually "savage" and vanquished Indians. This in itself communicated racism against the Indians. The Westerns were later succeeded by films that had no Indians in them but instead introduced a generation of superheroes and supervillians, as for example in the stories of *Batman, Star Wars, Rambo* and the like. While these stories do not include racism as such, they have continued to articulate, in an even more powerful manner, the idea of the good guys and the bad guys, and with it, the idea of us and them, with us being always the superior winner. While this in itself may not be prejudice and may not necessarily stimulate prejudicial feelings against any group, it nevertheless can lay the conceptual foundations for prejudice in the mind and the psyche of young people. The iconoclastic lyrics of popular music can likewise contribute to the conditions that in cases of interethnic conflict may evoke prejudice and racism.

• Structure of Society Theories

Another approach in trying to locate the factors of emergence and maintenance of prejudice has been the **structural approach**. According to this approach, prejudice is derived from the fact that society comes to be divided between those who have power and those who do not, or between the rich and the poor. In the first case, the division is between the *elites and non-elites*. The elites will always have a conception of ethnicities other than their own as being at least somewhat inferior to their own. The fact that they themselves are at the top of society's power structure is proof to them that they are at least in some way superior to those who are not. John Porter (1965: 60-68) points out that, to the majority elite who were in charge of establishing and developing Canada, this was an obvious fact. The idea of the English and French being the "Charter groups" in Canada was a way of legitimizing the elite ethnicities' superiority in the face of other ethnicities that existed in the country or were coming to Canada as immigrants, with a concession to the French.

In a society that invites new members from the outside because it needs their labour, the majority elites also have positive conceptions of the immigrant ethnicities. However, these conceptions relate to the qualities that are useful for the work the elite wants the immigrants to do, and as was pointed out previously, it is usually work that is less important than that of the elite. The most important work, such as the top levels of the government or top levels of the economic enterprise, is reserved for itself (Porter, 1965: 66)....

Another variant of the structural theory is the theory of the division of society between *the rich and the poor*. The rich are seen as always being prejudiced against the poor. In this case the poor are not perceived as a potential threat to the rich, but rather the rich are seen as having no interest in taking any responsibility for the poor. Prejudice becomes a way in which the rich dismiss their responsibility for the poor. Prejudice of the rich defines the poor as lazy, indolent, preferring to receive something for nothing (as, for example, welfare benefits), unwilling to take initiative in their own lives and the like. Prejudice is a way in which victims are blamed for their own lot. While it absolves the rich of any responsibility for this lot, it also masks the fact that the poor are poor because they are exploited by the rich. Ethnic groups are defined exclusively as minority groups and hence are seen as being in the category of the poor. Prejudice against them is part of the prejudice against the poor.

A different type of the structural theory is the theory of prejudice against the *middle-man minorities*. The structural position of the middle-man minorities is that between the majority group and other minority groups who are lower in status than the middle-man minority. In this position, the middle-man minority group serves as a broker between the majority group and the other minority groups. That is, it performs certain functions for both types of groups. It deals with members of other minority groups on behalf of the majority group, and it intervenes with the majority group on behalf of the other minority groups (Bonacich, 1973; Lieberson, 1970). The problem, however, is that the dissatisfactions of the majority group with the minorities and the dissatisfactions of the minority groups with the majority group are projected into the middle-man minority. That is, both sides, the majority group and the other minority groups, will tend to blame the middle-man minority group for their problems. Hence, the middle-man minority group becomes the subject of prejudice from both sides.

If my theory of relativity is proven correct, Germany will claim me as a German and France will declare that I am a citizen of the world. Should my theory prove untrue, France will say that I am a German and Germany will declare that I am a Jew.

Albert Einstein

• Interethnic Competition and Conflict Theory

Somewhat related to the structural theories but different from them are the theories that focus on **competition and conflict** between different ethnic groups. In social psychology, the theory is known as Realistic Group Conflict Theory (Brown, 1995: 163-179). According to this theory, prejudices are generated in the process of competition and conflict between ethnic groups. This can be competition for jobs, for influential positions, for political office, business competition for markets, competition for media attention, cultural competition, competition for recognition and the like. Some of these forms of competition will be discussed in the chapter on interethnic relations.

The theory holds that whenever the interests of groups are incompatible in intergroup relations, i.e., when the interests of one group are met at the expense of another, then the response of one group to another will tend to be negative and prejudicial. When the interests of the groups are complementary, i.e., if one group can gain with the assistance of another, then the response of that group will be positive and show little prejudice (Brown, 1995: 163).

• Social-Psychological Theories

A number of theories explain the emergence or persistence of prejudice in terms of **social-psychological dynamics.** They hold that a social phenomenon, such as war, increased crime rate, economic depression or recession, influx of new immigrants into the country and the like, produce psychological arousal in people. In their attempts to deal with these arousals, people often resort to psychological mechanisms that evoke prejudice.

Scapegoating is one such mechanism. In critical social situations, people often look for someone to blame for their problem and prejudice develops against those who become the subjects of the blame. Immigrants are one of the most common scapegoats. In periods of economic recession in North America, immigrants are often blamed for "taking jobs away from the people." With the development of hostility towards immigrants, pressure is put on the government to curtail immigration flow. A number of studies have tested the claim that immigrants take jobs away from the native-born

Aboriginal issues have been swept under the carpet for too long–self-government is overdue.

References

• Babad, Elisha. 1991. "Students as Judges of Teachers' Verbal and Nonverbal Behaviour." *American Educational Research Journal* 28: 211-34.

• Berkowitz, L. 1993. *Aggression: Its Causes, Consequences and Control.* New York: McGraw Hill.

• Bonacich, Edna. 1973. "A Theory of Middleman Minorities." *American Sociological Review* 38: 583-594.

• Brake, Michael. 1985. *Comparative Youth Culture: The Sociology of Youth Cultures and Youth Subcultures in America, Britain and Canada.* London: Routledge and Kegan Paul.

• Brown, Rupert. 1995. *Prejudice: Its Social Psychology.* Oxford: Blackwell Publishers.

• Canada. 1991. *Economic and Social Impacts of Immigration.* A research report prepared for the Economic Council of Canada. Ottawa: Canadian Communication Group Publishing.

• Economic Council of Canada. 1991. *Economic and Social Impacts of Immigration.* Ottawa: Minister of Supply and Services.

• Ehrlich, Howard J. 1973. *The Social Psychology of Prejudice.* New York: Wiley.

• Hansen, David T. 1993. "The Moral Importance of the Teacher's Style." *Journal of Curriculum Studies* 25: 397-421.

• Horowitz, E.L., and R.E. Horowitz. 1938. "Development of Social Attitudes in Children." In *Sociometry* 1: 301-338.

• Lieberson, Stanley. 1970 "Stratification and Ethnic Groups." *Sociological Inquiry* 40: 172-181.

• Liebert, R.M., J.N. Sprafkin, and E.S Davidson. 1989. *The Early Window: Effects of Television on Children and Youth.* 3rd ed. New York: Pergamon Press.

• Pineo, Peter C. 1977. "The Social Standing of Ethnic and Racial Groupings." *Canadian Review of Sociology and Anthropology* 14: 147-157.

• Porter, John. 1965. *The Vertical Mosaic.* Toronto: University of Toronto Press.

• Simon, Julian. 1989. *The Economic Consequences of Immigration.* London: Blackwell.

population and have concluded that this is not the case. The studies show that the contrary is true, that even in periods of recession, immigrants have no negative effect on the employment structure and often, in the long run, create new jobs through the businesses they establish (Simon, 1989; Economic Council of Canada, 1991). This conclusion shows that immigrants come to be blamed without any basis in fact. Rather they become an easy target for displaced blame.

Frustration-aggression hypothesis is closely related to the scapegoating theory and can be said to complement it. The hypothesis argues that frustration occurs when people are unexpectedly blocked from achieving a goal that they thought was within their grasp or was legitimately their due. The unexpected nature of frustration arouses a drive whose goal is that of harming some person or object (Berkowitz, 1993). Aggression resulting from frustration can be directed at the source of frustration, but it can also be directed at other persons or objects, unrelated to the source of frustration. The latter can particularly be the case when the source of frustration is difficult to change. If aggression is directed at other than the source of frustration, it will tend to fall on those who are the weakest and who will not readily strike back. This can explain why the groups that are most often prejudiced against are those that are the weakest in society. In Canada, the Native peoples were long seen to be the least prestigeful and most prejudiced against (Pineo, 1977). Until the 1970s, they were also a relatively powerless group. It is their own organizational and political activity that has raised their status and influence on the government and society.

The frustration-aggression hypothesis can also be useful in explaining the prejudices of members of minority groups against other minority groups or against the majority group itself. Many members of minority groups are frustrated by discrimination against them. On the job, in housing, but also politically and culturally, they often feel that they are blocked from what is their due or that they are not given the kind of rewards or recognition that they should be given for their work or as is their right in a democratic society. This produces aggressive and prejudicial feelings against the mainstream of society or against other minority groups.

"Threats to group identity" theory. This theory is related to the interethnic competition and conflict theory, since in the process of competition, ethnic groups may come to feel that their identity is threatened. It differs, however, from the competition and conflict theory because it does not focus on economic or political interests that the groups may compete for, but rather on symbolic interests. A group's identity is tied up with cultural symbols. These can be many, ranging from the group's language, various forms of art, religious expression and other elements of culture. When there is a challenge to the distinctiveness or dominance of any of these symbols, it comes to be seen as a challenge to the existence or dominance of the group itself. The response to this challenge is usually defensive, with group members attempting to reinstate the group by belittling those who speak for the challenging groups and/or reinforcing the distinctiveness or dominance of the group challenged.

In the United States, for example, the large presence of the Hispanic groups, mostly Mexican Americans, Puerto Ricans and Cubans, has made use of the Spanish language quite widespread in many areas of the country, particularly in large cities. Many official government forms are printed in two languages, English and Spanish, street signs are often in two languages and public schools teach Spanish. In the United States this unofficial bilingualism is a relatively new phenomenon. It has produced a strong reaction, however, among the dominant English-speaking population. In a number of states constitutional amendments have been passed, establishing English as the state's official language.

In Canada, a similar reaction has developed since the end of the 1980s against the policy of **multiculturalism** (Canada, 1991). In both the United States and Canada, the minority groups do not represent either a political or economic threat to the majority groups. They do, however, represent a symbolic threat to their hegemony, i.e., a threat to the symbols of their group identity. In turn, this threat evokes prejudicial reactions....

• Historical Legacy Theory

Historical legacy theories of prejudice are related to the competition and conflict theory, since they focus on particular historical events, usually those of political conflict, in which one group has caused injury or injustice to another group. However, it is not the events themselves that are seen as evoking prejudice among members of one group against another group, since these events have happened in the often remote past. What is important here is the memory of these events and the legacy these events have left for the members of a group. A legacy is a complex phenomenon. It includes feelings of obligation to righten the historical wrongs that members of a group share. But it also includes a certain mistrust of one group by another that is rooted in the original historical trauma. The legacy is transmitted through the socialization process, but it takes its place as part of the group's culture and is given a symbolic expression.

Many interethnic conflicts in the present are in some degree driven by a legacy of past events. This is true of the English-French and the Aboriginal-English relations in Canada. In the first case, the past event that evokes negative feelings of one group against the other is the conquest of New France that happened almost two and a half centuries ago. In the second case, the event is the treaties between the two that were agreed to in the past but can be determined to be still binding. Other cases abound: Catholic-Protestant relations in Northern Ireland, white-black relations in the United States, the legacy of apartheid in Africa, the Jewish Holocaust, man-made famine in the Ukraine, Spanish-Basque relations in Spain and so on and on.

KEY TERMS

- Prejudice and ethnocentrism
- Socialization theory
- "Structural" approach
- "Competition and conflict" theories
- Social-psychological dynamics
- Scapegoating
- "Frustration-aggression" hypothesis
- "Threats to group identity" theory
- Multiculturalism
- "Historical legacy" theories

REVIEW

1. Which of the five theories better explain the emergence of prejudice? Which better explain its persistence?

2. What mechanisms are used to deal with psychological arousal according to social-psychological theories of prejudice?

3. Allport's classification of theories of prejudice dates to 1954; Isajiw's, to 1999. How does this reflect on our ability to address this behaviour? How could study of these theories of prejudice affect our approach to this issue?

WORK IN A FAST-FOOD FACTORY

THE "NEW INFORMATION AGE"?

ESTER REITER

For office workers, the "new information age" has brought the advantages of computers, fax machines and other high-tech equipment. For workers in the service sector, such as the fast-food industry, this new technology has had quite a different impact.

PREVIEW

The introduction of new technology has affected all of our workplaces, but certain sectors of our economy have suffered its dehumanizing effects more than others. In comparing her work in a Burger King outlet to that in a factory, Reiter describes how the introduction of new technology has had a deleterious effect on the labour process. Ester Reiter is Programme Coordinator for Women's Studies at York University.

Fast-food workers, like factory workers, use expensive pieces of machinery to perform simple repetitive tasks under close supervision in an assembly line environment. Like factory workers, they have little scope for individual innovation and find their workplace set by the machines they tend. Any deviation from the routine prescribed by head office is forbidden since it would likely reduce efficiency.

But fast-food workers face an added burden: as **service workers** who meet the public, they become part of the package being sold. They are on display, so they must submit to having their personal appearance, speech and demeanour monitored, moulded and, as much as possible, standardized. An irregular personality, it seems, is every bit as unacceptable to the system as an underdone french fry or burnt burger.

This paper focuses on the technology and the **labour process** in the fast-food industry. Using Marx's description of the transitions from craft to manufacture to large-scale industry, it considers the changes in the restaurant industry brought about by the development of fast-food chains. The description of life in a fast-food factory is based on my experience working in a Burger King outlet in 1980/1.

Founded in 1954 by James McLamore and David Edgerton, Burger King became a wholly-owned subsidiary of Pillsbury in 1967. The company grew from 257 restaurants at the time of the merger to 3,022 by May 1981. About 130,000 people are employed in Burger Kings all over the world. By November 1982, there were 87 Burger King stores in Canada, 40 of them company owned.[1]...

In the fast-food industry, the machines, or the **instruments of labour**, assume a central place. Instead of assisting workers, the machines are dominant. [Karl] Marx described this as transition from "manufacture" to "large-scale industry."[2] Since the motion of the factory proceeds from the machinery and not from the worker, working personnel can continually be replaced. Frequent change in workers will not disrupt the labour process—a shift in organization applauded by Harvard Business Review contributor, Theodore Levitt.[3] According to Levitt, this new model is intended to replace the "humanistic concept of service" with the kind of technocratic thinking that in other fields has replaced "the high cost and erratic elegance of the artisan with the low-cost munificence of the manufacturer."

The labour process admired by Levitt has been adopted by many of the large fast-food companies including Burger King.

The brain centre of all Burger King outlets lies in Burger King headquarters in Miami, Florida. There the Burger King bible, the *Manual of Operating Data*, is prepared. The procedures laid down in the manual must be followed to the letter by all Burger King stores. To ensure procedures are followed, each outlet is investigated and graded twice yearly by a team from regional headquarters.

In order to maximize volume and minimize labour costs, there is tremendous emphasis on what Burger King management calls speed of service. Demand is at its peak during the lunch hour, which accounts for about 20 percent of sales for the day; the more people served during the hour of twelve to one, the higher the sales volume in the store.

Ideally, service time should never exceed three minutes.[4] Labour costs are also kept down by minimizing the use of full-time workers and by hiring minimum-wage part-time workers. Workers fill out an availability sheet when they are hired, indicating the hours they can work. Particularly when students are involved, management pressures them to make themselves as available as possible, though no guarantees are provided for how many hours a week of work they will be given, or on which days they will be asked to work.

Scheduling is done each week for the coming week and workers are expected to check the schedule each week to see when they are supposed to show up. *The Manual of Operating Data* recommends as many short shifts as possible be assigned, so that few breaks will be required.

Food and paper costs make up about 40 percent of the cost of sales in Burger King outlets. These costs are essentially fixed, owing to company requirements that all Burger King outlets buy their stock from approved distributors. In effect, individual stores have control over food costs in only two areas—"waste" of food and meals provided to employees. Both together make up less than four percent of the cost of sales.

Store operations are designed from head office in Miami. By late 1981, it was possible to provide store managers not only with a staffing chart for hourly sales—indicating how many people should be on the floor given the predicted volume of business for that hour—but also where they should be positioned, based on the type of kitchen design. Thus, what discretion managers formerly had in assigning and utilizing workers has been eliminated.

Having determined precisely what workers are supposed to be doing and how quickly they should be doing it, the only remaining issue is getting them to perform to specifications. "Burger King University," located at headquarters in Miami was set up to achieve this goal. Burger King trains its staff to do things "not well, but right," the Burger King way.[5] Tight control over Burger King restaurants throughout the world rests on **standardizing operations**—doing things the "right" way—so that outcomes are predictable....

As with the production of hamburgers, the cooking of french fries involves virtually no worker discretion. The worker, following directions laid out in the *Manual of Operating Data*, empties the frozen, pre-cut, bagged fries into fry baskets about two hours before they will be needed. When cooked fries are needed, the worker takes a fry basket from the rack and places it on a raised arm above the hot oil, and presses the "on" button. The arm holding the fry basket descends into the oil, and emerges two minutes and twenty seconds later; a buzzer goes off and the worker dumps the fries into the fry station tray where they are kept warm by an overhead light. To ensure the proper portions are placed into bags, a specially designed tool is used to scoop the fries up from the warming table.

Even at this station, though, management is concerned about **limiting worker discretion**. Despite the use of a specially designed scoop to control the portions each customer is given, a sign placed in the crew room for a few weeks admonished crew about being too generous with fry portions.

At the cash register, the "counter hostess" takes the order and rings it up on the computerized register. The "documentor" contains 88 colour coded items, ensuring that all variations of an order are automatically priced. As a menu item is punched in at the counter, it will appear on printers in the appropriate location in the kitchen. In this manner, the worker at sandwiches, for example, can look up at the printer and check what kind of sandwich is required. When the customer hands over the money, the cashier ring in "amount tendered" and the correct amount of change to be returned to the customer is rung up. Thus, cashiers need only remember to smile and ask customers to come again.

The computerized cash register not only simplifies ordering and payment, but is used to monitor sales and thus assist in staffing. If sales are running lower than expected, some workers will be asked to leave early. Output at each station is also monitored through the cash register. Finally, the computer at all company stores is linked through a modem to the head office in Miami. Top management has access to information on the performance of each store on a daily basis, and this information is routed back to the Canadian division headquarters in Mississauga.

Skill levels required in a Burger King have been reduced to a common denominator. The goal is to reduce all skills to a common, easily learned level and to provide for cross-training. At the completion of the ten-hour training program, each worker is able to work at a few stations. Skills for any of the stations can be learned in a matter of hours; the simplest jobs, such as filling cups with drinks, or placing the hamburgers and buns on the conveyor belt, can be learned in minutes. As a result, although labour turnover cuts into the pace of making hamburgers, adequate functioning of the restaurant is never threatened by people leaving. However, if workers are to be as replaceable as possible, they must be taught not only to perform their jobs in the same way, but also to resemble each other in attitudes, disposition, and appearance. Thus, workers are also drilled on personal hygiene, dress (shoes should be brown leather or vinyl, not suede), coiffure (hair tied up for girls and not too long for boys), and personality. Rule 17 of the handout to new employees underlines the importance of smiling: "Smile at all times, your smile is the key to our success."

While management seeks to make workers into interchangeable tools, workers themselves are expected to make a strong commitment to the store. If they wish to keep jobs at Burger King, they must abide by the labour schedule. Workers, especially teenagers, are expected to adjust their activities to the requirements of Burger King….

The daytime workers—the remaining 25 percent of the work force—were primarily married women of mixed economic backgrounds. Consistent with a recent study of part-time workers in Canada, most of these women contributed their wages to the family budget.[6] Although they were all working primarily because their families needed the money, a few expressed their relief at getting out of the house, even to come to Burger King. One woman said: "At least when I come here, I'm appreciated. If I do a good job, a manager will say something to me. Here, I feel like a person. I'm sociable and I like being amongst people. At home, I'm always cleaning up after everybody and nobody ever notices!"[7]

Common to both the teenagers and the housewives was the view that working at Burger King was peripheral to their major commitments and responsibilities; the **part-time nature of the work** contributed to this attitude. Workers saw the alterative available to them as putting up with the demands of Burger King or leaving; in fact, leaving seemed to be the dominant form of protest. During my period in the store, on average, eleven people out of ninety-four hourly employees quit at each two-week pay period. While a few workers had stayed at Burger King for a few years, many did not last through the first two weeks. The need for workers is constant.

Burger King's ability to cope with high staff turnover means virtually no concessions are offered to workers to entice them to remain at Burger King. In fact, more attention is paid to the maintenance of the machinery than to "maintaining" the workers; time is regularly scheduled for cleaning and servicing the equipment, but workers may not leave the kitchen to take a drink or use the bathroom during the lunch and dinner rushes.

The dominant form—in the circumstances, the only easily accessible form—of opposition to the Burger King labour process is, then, the act of quitting. Management attempts to head off any other form of protest by insisting on an appropriate "attitude" on the part of the workers. Crew members must constantly demonstrate their satisfaction with working at Burger King by smiling at all times. However, as one worker remarked, "Why should I smile? There's nothing funny around here. I do my job and

It is too difficult to think nobly when one thinks only of earning a living.

Jean-Jacques Rousseau, philosopher

that should be good enough for them." It was not, however, and this worker soon quit. Another woman who had worked in the store for over a year also left. A crew member informed me that she had been fired for having a "poor attitude."

Management control and lack of worker opposition is further explained by the fact that other jobs open to teenagers are no better, and in some cases are worse, than the jobs at Burger King. The workers all agreed that any job that paid the full rather than the student minimum wage would be preferable to a job at Burger King; but they also recognized that their real alternatives would often be worse. Work at a donut shop, for example, also paid student minimum wage, under conditions of greater social isolation; baby sitting was paid poorly; and the hours for a paper route were terrible. Work at Burger King was a first job for many of the teenagers, and they enjoyed their first experience of earning their own money. And at Burger King, these young men and women were in the position of meeting the public, even if the forms of contact were limited by a vocabulary developed in Burger King headquarters: "Hello. Welcome to Burger King. May I take your order?" Interaction with customers had some intrinsic interest.

In sum, workers at Burger King are confronted with a labour process that puts management in complete control. Furnished with **state-of-the-art restaurant technology**, Burger King outlets employ vast numbers of teenagers and married women—a population with few skills and little commitment to working at Burger King. In fact, this lack of commitment is understood through reference to a labour process that offers little room for work satisfaction. Most jobs can be learned in a very short time (a matter of minutes for some) and workers are required to learn every job, a fact that underlines the interchangeable nature of the jobs and the workers who do them. The work is most interesting when the store is busy. Paradoxically, work intensity, Burger King's main form of assault on labour costs, remains the only aspect of the job that can provide any challenge for the worker. Workers would remark with pride how they "didn't fall behind at all," despite a busy lunch or dinner hour.

It would be reassuring to dismiss the fast-food industry as an anomaly in the workplace; teenagers will eventually finish school and become "real workers," while housewives with families are actually domestic workers, also not to be compared with adult males in more skilled jobs. Unfortunately, there are indications that the teenagers and women who work in this type of job represent an increasingly typical kind of worker, in the one area of the economy that continues to grow—the **service sector**. The fast-food industry represents a model for other industries in which the introduction of technology will permit the employment of low-skilled, cheap, and plentiful workers. In this sense, it is easy to be pessimistic and agree with Andre Gorz's depressing formulation of the idea of work:

> The terms "work" and "job" have become interchangeable: work is no longer something that one does but something that one has. Workers no longer "produce" society through the mediation of the relations of production; instead, the machin-

Notes

[1] Promotional material from Burger King Canada head office in Mississauga, Ontario.

[2] Karl Marx, *Capital*, vol.1 ([1867]; New York: 1977), ch. xv.

[3] Theodore Levitt, "Production Line Approach to Service," *Harvard Business Review* 50, no.1 (Sept./Oct. 1972): 51–2.

[4] A "Shape Up" campaign instituted at the beginning of 1982 attempted to set a new goal of a 2 ½-minute service time.

[5] Personal communication, Burger King "professor," 4 January 1982.

[6] Labour Canada, *Commission of Inquiry into Part-Time Work* (Ottawa: 1983) [Wallace commission].

[7] Personal communication, Burger King worker, 8 August 1981.

[8] Andre Gorz, *Farewell to the Working Class* (Boston: 1982), 71.

ery of social production as a whole produces "work" and imposes it in a random way upon random, interchangeable individuals.[8]

The Burger King system represents a major triumph for capital. However the reduction of the worker to a simple component of capital requires more than introduction of a technology; workers' autonomous culture must be eliminated as well, including the relationships among workers, their skills, and their loyalties to one another. The smiling, willing, homogeneous worker must be produced and placed on the Burger King assembly line.

While working at Burger King, I saw the extent to which Burger King has succeeded in reducing its work force to a set of interchangeable pieces. However, I also saw how insistently the liveliness and decency of the workers emerged in the informal interaction that occurred. Open resistance is made virtually impossible by the difficulty of identifying who is responsible for the rules that govern the workplace: the workers know that managers follow orders from higher up. The very high turnover of employees indicates workers understand that their interests and Burger King's are not the same. As young people and women realize that their jobs in the fast-food industry are not waystations en route to more fulfilling work, they will perhaps blow the whistle on the Burger King "team." The mould for the creation of the **homogeneous worker** assembling the standardized meal for the homogeneous consumer is not quite perfected.

KEY TERMS

- Service workers
- The labour process
- Instruments of labour
- Labour costs
- Standardizing operations
- Limiting worker discretion
- Skill levels
- Part-time work force
- State-of-the-art technology
- The service sector
- Homogeneous worker

REVIEW

1. How are fast-food workers like factory workers? How have the workplaces of both been affected by new technology?

2. What action do most workers take if they are dissatisfied with the labour process at Burger King? What other options are open to them?

3. In 1982, Andre Gorz wrote that the terms "work" and "job" were interchangeable. Is this still true today? In what way has it changed?

MAC ATTACK

UNIONIZING AT McDONALD'S

SARAH INGLIS

Sarah Inglis liked her job at McDonald's until a new owner arrived, and things began to change. Working conditions worsened, and with "respect, dignity, and job security" at stake, Sarah decided to organize a union.

PREVIEW

In this selection, Sarah Inglis tells the story of her attempt, at the age of 16, to organize a union at her local McDonald's in Orangeville. A part-time employee, Sarah refused to tolerate poor working conditions, contacted the Service Employees International Union, and began her campaign to win over employees of the union-shy fast-food industry.

People say I tried to organize McDonald's in Orangeville because my dad is president of an auto workers' union local. I don't really think that because my dad and I, we didn't talk a lot about unions until after I had found one. I mean, sure, I've got some values from him—but he didn't do any of the organizing. I told him I wanted to do it. I guess he was a little shocked.

My grandmother was an activist. She was a feminist. I'm a feminist. Maybe I get some of my spunk from her.

Working at McDonald's was my first job. I stared in April of 1991. I was 14. The first thing I was trained on was the counter—orienting the food on the tray, and making the customers happy, and smiling. There's a lot more to a counterperson's job than what you see. They don't let you rest. As soon as you're done with your customer you can help somebody else out with another order, or you can stock up, or you can clean, but *just don't stop*. It's like you're a robot.

Under the management that was there when I first went to work at McDonald's, it was fine. You were treated with respect. Things were done as fairly as they possibly could be done. And when Cam Ballantyne—the second owner—first came in, I had a good rapport with him. I don't know why, but he liked me. But when I noticed what he was doing to the other employees, I was thinking, well, why the hell not me?

He fired a woman because she called a manager a bitch. She didn't call her a bitch, actually. I mean, she was friends with the manager, and she said: "Tone it down, people are kind of thinking that you're getting a little bit bitchy. I'd watch your ass around here." The manager put on Niagara Falls—I mean, she started crying—went and told Cam, and this employee was fired in the next three or four days—an employee that had been there for six years. I mean, that's not a just cause.

When Cam came in, the day staff were getting six-and-a-half to eight-hour days, five days a week. And he came in and slashed them down to about four-and-a-half. You still get a break for that. And then he slashed them down to three-and-a-half, which you don't get a break for. That's disgusting. I mean, they need that money. Pay rates are anything from minimum wage to, I guess, up to 12 bucks for a handful of people who've been there since the restaurant opened.

There were a lot of people talking about problems at work. Even this one girl–who is a major anti-union supporter now–was a total union supporter in the beginning. I remember her telling me that she had two jobs because Cam wouldn't give her enough hours. So she had to take another job at Northern Reflections at the mall. And when Cam found out, he threatened her. She told me he said, "I want to either see your resignation to Northern Reflections or your resignation here, because I don't believe you're being loyal to us." I mean, what law says you can only have one job?

At first I didn't talk about **organizing** to anybody. I heard about this new Bill 40, and I was thinking about that. I waited for it. Everything about Bill 40 made it easier for us to unionize. So in January 1993, my friend and I tried to organize with the Canadian Auto Workers' union. They seemed pretty positive, and we had the cards, and then they called us and said no. I don't think they ever told really told me what their reasons were.

Then I went camping in the summer and when I got back, I started trying to organize again. This was just after I had been taken off "drive-thru" because I don't smile enough.

So I called the Teamsters; I called the Hotel Employees and Restaurant Employees' union; I called a couple of other ones, and finally the Service Employees International Union. I just said, I want to speak to an organizer. All the other ones, when I spoke to them they'd say: well , how old are you? Or I'd tell them how old I was. But with the SEIU I said to myself, screw it. I'm not going to tell them, because it seemed to be making a difference. I think that maybe they didn't take me seriously enough.

When the SEIU called me back, I remember thinking Rui Amorim, the organizer, was some rough, tough business man–just because of his voice–and I was thinking, oh my God, what am I getting into? So he showed up at my door and met three other people who were interested in doing this, and he said, "Well, OK, you don't have to convince me, I'm sold on the idea. You've got to convince the director of organizing." So we had to get more numbers and invite them to an August 25 meeting to show, hey, we can do this. They came, and we got the cards. Things just started from there. We knew what we had to do.

Signing people up was like, for me, getting up at six in the morning and going to bed at four in the morning. It totally wrecked your normal day. We signed 67 out of 102 people.

It was difficult sometimes. Some people didn't understand what a union meant, so you had to go back to the very beginning and explain. Some of them were totally anti-union. And some of them signed as soon as they heard it. Some people thought that a union was just a money-hungry company that wanted to take you for everything you had. I mean, 18 cents an hour isn't taking you for everything you have, guys. Especially when unions put in hundreds of thousands of dollars in legal fees.

We applied for **certification** on October 1, and I don't know what the hell happened. The company sent people from McDonald's and they interviewed staff one at a time. There was an anti-union petition going around. Some of the anti-union people called the day staff and said, lookit, Cam knows who's signed cards, so you'd better hurry up and sign this petition or else he's going to think that you're not loyal to him. They didn't call me.

Cam held a crew meeting when he found out about the union, and I went to it. He tried to intimidate me there. He was saying that unions weren't good things, that they would destroy our big happy family, and take everything away we had now. "We give you enough," he was saying. "We give you half-price food, we give you free uniforms, we pay for your breaks." You know, that sort of thing. "We have flexible scheduling." They don't schedule anyone enough hours. I mean, what could be more flexible than that?

A lot of people were asking him questions about the union, so he said, why don't you let Sarah answer your questions? Well, we were holding a **union meeting** the same night. I said well, if you have questions, you can go to such-and-such a place and we'll be happy to answer them there. And then somebody said, well, why do you want a union here?

I said, "For respect, dignity, and job security."

And they said, "Who doesn't give you respect?"

I said, "The managers don't." And I said, "I'm sure that some of you must agree with that." Then Cam piped up and said, "What managers? What don't you like about them?"

"I've already tried to tell you," I said, "and it hasn't worked."

And he says, "Well, why don't you meet me tomorrow after school?"

"Nope, sorry I'm busy." I said, "Cam, why don't you get back to me about this?" Because he always told people to get back to him about things. So I sort of turned it around. It was beautiful.

Then he started talking about full-time benefits, and how they have packages for part-time workers, and one lady said, "What package? I've been working here for a year and I haven't seen any benefits." So then he says, "Get back to me about that." It was sort of a stupid meeting.

All the way through this I was in school. I had two jobs: one after school and then McDonald's on weekends. I worked until 8 or 9 at my other job about three or four times during the week, and then I'd come home and I'd do union stuff for about two or three hours. I'd be on the phone with the lawyers, and then I tried to do homework, but it didn't work. I was too tired to do anything. School suffered. My marks dropped. My social life took a new twist. I started hanging around with my committee more.

I guess I met with the lawyers just after October 1. I felt good about these guys. They seemed to know what they were doing. It freaked me out the first day I went to the **labour board** and saw my employer sitting across from me. It was a little bit intimidating. There were allegations of me locking people in my car. In my car the locks don't even work! There were charges of me intimidating this 300-pound guy.

The union was there to answer my questions, but I guess I needed more than that. I don't think they had a strategy planned about how to organize this place. I mean, that's really important, because there are so many loops and turns put into organizing a place like this. I don't think anybody really understands how to organize the fast-food industry right now.

I don't think the majority of the staff understood the significance of this case. And how it's going to go down in history, and how it's going to change the labour movement slightly and open the doors for all fast food restaurants to organize. I just don't think people understood totally what rights they exactly did have.

The day after we signed the vote agreement, I went on nation-wide TV, on *Front Page Challenge*. That was really neat. One of the lawyers faxed me some stuff the morning before the show on what I could and couldn't talk about, and gave me some good ideas. That helped me out a bit.

Preston Manning was on before me via satellite. I was behind the stage getting ready to go on, and they were killing him with questions and making him look like a real jackass. I thought, oh God, they're just getting warmed up for me, but they were really nice and pleasant. I don't know if it was just because of my age, or whether they agreed with what I was doing, or what.

When I got back to Orangeville, I tried to keep everybody as pumped up as I possibly could. The lawyers sent me flyers and so on, but there's only so much that you can make people read. You need some sort of flashy stuff to keep people's attention, especially the youth. Cam had all these juvenile cartoon drawings. I'm surprised that people didn't feel sort of insulted by the way that he presented the work atmosphere at McDonald's. It was like you were in grade one or two.

We held a couple of committee meetings with a business agent from the union, a week before the vote. We tried to do house calls, and spread literature out, and call people, and do whatever we possibly could to educate them and make them aware of what a union really is—in case they'd forgotten or management had twisted it in their minds.

Rui was up here for that. He headed a couple of meetings, from a week before the vote until the day before. Those all seemed to go very well, because he could talk to youth on their level. He became a friend. He was there to try to support people. He always said: "What it all boils down to is, do you personally want a union or not? It's up to you." He got people thinking for themselves.

The night before the vote, the company organized a crew rally to motivate people to vote No. Cam was saying a speech. I got there late, and when I walked in the door Cam started stumbling over all his words. I felt great. I

With all their faults, trade-unions have done more for humanity than any other organization of men that ever existed. They have done more for decency, for honesty, for education, for the betterment of the race, for the developing of character in man, than any other association of men.

Clarence Darrow, lawyer

mean, now he knows what it's like to feel intimidated, and how he made the crew feel. I got great satisfaction out of that.

After Cam's speech there was a slide show—which they played twice—with "Just Say No" buttons and everybody goofing off at work. People *wanted* to change their minds about the union, because they were scared of losing their jobs. People were very intimidated, and scared—and brainwashed, too. The slide show was synchronized with background music like "Shiny Happy People" and "It's a Wonderful World." It's a psychological thing that McDonald's seems to have the power to be able to do. I think McDonald's has this ability to make you think that there's nothing wrong, everything's beautiful. Just bring back good memories, not the bad. That's total bullshit.

I stood at the bottom of the steps of the church where the slide show was being held. As people were going out, I was trying to tell them about a union meeting we were having that night. Cam came down and stood almost right beside me and then people wouldn't speak to me or even look at me. I think it just shows you what management can do. How they can intimidate people. They wouldn't even look at me.

On the day of the vote I didn't know what I was supposed to be doing, so I went out for breakfast with my committee. Then I got on the phone with one of the lawyers, and he said, you'd better be on the phone with people, making sure that they have rides, especially the ones who you think are going to vote Yes. So I was trying to do that, but the media just flooded my house, and my phone, and I couldn't seem to get anything done. So we went down to McDonald's.

There was quite a bit of media down there the first time, so we went away and came back down in the afternoon to vote. The media was there, bigger than ever. Whenever I took a step somewhere they'd jump out in front of me, and then I'd take a step somewhere else, trying to psych them out, and they'd jump out in front of me again. It was pretty fun, actually.

I didn't really tell the media anything except I thought that we could win, and tried to stay as positive as I could, and give my committee as much support as I could.

I said, even if we don't win, we've already put ourselves into a win-win situation. Because **working conditions** have changed. McDonald's treated us like gold. It was unbelievable how they reacted to the union coming in.

I think the media were very fair. The CBC was the best. They just presented it as it was. I always had it in the back of my mind that if I was rude to the media then they may not be on my side any more and they may take a different angle. So I tried to be as polite as I possibly could.

I didn't want to find out the results of the vote in front of the media. I think by then everybody knew that it was going to end the way it did, and I didn't want our immediate reaction to be public—because I thought maybe there would be tears. We decided to drive around to a dark, empty Dairy Queen parking lot and find out the vote results by car phone.

While we were waiting, we got out of the car and sort of tried to clear our heads about the whole thing, which wasn't easy. My committee and I just started jumping around, joking around, goofing off–like regular teenage kids do. Then the organizing director got out of the car and said, "We lost. Get in."

There was like a three-second silence that seemed like an eternity. I don't think it really hit me. Then everybody just congratulated each other. We said: "We did it. We still won, in a way."

Then we found out the actual numbers in front of the press, and that was tough. I think that we were very strong, actually. Nobody really cried. We just said we did the best we could and we were just tight.

When we got back to my house, I didn't know what I wanted to do. There's no way to explain how I felt. There was an empty feeling inside of me. We deserved to win. We should have won the numbers.

A week after, one of my committee people, Courtney, was pushed by a manager. I wanted to cry when I heard that. You would have figured that the results of this union threat would have lasted a little bit longer than a week. She told me she was on her way to the washroom when the manager came up to her and said, "Who did you ask to go to the washroom?" She said, "Nobody. There was nobody around." And he pushed her and told her to get back up to the front of the store. I mean, Courtney's about five feet and the manager is about six feet. There's quite a difference.

I don't know what we should do about that any more. It all just seems like a waste. I mean, what did I do this for if it was going to last a week?

KEY TERMS

• Union organizing
• Union certification
• Union meeting
• Labour board
• Working conditions
• Workers' rights
• Companies' responsibilities

REVIEW

1. What response did Inglis receive from her fellow employees when she urged them to sign up with the SEIU?

2. How did Sarah campaign for the union? How did the management at McDonald's respond?

3. Sarah Inglis failed in her attempt to organize a union at McDonald's. What factors might have contributed to this failure?

But looking back, it was worth the effort. Even if things change back now, those people down there had it good for about four months. And once they begin to be treated as usual–as it was before the union came along–I think people will start to realize, "Look at what I've done. I voted against myself."

What advice would I have for other people trying to unionize in the fast-food industry? Go through the system. See what you can do on the inside first, and if it doesn't work, your ultimate choice is to unionize.

Read Mary Cornish's book, *Organizing Unions.* Honestly, I mean, it's got everything in it that you need to know about organizing a union, from approaching a union, to what you should ask them, to what you should research, to how you sign the cards.

From any union or organization I would be looking for support. I think I'd look at past practices, and how they organized places. I'd also be looking for a commitment to sort of stand with me and hold my hand–and all the employees' hands–through the whole process and have some support system.

I'd ask: What is the union offering? And maybe even have a contract between the committee and the union about a strategic plan of how you're going to organize. There has to be a plan to deal with all the loops and turns of the fast-food industry.

It would also be good to have other unions in your community support you and help you. After all the card-signing's done, have them make it public to the community, and try to help people not be intimidated, or to be at least *less* intimidated. They should be saying, "Lookit, it's OK, it's your right to do this, you have every right under the law to organize. If they're going to fire you, let them, and we'll fight for your job back." I know it's hard for people to do that, but I mean, you have to stand up for your rights. Otherwise, you're back in the 1800s.

I think the youth have to be educated about their rights, and I also think adults need to be educated about their rights. Maybe it's not just the union's job, but it's Canada's job to enforce **workers' rights** and **companies' responsibilities**. Because there's so much illegal activity that goes on. I mean, there's sexual harassment, verbal harassment....

People need more say over their livelihood. They should have some rights when negotiating with their employers, and not let employers have the last word all of the time, and not give them the right to make up the rules as they go along.

People want to feel there's somebody out there who's on their side, so that they won't be one against a giant corporation. People want to have respect and dignity. People want to be treated like human beings. Not dogs. And not children.

Body Ritual among the "Nacirema"

A Magical Mystery Tour

HORACE MINER

What is the purpose of a "charm-box"? What role is played by "holy-mouth-men"? Welcome to the magical world of the Nacirema, whose beliefs and rituals so mirror our own!

The **anthropologist** has become so familiar with the diversity of ways in which different peoples behave in similar situations that he is not apt to be surprised by even the most exotic customs. In fact, if all of the logically possible combinations of behaviour have not been found somewhere in the world, he is apt to suspect that they must be present in some yet undescribed tribe. This point has, in fact, been expressed with respect to clan organization by [George] Murdock. In this light, the magical beliefs and practices of the Nacirema present such unusual aspects that it seems desirable to describe them as an example of the extremes to which human behaviour can go.

Professor [Ralph] Linton first brought the ritual of the Nacirema to the attention of anthropologists twenty years ago, but the culture of this people is still very poorly understood. They are a North American group living in the territory between the Canadian Cree, the Yaqui and Tarahumare of Mexico, and the Carib and Arawak of the Antilles. Little is known of their origin, although tradition states that they came from the east. According to Nacirema mythology, their nation was originated by a culture hero, Notgnihsaw, who is otherwise known for two great feats of strength—the throwing of a piece of wampum across the river Pa-To-Mac and the chopping down of a cherry tree in which the spirit of Truth reside.

Nacirema culture is characterized by a highly developed **market economy** which has evolved in a rich natural habitat. While much of the people's time is devoted to economic pursuits, a large part of the fruits of these labours and a considerable portion of the day are spent in **ritual activity**. The focus of this activity is the human body, the appearance and health of which loom as a dominant concern in the ethos of the people. While such a concern is certainly not unusual, its ceremonial aspects and associated philosophy are unique.

PREVIEW

In this article, anthropologist Horace Miner takes a satirical look at the "Nacirema," a people whose culture is riddled with magic, and whose everyday lives are based on superstition and the supernatural. Miner subtly sensitizes the reader to his or her own ethnocentricity, and presses the reader to recognize that the primitive and the magical are less a matter of specific practices than the assumptions that we draw upon to interpret those practices.

The fundamental belief underlying the whole system appears to be that the human body is ugly and that its natural tendency is to debility and disease. Incarcerated in such a body, man's only hope is to avert these characteristics through the use of the powerful influences of ritual and ceremony. Every household has one or more shrines devoted to this purpose. The more powerful individuals in the society have several shrines in their houses and, in fact, the opulence of the house is often referred to in terms of the number of such ritual centres it possesses. Most houses are of wattle and daub construction, but the shrine rooms of the more wealthy are walled with stone. Poorer families imitate the rich by applying pottery plaques to their shrine walls.

While each family has at least one such shrine, the rituals associated with it are not family ceremonies but are private and secret. The rites are normally only discussed with children, and then only during the period when they are being initiated into these mysteries. I was able, however, to establish sufficient rapport with the natives to examine these shrines and to have the rituals described to me.

The focal point of the shrine is a box or chest which is built into the wall. In this chest are kept the many charms and magical potions without which no native believes he could live. These preparations are secured from a variety of specialized practitioners. The most powerful of these are the medicine men, whose assistance must be rewarded with substantial gifts. However, the medicine men do not provide the curative potions for their clients, but decide what the ingredients should be and then write them down in an ancient and secret language. This writing is understood only by the medicine men and by the herbalists who, for another gift, provide the required charm.

The charm is not disposed of after it has served its purpose, but is placed in the charm-box of the household shrine. As these magical materials are specific for certain ills, and the real or imagined maladies of the people are many, the charm-box is usually full to overflowing. The magical packets are so numerous that people forget what their purposes were and fear to use them again. While the natives are very vague on this point, we can only assume that the idea in retaining all the old magical materials is that their presence in the charm-box, before which the body rituals are conducted, will in some way protect the worshipper.

Beneath the charm-box is a small font. Each day every member of the family, in succession, enters the shrine room, bows his head before the charm-box, mingle different sorts of holy water in the font, and proceeds with a brief rite of ablution. The holy waters are secured from the Water Temple of the community, where the priests conduct elaborate ceremonies to make the liquid ritually pure.

In the hierarchy of magical practitioners, and below the medicine men in prestige, are specialists whose designation is best translated "holy-mouth-men." The Nacirema have an almost pathological horror of and fascination with the mouth, the condition of which is believed to have a supernatural influence on all social relationships. Were it not for the rituals of the mouth, they believe that their teeth would fall out, their gums bleed, their jaws shrink, their friends desert them, and their lovers reject them. They also believe that a strong relationship exists between oral and moral characteristics. For example, there is a ritual ablution of the mouth for children which is supposed to improve their moral fibre.

The daily body ritual performed by everyone includes a mouth-rite. Despite the fact that these people are so punctilious about care of the mouth, this rite involves a practice which strikes the uninitiated stranger as revolting. It was reported to me that the ritual consists of inserting a small bundle of hog hairs into the mouth, along with certain magical powders, and them moving the bundle in a highly formalized series of gestures.

In addition to the private mouth-rite, the people seek out a holy-mouth-man once or twice a year. These practitioners have an impressive set of paraphernalia, consisting of a variety of augers, awls, probes, and prods. The use of these objects in the exorcism of the evils of the mouth involves almost unbelievable ritual torture of the client. The holy-mouth-man opens the client's mouth and, using the above mentioned tools, enlarges any holes which decay may have created in the teeth. Magical materials are put into these holes. If there are no naturally occurring holes in the teeth, large sections of one or more teeth are gouged out so that the supernatural substance can be applied. In the client's view, the purpose of these ministrations is to arrest decay and to draw new friends. The extremely sacred and traditional character of the rite is evident in the fact that the natives return to the holy-mouth-men year after year, despite the fact that their teeth continue to decay.

It is to be hoped that, when a thorough study of the Nacirema is made, there will be careful inquiry into the personality structure of these people. One has but to watch the gleam in the eye of a holy-mouth-man, as he jabs an awl into an exposed nerve, to suspect that a certain amount of sadism is involved. If this can be established, a very interesting pattern emerges, for most of the population shows definite masochistic tendencies. It was to these that professor Linton referred in discussing a distinctive part of the daily body ritual which is performed only by men. This part of the rite involves scraping and lacerating the surface of the face with a sharp instrument. Special women's rites are performed only four times during each lunar month, but what they lack in frequency is made up in barbarity. As part of this ceremony, women bake their heads in small ovens for about an hour. The theoretically interesting point is that what seems to be a preponderantly masochistic people have developed sadistic specialties.

The medicine men have an imposing temple, or *latipso*, in every community of any size. The more elaborate ceremonies required to treat very sick patients can only be performed at this temple. These ceremonies involve not only the thaumaturge but a permanent group of vestal maidens who move sedately about the temple chambers in distinctive costume and headdress.

Anthropology is the science which tells us that people are the same the whole world over—except when they are different.

Nancy Banks-Smith, British columnist

The *latipso* ceremonies are so harsh that it is phenomenal that a fair proportion of the really sick natives who enter the temple ever recover. Small children whose indoctrination is still incomplete have been known to resist attempts to take them to the temple because "that is where you go to die." Despite this fact, sick adults are not only willing but eager to undergo the protracted ritual purification, if they can afford to do so. No matter how ill the supplicant or how grave the emergency, the guardians of many temples will not admit a client if he cannot give a rich gift to the custodian. Even after one has gained admission and survived the ceremonies, the guardians will not permit the neophyte to leave until he makes another gift.

The supplicant entering the temple is first stripped of all his or her clothes. In every-day life the Nacirema avoids exposure of his body and its natural functions. Bathing and excretory acts are performed only in the secrecy of the household shrine, where they are ritualized as part of the body-rites. Psychological shock results form the fact that the body secrecy is suddenly lost upon entry into the *latipso*. A man, whose own wife has never seen him in an excretory act, suddenly finds himself naked and assisted by a vestal maiden while he performs his natural functions into a sacred vessel. This sort of ceremonial treatment is necessitated by the fact that the excreta are used by a diviner to ascertain the course and nature of the client's sickness. Female clients, on the other hand, find their naked bodies are subjected to the scrutiny, manipulation and prodding of the medicine men.

Few supplicants in the temple are well enough to do anything but lie on their hard beds. The daily ceremonies, like the rites of the holy-mouth-men, involve discomfort and torture. With ritual precision, the vestals awaken their miserable charges each dawn and roll them about on their beds of pain while performing ablutions, in the formal movements of which the maidens are highly trained. At other times they insert magic wands in the supplicant's mouth or force him to eat substances which are supposed to be healing. From time to time the medicine men come to their clients and jab magically treated needles into their flesh. The fact that these temple ceremonies may not cure, and may even kill the neophyte, in no way decreases the people's faith in the medicine men.

There remains one other kind of **practitioner**, known as a "listener." This witch-doctor has the power to exorcise devils that lodge in the heads of people who have been bewitched. The Nacirema believe that parents bewitch their own children. Mothers are particularly suspected of putting a curse on children while teaching them the secret body rituals. The counter-magic of the witch-doctor is unusual in its lack of ritual. The patient simply tells the "listener" all his troubles and fears, beginning with the earliest difficulties he can remember. The memory displayed by the Nacirema in these exorcism sessions is truly remarkable. It is not uncommon for the patient to bemoan the rejection he felt upon being weaned as a babe, and a few individuals even see their troubles as going back to the traumatic effects of their own birth.

In conclusion, mention must be made of certain practices which have their base in native aesthetics but which depend upon the pervasive aversion to the natural body and its functions. There are ritual fasts to make fat people thin and ceremonial feasts to make thin people fat. Still other rites are used to make women's breasts larger if they are small, and smaller if they are large. General dissatisfaction with breast shape is symbolized in the fact that the ideal form is virtually outside the range of human variation. A few women afflicted with almost inhuman hypermammary development are so idolized that they make a handsome living simply going from village to village and permitting the natives to stare at them for a fee.

Reference has already been made to the fact that excretory functions are ritualized, routinized, and relegated to secrecy. Natural reproductive functions are similarly distorted. Intercourse is taboo as a topic and scheduled as an act. Efforts are made to avoid pregnancy by the use of magical materials or by limiting intercourse to certain phases of the moon. Conception is actually very infrequent. When pregnant, women dress so as to hide their condition. Parturition takes place in secret, without friends or relatives to assist, and the majority of women do not nurse their infants.

Our review of the ritual life of the Nacirema has certainly shown them to be a magic-ridden people. It is hard to understand how they have managed to exist so long under the burdens which they have imposed upon themselves. But even such exotic customs as these take on real meaning when they are viewed with the insight provided by [Bronislaw] Malinowski when he wrote:

> Looking from far and above, from our high places of safety in the developed civilization, it is easy to see all the crudity and irrelevance of magic. But without its power and guidance early man could not have mastered his practical difficulties as he has done, nor could man have advanced to the higher stages of civilization.

KEY TERMS

- Anthropologist
- Market economy
- Ritual activity
- Practitioners

REVIEW

1. What is the first clue author Horace Miner provides that indicates that the "Nacirema" are actually the subject of a satirical article? What is the main danger of using satire as a means of social criticism?

2. What techniques does Miner use to make this piece seem like a legitimate scholarly article? Is he successful in deceiving the reader to a certain extent?

3. What does Miner's approach teach us about our assumptions concerning the practices of other cultures?

Living Together

"Ethnic Cleansing" and Other Abominations

BOB RAE

By any reasonable criteria, ethnic differences—differences based on colour, religion or ancestry—should play a relatively minor role in world affairs. Yet they have recently assumed an enormous importance. Can we learn to respect others and live together in harmony? Is there an alternative to continuing ethnic conflict?

PREVIEW

In this brief essay, author Bob Rae posits good government and the principles of federalism as partial solutions to the nationalist excesses of this century, witnessed most recently in Kosovo. The effects of globalization have heightened the irrational longing for homogenous nations, and the words of Thomas McGee, one of the Fathers of Confederation, on federalism may well contain some much-needed wisdom. Rae was premier of Ontario from 1990-95 and is now a lawyer with Goodman Phillips & Vineberg in Toronto.

I write these words in the shadow of the tragedy of Kosovo. A few years ago it would have been in the wake of the slaughter in Rwanda. We are coming to the end of the bloodiest and most destructive century in world history. Those who believe in the natural evolution of mankind to some higher level of civilization have to ask themselves how far we have really advanced.

This century has also seen a greater degree of integration of the world economy; the word **"globalization"** is everywhere in our consciousness. Technology and the economies in which we all live and work are making us more interconnected by the day.

At a human level, globalization creates several dynamics. People move, and societies that might have thought of themselves as more or less homogeneous have necessarily become more diverse. For anyone travelling on the subway in Toronto, it is impossible not to think of our having become the world in one country or even one street.

Governance matters. How people govern themselves, live with each other, educate their children, create institutions of civil society, treat their neighbours—all these things have great consequences for the well-being of people.

Federalism is not a magic formula for solving the world's problems, but Thomas D'Arcy McGee, one of the Fathers of Confederation, was surely right when he said that federalism implies something deep in human nature itself. (It was McGee's birthday yesterday, so it's a good idea to remember him.)

There have always been ethnic tensions whenever people who live differently live side by side. The answer to these tensions is not to eliminate the people who are different from ourselves, or to insist that they become just like us. That is the way to permanent conflict and war. It is terrible to realize that "ethnic cleansing" has now joined the Orwellian lexicon of the 20th century.

Nor should we accept the argument that every separate nationality requires its own sovereign state. As Ernest Renan pointed out more than 100 years ago, the notion that there is such a thing as a homogeneous nation, be it culturally, racially, religiously or linguistically, is nonsense, a fiction that can only be created by blocking out the truth of inevitable diversity. A nation is a political construct, based on common interests and a sense of shared experience. It is not "normal," as one Quebec politician keeps putting it, for a state to be entirely homogeneous.

A healthy dose of federalism, then, is required to deal with the excess of nationalism that has been a tragic feature of the 20th century. Europe is discovering this, although the "f" word dare not always speak its name.

Our own history as Canadians has taught us the value of federalism, and the dangers of ignoring its principles. When the interests of minorities were ignored, or when the values of a nationality were dismissed, we created the conditions for internal conflict. By the same token, the vitality of a decentralized federation with a considerable degree of provincial autonomy, but with enough central capacity to coordinate and lead, has been an important element of our recent successes. While Canada's two recent attempts at more comprehensive constitutional reform–Meech and Charlottetown–did not succeed in getting ratified, we have been more successful recently at making smaller steps. The Agreement on Internal Trade and the Social Union are good examples. While Quebec's absence from the latter is to be regretted, it is not unrealistic to expect that a provincial government more committed to the renewal of Canadian federalism will be able to improve the practical running of the federation even more.

McGee would have become a much more widely known and appreciated man if his life had not been cut short by an assassin's bullet in 1868, a year after Confederation. Here is McGee:

> There is something in the frequent, fond recurrence of mankind to this principle [of federalism], among the freest people, in their best times and in their worst dangers, which leads me to believe, that it has a very deep hold in human nature itself – an excellent basis for a government to have.… The principle of Federation is a generous one. It is a principle that gives men local duties to discharge, and invests them at the same time with a general supervision, that excites a healthy sense of responsibility and comprehension.… It is a principle eminently favourable to liberty, because local affairs are left to be dealt with by local bodies, and cannot be interfered with by those who have no local interest in them, while matters of a general character are left exclusively to a General Government.

Choose the words of McGee over the words of victimhood, of regional spite, of ethnic anxiety.

KEY TERMS

- Ethnic cleansing
- Globalization
- Governance
- Federalism
- Sovereign state
- Nation
- Constitutional reform

REVIEW

1. How has globalization affected the social fabric of Canada? What tensions have resulted?

2. According to Thomas McGee, what principles are embodied by federalism?

3. What role has nationalism played in the tragedy of Kosovo? How could "a healthy dose of federalism" combat the effects of nationalism?

Six Degrees of Separation

It's a Small World, Isn't It?

POLLY SHULMAN

How far removed are you from Michael Jordan or Céline Dion? Chances are you know someone who knows someone who knows someone who knows someone who knows someone who knows those people.

PREVIEW

Mathematicians Strogatz and Watts have proposed a "small world" theory in which there are only six people separating any two of us. The small world theory applies not only to social networks but also to those found throughout nature and technology, and its proponents eagerly await its application in other fields. Polly Shulman is a senior editor at "Discover" magazine.

When Duncan Watts was pursuing his Ph.D, his adviser was Steven Strogatz, who has written scientific papers with Rennie Mirollo, who was a teaching assistant for Steve Maurer, whose mother used to live down the hall from my Grandma Rose in a high-rise in Hackensack, New Jersey. Small world, right?

Such coincidences crop up a lot. According to cocktail-party lore, every pair of people on the planet—a randomly chosen Inuk and a Parisian, a Solomon Islander and a dude from Nebraska—are connected by a chain of at most six acquaintances. Personally, I am—to drop only a few names—two steps from Prince Charles and Stephen Hawking, three steps from Marilyn Monroe and King Carl XVI Gustaf of Sweden, four steps from King Juan Carlos of Spain, and close friends with the brother of a childhood buddy of the Dutch crown prince. And chances are you, too, have similar connections.

Dr. Strogatz and Dr. Watts study "small worlds"—networks that consist of lots of little cliques but in which a few members of each clique have connections to other, more distant parts of the network.

"The small-world effect is not just a curiosity about **social networks**," says Dr. Strogatz, an applied mathematician at Cornell. "It occurs in many different kinds of networks throughout nature and technology." The small-world effect could have a lot to do with how diseases such as AIDS spread, for example: The idea that everyone is at most six degrees apart takes on a sinister significance when we look for shared sexual partners instead of shared acquaintances. It also could explain how rumours spread, says Dr. Watts, now a postdoctoral fellow at the Santa Fe Institute.

Mathematically minded people, Dr. Strogatz says, often approach the small-world question with a simple calculation: Suppose I have 100 friends, each of whom also has 100 friends. A hundred times 100 makes 10,000 friends of my friends. If each of those 10,000 people has 100 friends, there will be one million people three degrees away from me. Five steps away, there are 10 billion.

"So a lot of people would say it's not surprising that the **degree of separation** is small," concludes Dr. Strogatz, "because within five steps you've done the whole planet."

But that calculation presumes that each 100 friends are 100 new people. In the real world, many of one's friends know each other. And it's easy to imagine a very exclusive clique of 100 people in Greenwich, Conn., say, who know only one another and wouldn't dream of associating with anyone outside their circle. Conceivably, no chain of acquaintances connects you or me with any member of that clique.

"So how do you even begin to think about these sorts of networks?" Dr. Watts asks.

Dr. Watts and Dr. Strogatz began with a beautifully structured network called a **ring graph**.

"Think of a lot of people standing in a circle holding hands," Dr. Watts says. "Say there are a million people and you know 100 of them. You know 50 people on your left and 50 people on your right, and they are the only ones you can communicate with. What if you want to get a message to person number 500,000 on the other side of the circle–how do you do that? Well, you shout the message to your farthest friend, number 50 to your left side, and say, 'Pass it on.' The best they can do is shout to their 50th friend to the left, and so on." On average, there are 5,000 steps between pairs of people in this world. And 5,000 degrees of separation, as Dr. Watts points out, is an awful lot.

Now imagine the same million people standing in the same circle. Each still has 100 friends. But instead of knowing only the 50 people to the left and the 50 to the right, everyone chooses friends at random from the million people available. Now when he and Dr. Strogatz calculate the average degree of separation between two people, it comes out to about four.

What happens between the **orderly world** and the **random one**? To find out, Dr. Watts and Dr. Strogatz started with an orderly model and carefully messed it up, making worlds that were progressively more random. So instead of knowing the 50 people to your right and the 50 to your left, you might know the 50 to your right, and 49 of the 50 to your left. But number 17 to your left is a stranger; instead, you're close friends with number 307,411.

These new connections quickly bring the world closer together, Dr. Watts says. In fact, it takes only a tiny number of rewirings–less than 1 percent of the total connections–to bring the average degree of separation down from 5,000 to just over four, close to the average degree of separation of a random world.

How common are these small worlds in nature? Dr. Strogatz and Dr. Watts began looking for networks in which every connection was known, allowing them to determine the shortest possible path between any two points. Such networks were hard to find, but they turned up three: the neural network of a nematode worm; the power grid of the western U.S.; and the Hollywood graph, a database of everyone who has ever acted in a feature film. People use this very database (available on the Web at www.cs.virginia.edu/~bct7m/bacon.html) to play a game called Six Degrees of Kevin Bacon, tracing connections between the *Footloose* thespian and other Hollywood luminaries.

Although Dr. Watts and Dr. Strogatz chose those three examples because they were the only networks they could find in which all the connections were known, all turned out to be small worlds.

"Is this as widespread a phenomenon as we guess it is?" Dr. Strogatz asks. "I would look forward to work by, say, neurologists mapping out brain networks. The people who study ecology could study food webs–which organisms are eating each other. In economics, it would be interesting to trace out networks of markets and consumers and buyers and sellers. I'm sure, there are people who are thinking about **network theory** in economics and in finance–it could be at the level of whole nations interacting, or even just individual people."

And chances are you know someone who knows someone who knows someone who knows someone who knows someone who knows those people.

PART 4
The Arts and Humanities

O, had I but followed the arts!

William Shakespeare's Sir Andrew Aguecheek, in Twelfth Night, Act 1, Sc. 3, bemoaning the time he spent in "fencing, dancing, and bear-baiting."

The Arts and Humanities

An Introduction

The appearance of modern humans, homo sapiens, appears to have coincided with the appearance of art as we know it, perhaps as recently as 35,000 years ago. What is it about art that conjures up basic human passions? This unit explores the finer points of human life.

In an article in an earlier section, Marie Curie, the co-discoverer of plutonium and radium, made a plea that the scientist should be allowed to do "science for science's sake." Though perhaps a little controversial to non-scientists, most scientists would probably agree. However, it is unlikely that any artist or even any layperson would dispute the notion that, above all, we must champion "**art for art's sake.**" Few things irritate people more than when artists are subjected to political constraints, when artistic freedom is curtailed, or when what claims to be art is really just commercial advertising or political propaganda. What is it, then, about art that turns on people's basic passions?

FUNDAMENTAL TRUTHS

Art is obviously not science. To enjoy art, or to "do" art, you must come up with a **subjective interpretation** based on your own perception of things. The formal rules of scientific experimentation, hypothesis testing, and so on, do not apply. Art summons up emotions. It can disturb us, enlighten us and even threaten us as we seek to understand the intended message of the artist. Moreover, since we all initially perceive works of art as individuals, what one person sees in a painting, for example, might or might not be seen by others. The mere fact that you cannot see things exactly the same way others do is of no matter in the arts—it is the viewer who matters most, for art is subjective by its very nature.

Yet, art is not entirely individualistic. "As the unity of the modern world becomes increasingly a technological rather than a social affair," wrote Marshall McLuhan, Canadian communications theorist, "the techniques of the arts provide the most valuable means of insight into the real direction of our own collective purposes." In other words, great literature, painting, drama and music open up doors to **fundamental truths**.

It is the combination of these two aspects—the intense individual subjectivity and the search for fundamental truths—that defines the arts and necessitates "art for art's sake." As an individual begins to relate to himself or herself through art, there occurs a deepening personal enrichment that goes beyond the bounds of simple perception. There is a sense of disclosure by the artist, no matter what form his or her work takes, that speaks to us all.

What do we know about the origins of art? We have been fabricating artifacts for at least 2.5 million years, but for most of that time those artifacts were merely undecorated stone tools. The flowering of ancient art happened quite recently. The oldest known artistic manifestations in Western Europe date from as recently as 35,000 years ago. This was the time when modern people were replacing Neanderthals in that part of the world. Art objects such as jewelry (beads and pendants) began to appear, as did the spectacular cave paintings of Spain and France. That same pattern is repeated elsewhere. Thus, the appearance of art as we know it coincides with the appearance of modern humans, **homo sapiens**. The older species that were displaced appear to have showed little inclination to pick up a paint brush.

KEY TERMS

• Art for art's sake
• Subjective interpretation
• Fundamental truths
• Homo sapiens

COMING TO A THEATRE NEAR YOU

Great works of art traverse continents and centuries. Today, the large galleries around the world pay ever-spiralling amounts for a painting by Rembrandt or a sculpture by Renoir. Even literature that has long been in the public domain has a way of finding its way to market. Witness the William Shakespeare revival—as the new millennium begins there are several new Hollywood versions of his plays (*Romeo and Juliet* and *A Midsummer Night's Dream*, to name just two) and one award-winning movie about the bard himself (*Shakespeare in Love*). Such is the power of art.

Artistic work, then, though highly individualistic in many respects, is social activity *par excellence* insofar as it very much depends on there being, somewhere, an "audience." Artists seek to uncover "fundamental truths" that give meaning to life and capture the essence of what it means to be human. With stakes as high as these, it is no wonder that artists insist on their right to do "art for art's sake" and to be free from censorship of all kinds.

This unit focuses on a broad foundation of both the expressive and reflective arts. A range of artistic forms and points of view are represented. Several articles towards the end address philosophical and spiritual issues, which are also included under the broader heading of "the humanities." The arts and humanities can open inner doors of discovery and wonder. It is hoped that this section of the book will encourage a deeper interest in them.

Painting is a blind man's profession. He paints not what he sees, but what he feels, what he tells himself about what he has seen.

Pablo Picasso, Spanish artist

Portrait of the Arts

Art for Art's Sake

MORTON RITTS

The arts "show" us the truth of the human condition, a truth that is greater than the truth we are "told" by science. Artists, motivated by their need for self-actualization and their desire, perhaps, for immortality, serve as our truth's chroniclers.

PREVIEW

What is the place of art in our daily lives? How does an artistic work differ from a scientific work? In this short but insightful essay, Canadian author and educator Morton Ritts explores the relevance of art and concludes that the artist has a special place in our world: he or she helps to redraw and enlarge the boundaries of our emotional and intellectual experience.

Let us examine the role of the arts. Sometimes it's harder to say what art is than what it isn't. Art, for example, isn't science. **Science** is factual and propositional. It tries to provide knowledge that is objective and clear, with verifiable observations based on a rigorous method of enquiry.

Art, on the other hand, tends to be ambiguous and problematic. It is both factual and fictional. Indeed, on one level, narrative arts like literature and film proclaim themselves to be not "true" at all, to be "made-up." How can something that's made up be true? And yet, we know from our own experience that when we read certain novels or see certain films we're struck by just how "true to life" they are.

There is a profound paradox here. Characters in novels and films who are invented, who are fictions, often reveal more about human nature than real people. Fiction, in other words, has the capacity to provide us with greater insight to truth than truth. But fiction is just another kind of truth. All art is.

Of course, psychology and biology also provide us with truth. But their focus is always general, while art portrays the particular. For example, as a psychological theory, Sigmund Freud's "oedipal complex" is universal and abstract. But in his novel *Sons and Lovers*, D.H. Lawrence gives this theory specific, concrete form by creating a rich and complex character whose intense, troubled relationship with his mother dominates his life.

For another example compare the description of anxiety and fear in a psychology textbook with how these same emotions are depicted in a novel or film. The textbook account is analytical, factual. This is fine, but such an account doesn't convey to us what anxiety and fear "feel" like. A well-written novel or well-made film does, however, by locating these emotions in actions that compel our interest. This difference between fact and fiction is the difference between science and the arts. Science and the social sciences "tell" whereas the arts "show."

Vincent van Gogh, *Starry Night*, (1889), oil on canvas; 73.7 x 92.1 cm.

Vincent van Gogh (1853-1890) was a Dutch post-impressionist painter, whose work represents the archetype of expressionism, the idea of emotional spontaneity in painting.

Courtesy of the Museum of Modern Art, New York. Photograph © 1995.

We've said that the arts "show" by giving us knowledge of the particular. As the *Sons and Lovers* example suggests, we come to know an important universal relationship (mothers and sons) in the depiction of a specific relationship.

The arts "show" by way of creativity, discipline, expressiveness. They give form to our experience. Sometimes the result is indirect, as in expressionist painting. Sometimes it's brutally direct, as in *The Killing Fields*, a powerful film about the genocide that occurred in Cambodia in the 1970s. Different as they are, both examples represent some important aspect of truth....

In his play, *A Midsummer Night's Dream*, William Shakespeare compared artists (poets) to lovers and lunatics. What connects them, he suggests, is precisely this power of the imagination:

> And, as imagination bodies forth,
> The form of things unknown, the poet's pen
> Turns them to shapes, and gives to airy nothing
> A local habitation and a name.

The artist, then, is someone whose imagination makes the unknown known, the invisible visible and the unconscious conscious—which is very close to the therapeutic process of Freudian psychoanalysis. Art itself is a way of exploring the mysteries of **the human condition**, not in the linear fashion of scientific enquiry but in the associative, circular manner of therapy. "We shed our sicknesses in books," D.H. Lawrence wrote. Art, he meant, heals.

REVIEW

1. What does the author mean when he says "fiction is just another kind of truth"?

2. The author argues that the tools the artist uses are different from those used by scientists. What are the main tools of the artist?

3. In this article, the author refers to the work of psychologist Abraham Maslow. What were the different levels of human needs Maslow distinguished and where does art fit in Maslow's hierarchy of needs?

That's perhaps one reason why people feel the need to write, paint, play an instrument or sing. Another reason, we've suggested, is the desire to leave some sign, some evidence of our existence. As children we seek even the most trivial kind of immortality, nothing more sometimes than carving our initials into the trunk of a tree or printing our name in the fresh concrete of a sidewalk.

The **humanistic psychologist** Abraham Maslow offers still another way of looking at the desire to create. We may recall that in his **hierarchy of needs**, Maslow speculates that physical survival is basic. Someone who lacks the requirements for physiological well-being, including food and shelter, isn't much interested in writing novels or painting landscapes.

But once these basic needs are satisfied, we often ask ourselves, "What more is there to life?" What's more, Maslow says, are the higher level needs for love, esteem and, above all, **self-actualization**. More than most people, artists are obsessed by the need to self-actualize, to be the best they can at whatever they are. A tale about two modern painters, Amadeo Modigliani and Chaim Soutine, illustrates this point.

Modigliani and Soutine were friends who shared a studio in a small garret in Paris at the turn of the century. They were almost stereotypes of the starving artist, deprived of material comforts but endowed with rich and productive imaginations.

One day, the story goes, they bought a chicken at the local butcher shop, as the subject for a "still life." They hung it from the rafters in their studio and set up their easels. In the midst of their preparation, however, it occurred to them that they hadn't had a decent meal in weeks. They'd spent their last francs on a chicken, but incredibly—foolishly, it seemed at that moment—they were intending to paint it, not eat it.

Maslow might explain their dilemma this way: If the two friends cooked the chicken, they'd satisfy their basic survival needs but not their need for art. On the other hand, if they painted the chicken, they'd satisfy their need for self-actualization, but might starve to death in the process. What to do? In fact, they arrived at one of those inspired compromises that are the mark of true genius—they painted very quickly (while the chicken was still fresh).

The story is a good example of the struggle between the demands of life and those of art. Someone once asked the great artist Picasso whether, if his house caught fire, he'd rescue his cat first or his paintings. He answered his cat. Picasso's point was that artists draw their inspiration from life. Without life there can be no art.

THE STATE OF THE ARTS

CANADIAN ARTS AT THE MILLENNIUM

CANADA YEARBOOK

Many of Canada's artists have achieved dazzling success, especially in recent years. Yet, it is difficult to maintain and express our distinct Canadian voice against the barrage of American culture. The survival of our arts depends not only on our talent base but on private donations, corporate sponsorship and government support.

The 1990s have been years of almost mesmerizing success for Canadian writers, singers and movie makers alike. Anne Michaels' novel *Fugitive Pieces* won international praise with Britain's Orange Prize and the American Lannan Literary Award, and domestic acclaim with Ontario's Trillium Prize.

Margaret Atwood's *Alias Grace* and Rohinton Mistry's *A Fine Balance* were in the running for Britain's Booker Prize, and Nancy Huston's *Instruments des ténèbres* was short-listed for France's Prix Goncourt. Quebec's Ying Chen was shortlisted for le prix Fémina and Kathy Reichs, also from Quebec, made Canadian and American best-seller lists with her novel *Déja Dead*. Last but not least, Michel Tremblay's most recent novel, *Un objet de beauté*, won accolades both in Quebec and France.

Canada's musical artists have followed suit. In the 1990s, Céline Dion, Shania Twain and Alanis Morissette together sold more than 56 million albums.

In 1997, the film version of Michael Ondaatje's novel *The English Patient* swept the Oscars, winning a total of nine Academy Awards. Atom Egoyan was awarded the Cannes International Critics' prize for *The Sweet Hereafter.*

Fittingly, a point of reference for all this success is found in Anne Michaels' novel *Fugitive Pieces*. "Nothing is sudden," she writes. "Just as the earth invisibly prepares its cataclysms, so history is the gradual instant." In Canada, the "gradual instant" has much historic precedent. We can go back to the turn of the century and the days of the famed Mary Pickford, a Canadian from Toronto, to find our roots in cinematic performance, literary pursuits and drama.

As early as 1797, the Halifax Chess, Pencil and Brush Club encouraged its members in the activities its title suggested, while in St. John's in 1880, book lovers had to join a waiting list before they could get into the Eclectic Reading Club. In Saint Boniface, Manitoba, in 1925, le Cercle Molière began presenting plays in French and continues to do so today....

PREVIEW

The past decade has brought phenomenal success to some Canadian artists, who have garnered both national and international praise. According to data provided in the government's own "Canada Yearbook," however, the general state of the arts in Canada does not mirror this success. While our government has made efforts to protect our cultural heritage, by imposing revenue taxes and regulating Canadian content and control, many of our artistic companies struggle to break even at the box office.

GOVERNMENT SUPPORT

In 1951, one of Canada's foremost literary figures, Robertson Davies, issued a warning to a government commission on cultural activity: "Canada will not become great by a continued display of her virtues for virtues are–let us face it–dull. It must have art if it is to be great." The Massey commission eventually concluded that government had a role to play in the support of arts and leisure. One direct result was the creation, in 1957, of the Canada Council, now known as the **Canada Council for the Arts**.

Today, all levels of government in Canada support culture. The federal government helps through grants, tax measures and through the support of special programs like those of the Canada Council. Since 1989-90, total federal spending on culture has been about $2.9 billion a year, or just under $100 a year for every Canadian.

In recent years, there have been internal shifts in how this money is spent. Between 1990 and 1996, federal support for the literary arts declined almost two-fifths, from $239 million to $146 million. During the same period, support for cultural industries (these include broadcasting, film and video, sound recording and publishing) increased about 5% to just over $2 billion....

THE ARTISTS

"What do you want, Frances?"
"A job."
He starts to laugh again but Frances just looks him steady in the eye.
He shuts up and asks, "What can you do?"
"I can dance. I can sing and play piano."
He looks her up and down. "What else?"
She twists her mouth into a sneer she hopes is hard as nails.
"I can do anything."
He gives a short chuckle. Then another, and nods.
"You're all right, Frances."

In Canada, culture is both created and consumed daily. The result of our encounters with each other, with the land and with the vagaries of our climate, it is also a way of life. In this excerpt from Ann-Marie MacDonald's *Fall on Your Knees*, we find a telling description of our artists: multitalented and often willing and able to work at more than one job at a time.

Artists in Canada write, perform, design, create, curate and teach. Many of them are well educated (50% are university graduates), about 60% are self-employed, and they are generally young (61% are under the age of 44). On average, Canadian artists earn about $24,000 a year, slightly below the national average of $29,000....

For a **cultural industry** to survive, there must be a market for its products. It would appear that the market is a fairly vigorous one in Canada, not

Culture is created and consumed daily–in our schools, our offices, our communities and our homes.

only in terms of what we are spending on recreation but also in our attendance at cultural events and heritage sites. In 1996, Canadian households spent an average of about $2,600, or 5% of the budget, on recreation, up 15% from 1992. Mostly, this spending shows our growing affinity for gadgets, be they computers, cameras or sports equipment. We also, however, like to step out. Spending on entertainment and performances rose more than one-third to $430 per household. While the main reason for the increase was due to cable television charges, there was also more spending on admissions to movie theatres and live performances such as concerts.

Through art we express our conception of what nature is not.

Pablo Picasso, Spanish artist

THE PERFORMERS

Since 1989, a chandelier weighing 600 kilograms has come crashing down on the stage at the Pantages Theatre in Toronto at every performance, bringing the first act of *The Phantom of the Opera* to a dramatic close. Eight years and 3,345 chandelier-falls later, the theatre has sold more than 6 million tickets for this spectacle, the Canadian cast recording has sold more than 800,000 copies, and the box office has taken in $565 million.

In 1997, in St. John's, two women produced the first St. John's Fringe Festival. With a one-time grant of $25,000, they staged 15 productions in five days–and box office receipts were to be kept by the performers. Canadian theatre exists somewhere between the Phantom and the fringe.

In fact, Canadian theatre accounts for nearly half the economic activity in the performing arts. Its recent history can be told in three acts. Act I is the founding of Ontario's Stratford Festival in 1953. Act II is the start of a network of regional theatres founded in the 1950s and 1960s. Act III is the development of a commercial theatre scene in large urban centres including Montréal, Toronto, and most recently, Vancouver. In fact, Toronto is now listed as the third-largest centre for English language theatre in the world, after New York's Broadway and London's West End.

In Quebec, a thriving theatre scene is also making international waves. There is the work of Normand Chaurette whose play *Les Reines* has found its way to France's famous Comédie-Française, in addition to charming audiences in capital cities throughout Europe and whose *Le Passage de l'Indiana* made a huge splash at the Avignon Festival in 1996. Carole Fréchette's play *Les Quatres Morts de Marie* is staged regularly in France, as are the works of Robert Lepage, Denis Marleau and Gilles Maheu.

In 1994-95, there were 293 not-for-profit theatre companies and Canadians were happy to see their productions, picking up 8.5 million tickets to do so. Total revenues were $183 million. Of these, half came from the box office, a third from public grants and the rest from private donations and corporate sponsors....

Michael Snow, *Race* (1984). Photograph and paint on board, 176 x 79 cm. Courtesy of Agnes Etherington Art Centre, Queen's University. Reprinted with the permission of Michael Snow.

MUSIC, DANCE AND OPERA

The colourful conductor of the Winnipeg Symphony Orchestra, Bramwell Tovey, has stated that to get even more people out to the symphony, there is work to be done on the image of classical music. "We're still wearing the tails of the 19th century," he says, "while the challenge is to create the audience of the 21st century." Yuli Turovski, who is the founder of Montréal's chamber orchestra I Musici, has written "just as much as the body requires food, so too does the soul require music."

Both sentiments find resonance in the statistics. In 1994-95, music organizations reported an attendance of 3.2 million people at more than 4,000 musical performances. Revenues came to $114 million: 42% from the box office, 37% from grants and the remaining 21% from private and corporate donations. With some 18 opera companies, another 111 music groups and 71 dance companies, Canadians have much choice in terms of cultural entertainment. (All of these groups are identified as not-for-profit.)

Canada's foremost classical and contemporary ballet companies are well established and include the Royal Winnipeg Ballet (founded in 1941), The National Ballet of Canada (1951) and Les Grands Ballets Canadiens (1958).

If the symphony isn't the ticket, there's always dance: in 1994-95, dance companies presented more than 2,100 performances, playing to audiences totalling more than 1. 1 million people.

In 1994-95, dance companies earned revenues of $56 million, of which box office income and grants each accounted for roughly 40%, while the remaining 20% came from corporate sponsors and private donations. Also in 1994-95, volunteers with Canada's dance companies actually outnumbered paid staff by 10% and these dance companies managed to produce a small surplus that year.

Meanwhile, in 1994-95, opera companies presented more than 900 performances, selling 750,000 tickets. Their expenses came to $40.3 million while total revenues were $40.5 million, almost half of which came from the box office. Grants accounted for 30%; donations and sponsorships made up the remainder. Overall, opera in Canada is a debt-free enterprise.

AT THE MOVIES

On June 27, 1896, in a darkened room at 78 rue Saint Laurent in Montréal, viewers witnessed something never seen before in Canada: a "moving picture." The *Cinématographe* was the invention of the Lumière brothers of Paris and this first audience saw a series of minute-long films, including footage of a train arriving at a station, a boat at sea, and the Lumière brothers playing cards.

In the years that followed, Canadian audiences were to see films of music-hall performances and circus acts, the trick photography of the Méliès Brothers from France, as well as Canadian news events such as the 1907 Québec Bridge disaster near Québec, shot by Leo-Ernest Ouimet, a major figure in the history of Canadian cinema.

The era of the great movie palaces began in the early 1900s. In 1906, Ouimet constructed the Ouimetoscope, the first permanent cinema in Montréal. In the 1920s, Jules and Jay Allen of Brantford, Ontario built a chain of 53 movie theatres across Canada, although in 1923, these theatres were acquired by an American company. Today, many of the picture palaces of the past have been converted into multiple-screen theatres or sit abandoned and drive-ins have all but disappeared.

The Canadian public has had an on-again, off-again love affair with the silver screen. In 1952, at the apex of cinema's popularity in Canada, there were some 256 million admissions to the movies and drive-ins. While the movies have not had this kind of draw since, and in fact have lost audiences in the intervening decades, Canadians appear now to be back in line at the box office. In 1995-96, movie admissions, including those for the few remaining drive-ins, came to 87 million, up some 15 million from the start of this decade....

Investment policy guidelines put in place in 1988 keep the distribution of movies in the hands of Canadian-owned companies by limiting what foreign-owned firms can distribute in Canada. In 1992-93, Canadian controlled distribution companies captured only 17% of the revenues from distributing films to movie theatres; by 1994-95, that share had increased to 24%.

Most of what Canadians see at the movies comes from other countries. Canadian films account for about 5% of the available screen time in Canadian cinemas.

In terms of production, Canadian feature films make up less than 1% of total Canadian film and video production, but they still make waves at

Canadian screen legend Mary Pickford played in such films as *The Poor Little Rich Girl* (1917).

international festivals, as filmmakers David Cronenberg, John Greyson, Atom Egoyan, Robert Lepage and others have experienced. In 1994-95, producers brought 38 feature films to production, 19 of them from Quebec.

Indeed, Quebec cinema is gaining international attention, as the numerous awards and nominations that its filmmakers have received readily attest. In recent years, the credits have rolled: Denys Arcand for his *The Decline of the American Empire* and *Jesus of Montréal*; Jean-Claude Lauzon for his *Léolo, Un Zoo, la nuit*; François Girard for *Le Dortoir, Thirty-Two Short Films About Glen Gould*; and Frédéric Back for *Crac* and *L'Homme qui plantait des arbres*, both animated films.

Canada's acclaimed **National Film Board** continues to adjust to reduced funding. In 1995-96, the Board received $77 million in government funding and with a work force of about 518 people, shot 110 productions, rented out almost 200,000 films and videos, and received 99 awards. In 1996-97, its parliamentary appropriation was cut to $72.8 million. Nonetheless, it produced 102 productions and co-productions in 1996-97 and received 104 awards. Almost 4,000 Canadian television broadcasts featured National Film Board productions.

Filmmaking is an increasingly international venture and Canadian participation in co-productions is growing. In the early 1980s, Canadian producers signed only five **co-production agreements**. By 1996, Canadian filmmakers were part of 32 co-production agreements involving 44 countries. Similarly, investment in the film industry is increasing. Between 1991-92 and 1994-95, Canadian investment in film and video production grew by a third, reaching $421 million, while foreign investment tripled to $212 million.

Canada exports film talent as well as films. Celebrated for their technical and creative know-how, graduates of Canada's animation programs at colleges, especially those in Ontario and British Columbia, are working in major international animation studios, as well as for animation studios in Canada. Canadian technical and creative expertise placed Tom Hanks alongside John F. Kennedy in *Forrest Gump*, changed the shape of Jim Carrey's face in *The Mask*, and created characters and other special effects for Disney's animated feature *The Hunchback of Notre Dame*.

RADIO AND TELEVISION

Two of the most powerful forces on the Canadian arts scene are generally found in the home: radio and television. In 1996, Canadians listened to an average of 20 hours of radio a week and watched an additional 23 hours of television. Generally, the programs were aired by a mix of publicly funded and commercial stations and networks.

Radio tastes vary. From 1991 to 1995, stations offering an easy-listening format lost 70% of their share of listeners, while album-oriented rock stations lost 42% of theirs. Where these listeners go is a matter of conjecture, but during the same period, talk radio experienced a 15% increase in its market share and country music, a 9% increase.

Television tastes are split between foreign and Canadian programming. In 1995, Canadians spent as much time watching foreign comedy and drama as we did watching all Canadian programming combined....

• The Canadian Broadcasting Corporation

At a cost of about $0.08 a day for every Canadian, the publicly funded **Canadian Broadcasting Corporation (CBC)** provides national radio and television services in English and French, a 24-hour cable news service in English and another in French, a Northern service in eight Aboriginal languages, and Radio Canada International, a shortwave radio service that broadcasts around the world in seven languages. In 1996-97, the CBC's federal government allocation was $855 million, a drop of $110 million from the previous year.

The CBC has been called the "ribbon of reason" that holds Canada together, just as the railway was once our "ribbon of steel." But the CBC, which includes some 22 television stations and 68 radio stations, has been under its own financial strain. Between 1994 and 1998, it faced an estimated shortfall of more than $400 million and between 1996 and 1997, cut 1,300 employees.

In 1997, the CBC celebrated 60 years of public broadcasting and in spite of its difficulties was able to boast a 90% Canadian television content schedule in prime time.

RECORDED MUSIC

In 1996, a four-CD compilation of Canadian pop music called *Oh What a Feeling* went straight into the top 10, selling more than 250,000 copies, and became the first boxed set in Canadian music history to receive "diamond" status. As a world supplier, Canada is the second-largest producer of French-language recordings after France, and the third-largest producer of English language recordings after the United States and the United Kingdom.

The United States and Europe are, not surprisingly, the key foreign markets for the Canadian music industry. France is the single most important market for the Quebec industry, which received an important boost when France introduced a quota requiring its radio stations to reserve 40% of their air time for French-language music of any nationality.

In 1993-94, Canada's record companies released 6,300 recordings and earned $860 million in revenues. Although only a very few record companies are owned by foreign companies, these latter earned 80% of all revenues.

From 1989 to 1994, releases with **Canadian content** increased in number by 17%, and in revenues by 155%. Interestingly, during this time period,

True science investigates and brings to human perception such truths and such knowledge as the people of a given time and society consider most important. Art transmits these truths from the region of perception to the region of emotion.

Leo Tolstoy, Russian author

Canadian creativity reaches across the land; some of the best is in the National Gallery, Ottawa.

the Canadian content share of total releases actually declined from 14% to 11%, given the faster pace of growth in foreign releases. Even so, more Canadian recordings are being released and they're selling well. The Canadian content share of total recording-related revenues almost doubled from 1989 to 1994, increasing from 6% to 11%.

THE PRINTED WORD

If you walked into a bookstore or visited a newsstand in Canada, you would see a surprising number of home-grown titles on the shelves. Publishers' profits are not always healthy, but interest in Canadian books and magazines is high, and **government policies and grants** lend support to these industries.

• Books

Quite apart from the creative vigour of Canada's writers and their successes of late, the business of book publishing tells another story. More than a quarter of Canadian publishing companies are unprofitable. In 1994-95, for all publishers, profits averaged 7.0% of revenues. This is an improvement over 1991-92, when profits averaged only 3.6%. In 1994-95, more than two-thirds of Canada's publishers received some form of government aid.

In 1994-95, sales in Canada by publishers and exclusive agents were $1.4 billion, while Canadian publishers earned an additional $370 million through exports and foreign sales. At the same time, Canada's readers could choose from 11,000 new and 7,477 reprinted titles published in Canada....

• Magazines

In 1995, the Canadian government imposed an 80% tax on revenues of magazines with an editorial content less than 80% Canadian. The following year, the U.S. government complained to the World Trade Organization that together with Canada's postal subsidies to magazines–approximately $58 million in 1996-97–this tax was a violation of the rules of international trade. In 1997, the World Trade Organization ruled in favour of the United States and Canada agreed to change its regulations.

The dispute revolved around what is called a **"split-run" edition** of a magazine: a magazine prepared in the United States but published as a "Canadian" edition, with virtually the same content as the American version, and with space dedicated for Canadian advertisers.

In addition to split-run magazines, Canada's readers have a choice of many home-grown magazines. In fact, there were about 1,404 periodicals published in 1994-95, mostly in English and French, with a few in Chinese or Punjabi, Portuguese, Italian and so on. Total revenues came to $860 million....

• Libraries

One of the most common cultural centres in Canadian communities is the public library. Public libraries have been supported with public funds since 1882, when Ontario's "free books for all" movement began to spread across the country. There is no official count on the number of Canadian libraries (recent estimates vary from almost 4,000 to more than 6,000).

Libraries in Canada are funded primarily by local government. In 1994-95, municipal governments spent $1.1 billion on libraries and provincial governments spent an additional $707 million. The federal government spent $38 million on libraries, including the National Library of Canada. **The National Library**, which was established in 1953, acquires every publication ever released in Canada.

HERITAGE

Canada's **heritage sites** form an important part of our culture. In 1995-96, these sites–some 2,390 institutions including museums, nature parks and historic sites–logged 113 million visits. Although one in three heritage sites charged admission, attendance still increased 2% from the year before....

In 1997, in France, the first ever "offshore" Canadian national historic sites were inaugurated to commemorate the Canadians who died in the First World War. Beaumont-Hamel honours the 1st Newfoundland Regiment, virtually wiped out at the Battle of the Somme on July 1, 1916, and the site at Vimy Ridge honours the more than 60, 000 Canadians who died in the First World War.

FESTIVALS

It seems that festivals beget festivals. In 1958, Miramichi, New Brunswick, established a traditional folk music festival. Orillia, Ontario, followed with the first Mariposa Festival in 1961, and Canada's largest folk festival, in Winnipeg, began in 1974. Edmonton staged Canada's first fringe theatre festival in 1982.

Now there is a circuit of fringe festivals from St. John's, Newfoundland, to Victoria, British Columbia. Some cities seem to be constantly in festival mode. Montréal, for example, hosts the Just for Laughs International Comedy Festival, the Fringe Festival and the Festival Internationale de Jazz, to name just a few of its annual offerings.

In 1994-95, some 150 of Canada's festivals received $83 million in federal support. The entertainment may feature jazz, buskers, comedy, visual art and dragon boats. It can range from such events as Gimli's *Íslendingadagurinn* to Edmonton's Heritage Days. In fact, these are just two of the more than 150 festivals that now take place in Canada.

KEY TERMS

• Canada Council for the Arts
• The cultural industries
• Investment policy guidelines
• The National Film Board
• Co-production agreements
• Canadian Broadcasting Corporation
• Canadian content
• Government policies and grants for the cultural industries
• "Split-run" editions
• The National Library
• Heritage sites

PREVIEW

1. Which literary figure told a government commission that Canada needed art in order to be great? How did the government respond to his argument?

2. How does the Canadian government support the arts in Canada? What steps have they taken to protect our culture?

3. Why do you think the Canadian arts must rely so heavily on donations, sponsorship and grants for financial support despite critical successes?

Rehanging the National Wallpaper

Canada's "Group of Seven"

DANIEL FRANCIS

Art lovers or not, we've all been exposed to the popular work of the Group of Seven painters, reproduced on everything from T-shirts to calendars. Daniel Francis tells us how this came to pass.

PREVIEW

A retrospective exhibition of the Group of Seven collection prompts journalist Daniel Francis to reflect on the role of the former "national school" of painters in Canadian history. In this in-depth exploration, he seeks to separate the facts from the myths that surround the group, myths propagated by the group itself.

When I lived in Ottawa in the 1970s, I used to enjoy passing lazy afternoons at the **National Gallery** looking at the pictures. I remember how surprised I was when I first encountered the Group of Seven collection. These paintings were completely familiar–I'd seen them in schoolbooks and on calendars, posters, T-shirts, everywhere–yet at the same time they were completely unexpected. I realized that I had never really seen them before. These were not the flat, insipid, washed-out images of the reproduction factories. Instead they were luminous and bright and spirited. In a word, they were beautiful–which was not a word I had thought to associate with the Group of Seven before.

Most people who see the G7 for the first time in person must experience similar sensations of discovery and recognition. Our sense of them has been so attenuated over the years by repeated exposure to wholesale reproduction–Robert Fulford has called them "our national wallpaper"–that only an encounter with the real thing can rehabilitate it. Such an encounter becomes more probable this year because the National Gallery has mounted a major exhibition to celebrate the seventy-fifth anniversary of the Group's formation. The show opened in Ottawa last October and travels to Montreal, Toronto and Vancouver throughout 1996. It is supplemented by a handsome book-cum-catalogue, *The Group of Seven: Art for a Nation*, by curator Charles Hill.

The new exhibition offers an excuse to think again about the place of the G7 in our history, a task made necessary by the myths which have surrounded the Group since its inception. For quite some time history remembered the G7 as a group of radicals who were forced to endure the vicious abuse of ignorant critics for daring to break with European tradition and to paint Canada in a bold, new way. This was the Group's own story, parlayed into legend by themselves and their admirers. It was appealing because it offered posterity that most irresistible of all pleasures, the chance to condescend to the past. How could the critics have been so stupid, we wonder? Couldn't they recognize the future when they bumped into it?

More recently the myth of the misunderstood modernists has been exposed for the half-truth it always was. The G7, it turns out, was not the victim of malign critics suffering from a colonial mentality. In fact, they won success almost immediately. They had wealthy **patrons**, including the National Gallery; most of the reviews of their shows were encouraging; they were chosen to represent Canada in major exhibitions abroad. Within a decade of its formation the Group was being hailed as Canada's "national school" of painters.

In which case the more appropriate question becomes: Why? Why did Canadians embrace the Group so easily? The answer is that for all their radical rhetoric, the G7 was essentially conservative. They gave Canadian art lovers a chance to dabble in what they thought was **Modernism** while remaining comfortably anti-modern at the same time. In other words, the G7 are the Red Tories, the Progressive Conservatives, of Canadian art, taking new ideas and dressing them down to suit the stodgy cultural environment in which they found themselves.

The **Group of Seven** began to coalesce in the years leading up to World War One. Appropriately enough, the prehistory of the Group begins with a painting. In 1911, A.Y. Jackson, a young Montreal painter, exhibited a canvas called *At the Edge of the Maple Wood* at the annual showing of the Ontario Society of Artists in Toronto. The painting depicted a familiar sugaring-off scene in rural Quebec, but its vigorous colour and texture made a strong impression on several painters who saw it in Toronto. Together these artists were just beginning to articulate a new approach to interpreting the Canadian landscape. The reclusive genius Tom Thomson, working as a photo-engraver with the commercial art firm Grip Ltd., later said that *Maple Wood* opened his eyes to the **Canadian landscape**. Thomson's colleagues at Grip, J.E.H. MacDonald and Arthur Lismer, both praised its fresh approach to a familiar subject. "Jackson's contribution was the beginning of a kinship and a movement in Canada," Lismer said. Lawren Harris wrote later that "it stood out from all the other paintings as an authentic, new expression."

Lawren Harris, wealthy son of an Ontario farm machinery manufacturer, did not forget Jackson's painting, and two years later he bought it from Jackson, thereby inaugurating a friendship which would transform Canadian art. The painting was a turning point, not just for the Group but for the country. "*The Edge of the Maple Wood* was to Canadian art what *Le Déjeuner sur l'Herbe* or *Les Demoiselles d'Avignon* was to French art," Harold Town has written. "Its plangent colour and effortless virtuosity, its sense of absolute Canadian place, galvanized a grumble of dissatisfaction into the tumble of revolt."

The sale of the painting occurred at a crucial moment for A.Y. Jackson, who had been contemplating a life in exile south of the border. Instead, he was persuaded by Harris to visit Toronto first, which he did in May 1913. Immediately he was swept up in the energy of the new movement of artists centred on the Arts and Letters Club. He spent that summer and fall sketching on Georgian Bay where he met James MacCallum, a Toronto ophthalmologist and art

The vitality of a new movement in Art must be gauged by the fury it arouses.

Logan Pearsall Smith, U.S. essayist

enthusiast who was becoming the patron of the new movement. MacCallum invited Jackson to use his comfortable cottage on Go Home Bay, then offered to pay all of his expenses if Jackson, instead of going to the States, remained in Toronto.

In Toronto Jackson, who was then thirty-one years old, found a group of artists who were ardently committed to an idea: the idea of painting Canada. "We lived in a continuous blaze of enthusiasm," Lawren Harris wrote. "We were at times very serious and concerned, at other times, hilarious and carefree. Above all, we loved this country, and loved exploring and painting it." When the Studio Building opened on Severn Street near Bloor and Yonge early in 1914, it became the clubhouse for the new movement. Several of the commercial artists from Grip worked at the building. One of them, Fred Varley, wrote his sister that "we are all working to one big end. We are endeavouring to knock out of us all of the preconceived ideas, emptying ourselves of everything except that nature is here in all its greatness, and we are here to gather it and understand it if only we will be clean enough, healthy enough, and humble enough to go to it willing to be taught."

"Every day was an adventure," Jackson recalled of this period. He shared a space with Thomson, another of Dr. MacCallum's protégés, and the two artists became friends. They painted together, went to the movies together, conspired to be famous together and began making sketching trips together to the bush country of Algonquin Park north of Toronto. Thomson had discovered this wilderness setting in the spring of 1912 and had spent the summer of 1913 camping out in the park at Canoe Lake. The following year two of Thomson's colleagues from Grip joined them: Fred Varley and Arthur Lismer. "The country is a revelation to me and completely bowled me over at first," Varley confided in a letter. Lismer was equally affected. "The first night spent in the north and the thrilling days after were turning points in my life," he wrote. A definite **Algonquin School of painting** was taking shape.

At this early stage Thomson provided the spark of inspiration. His style, with its audacious use of vivid colour and blunt brush strokes, seemed to embody the raw energy of the northern landscape. All the better that he was self-taught and completely ignorant of modern painting. The others considered him the prototype of what the new Canadian artist should be: an untutored genius, whose art sprang from an intuitive understanding of the land. They all came from cities, but Thomson was a country boy, raised on a farm near Georgian Bay where he learned to handle a paddle, a hunting rifle and a fishing rod with equal facility. His familiarity with the outdoors impressed his clumsier, less robust painting companions.

Things were different when winter forced Thomson out of the woods back to Toronto, where he lived like a fish out of water. Low on funds, he camped out in a shack behind the Studio Building, where he lived with a minimum of creature comfort, staying in all day, venturing out at night to tramp the snow-filled ravines of the Don Valley on snowshoes. It was here that he completed some of the most famous paintings in Canadian history, paintings such as *The West Wind* and *The Jack Pine*, paintings which have become iconic images by which Canadians recognize themselves.

All the elements were present as early as 1914 for the formation of the Group of Seven, though at this point it probably would have been called The Algonquin School. It did not happen, only because World War One happened first. The war scattered the Algonquin painters in several directions. Some enlisted, others remained at home. They were all stunned in the summer of 1917 by the unexpected death of Tom Thomson. In those horrible war years death itself was no surprise; it was the way Thomson died which was so shocking. He was renowned as a woodsman, an expert canoeist, someone who could paddle all day without rest. Yet apparently, on one of his frequent fishing trips in Algonquin Park, he fell out of his canoe and drowned.

While his death left Thomson's colleagues profoundly saddened, it seemed to stiffen their resolve to continue along the path they had chosen. World War One derailed the new movement temporarily, but it did not fundamentally alter its direction. Unlike their European counterparts, thrust by the spiritual crisis of the war into nihilistic experimentation, most evident in Dada and Surrealism, the Canadians regrouped in Toronto more determined than ever to paint the native landscape.

There is no account by any of the participants of the decisive meeting at Lawren Harris's house which led to the formation of the Group of Seven in mid-March 1920. The name was probably borrowed from similar groups which existed in New York (The Eight, or Ashcan School, organized the sensational Armory Show of 1913) and Berlin. The first use of the name was in a letter dated March 21 from Arthur Lismer to Eric Brown, director of the National Gallery in Ottawa. "Harris, Jackson, MacD[onald], Johnston, [Franklin] Carmichael, Varley and myself," Lismer ticked off the names of the founding members. "'Group of Seven' is the idea. There is to be no feeling of secession or antagonism in any way, but we hope to get a show together that will demonstrate the 'spirit' of painting in Canada." There was nothing like a formal vote or a decision to incorporate. The Group of Seven was a movement, not an organization. What bound the artists together was not membership in an exclusive club but a shared commitment to certain ideas about painting.

The first exhibition by the G7 opened at the Art Gallery of Toronto, May 7, 1920. Subsequently the Group and its supporters invented the legend that the new movement was besieged by adverse reviews and viciously negative criticism. According to Lawren Harris, they were "attacked from all sides." The initial exhibition created "an uproar," claimed Jackson many years later. "There was plenty of adverse criticism, little of it intelligent." In fact the response was favourable, if less enthusiastic than the painters had hoped for. Only about 100 people a day came to see the show, but for the most part critics were polite. The National Gallery purchased three of the canvases and helped to organize a smaller touring exhibition in the United States. The 1920 show did not receive the critical mugging which its participants claimed it did.

Art is not an imitation of anything or a daydream or a memory or a vision, it has a life of its own, an emotion we cannot get from anything in life outside it.

David Milne, Canadian artist

This should come as no surprise. Members of the G7, while they liked to see themselves as young rebels, were actually all established painters who by 1920 had been part of the Toronto art scene for a decade or more. MacDonald, the eldest, was forty-seven years old; he had been showing his paintings since before the war. So had Harris, Jackson and Lismer, all of whom were approaching middle age. Both the Ontario government and the National Gallery had purchased their work. Several of the Group made their living as commercial artists and their illustrations appeared in such mainstream magazines as *Maclean's* and *Canadian Magazine*. Wealthy patrons were expressing interest. Still, despite all this evidence of support, the Group insisted throughout its life, and for many years after, that critical opinion was overwhelmingly against it.

The Group's persecution complex began developing back before the war. It took human shape in the portly figure of Toronto critic Hector Charlesworth, contributor to *Saturday Night* and a fixture on the city's art scene. While most reviewers approved, or at least tolerated, the Algonquin painters' riotous landscapes, Charlesworth conceived an enduring dislike for them which he expressed with vehemence. His first run-in with a future Group member occurred in 1916 when J.E.H. MacDonald exhibited several paintings at the annual Ontario Society of Artists show. "MacDonald certainly does throw his paint pots in the public's face," Charlesworth wrote. He went on to say that MacDonald's "crude" depictions of the Shield country could more aptly be titled "Hungarian Goulash and Drunkard's Stomach." MacDonald responded in a letter to the *Globe* newspaper in which he berated Charlesworth's ignorance and superficiality, and accused him of libel.

This skirmish has become one of the most celebrated incidents in Canadian art history, obscuring the fact that the Algonquin work actually received a pretty favourable reception. Charlesworth himself shied away from further confrontation for several years. He did not review the Group's inaugural show in 1920, nor did he take much notice of the flurry of exhibitions which followed over the next two years. But as public acceptance of the Group's work increased, he could not keep silent, bursting back into print in 1922 with an attack on the National Gallery for what he thought was its excessive patronage of the Group, "those theatrical scene painters." Charlesworth would never be reconciled to the new movement. He was particularly irritated by its claim to be the first painters to develop a distinctively "Canadian" approach to their art. He saw himself as the defender of an earlier generation of artists who were just as committed to "independent expression" as the Group, but got no credit for it. When British critics also praised the Group's work following a large exhibition of Canadian paintings in Wembley, England, in the spring of 1924, Charlesworth became even angrier. He had already gone on record as calling the Group's style "freakish" and "violent." Following Wembley, invective took over completely. Members of the Group were a bunch of "paint slingers" devoted to the "cult of ugliness."

In retrospect it is clear that the dustup with Charlesworth worked to the Group's advantage. The controversy kept the G7 in the public eye, never a bad thing for artists struggling to find buyers for their work. More important, it

Tom Thomson, *Autumn Foliage* (1916). Oil on wood, 26.7 X 21.5 cm.

Tom Thomson,
The Jack Pine (1916-17).
Oil on canvas,
127.9 X 139.8 cm.

Tom Thomson (1877-1917) died before the Group of Seven was founded, but he was the Group's main artistic inspiration. His famous works, capturing the northern part of Algonquin Park, include *Spring Ice* (1916), *Autumn Foliage* (1916) and *The Jack Pine* (1916-17).

Tom Thomson,
Spring Ice (1916).
Oil on canvas,
72.0 X 102.3 cm.

Lawren S. Harris, *North Shore. Lake Superior* (1926). Oil on canvas, 102.2 X 128.3 cm.

Lawren S. Harris (1885-1970) was a founding member of the Group of Seven and a powerful force in Canadian art, continually inspiring others.

Looking back on the Group of Seven years, A.Y. Jackson wrote, "While we rather prided ourselves that the Group had no leader, without Harris there would have been no Group of Seven. He provided the stimulus; it was he who encouraged us always to take the bolder course, to find new trails."

Lawren S. Harris, *Shacks* (1919). Oil on canvas, 107.9 X 128.3 cm.

A.Y. Jackson, *The Edge of Maple Wood* (1910). Oil on canvas, 54.6 X 65.4 cm.

A.Y. Jackson (1882-1974) was a central force in the formation of the Group of Seven as well as in the formation of its successor, the Canadian Group of Painters, in 1933.

Ironically, just prior to joining the Group of Seven, Jackson wrote that the Ontario northland was "a great country to have a holiday in ... but it's nothing but little islands covered with scrub and pine trees, and not quite paintable.... Sketching simply won't go."

A.Y. Jackson, *Terre Sauvage* (1913). Oil on canvas, 128.8 X 154.4 cm.

Frederick H. Varley, *Squally Weather, Georgian Bay* (1920). Oil on canvas, 30 X 40.9 cm.

Frederick Varley (1881-1969) was a founding member of the Group of Seven, but his perspective was broader, extending back to the European traditions, and was as committed to the human figure as to the landscape.

Varley once defined the artist as "an outsider, beyond the materialism of his age, one who sees differently–a bloody fool, he cannot be changed. He serves as a foil to others' sanity."

Frederick H. Varley, *Three Clouds and a Tree* (c.1935). Oil on wood, 30.1 X 38.0 cm.

J.E.H. MacDonald,
The Solemn Land (1921).
Oil on canvas,
122.5 x 153.5 cm.

J.E.H. MacDonald
(1873-1932) was the
oldest member in the
Group of Seven and a
leading founding member.
He was particularly
insistent on acknowledging
the historical context of the
Group, tracing its origins
to earlier painters in
Canada. One such early
painter, C.W. Jeffreys,
remarked that
"MacDonald's art is
native–as native as the
rocks, or the snow, or the
pine trees, or the lumber
that are so largely his
themes." MacDonald and
Lawren Harris were drawn
together early and were
the nucleus of the Group
of Seven.

J.E.H. MacDonald,
The Tangled Garden
(1916). Oil on
beaverboard,
121.4 X 152.4 cm.

Arthur Lismer,
The Guide's Home (1914).
Oil on canvas,
102.4 X 114.4 cm.

Arthur Lismer (1885-1969)
arrived in Canada from
England in 1911 and soon
was working alongside
J.E.H. MacDonald, Tom
Thomson and Frank
Carmichael. By 1913, he,
too, was travelling to
Georgian Bay and
Algonquin Park on
sketching trips. His early
works, such as *The
Guide's Home,* portray the
rugged northern Canadian
landscapes within the
broad style of European
impressionism.

Arthur Lismer,
*September Gale,
Georgian Bay* (1921).
Oil on canvas,
122.4 X 163.0 cm.

Franz H. Johnston,
Fire-swept, Algoma (1920).
Oil on canvas,
127.5 X 167.5 cm.

Franz Johnson (1888-1949) participated in the first exhibition of the Group of Seven in 1920, but in 1924 he was reported to have resigned from the Group: "I was never a member of the school of seven in the sense of taking a formal oath of allegiance to an art brotherhood or of subscribing to rigid doctrines. They were my friends. I shared their enthusiasm for new ideas and new methods." Johnston's most successful work, *Fire-swept, Algoma,* of 1920 was one of a number of paintings resulting from three trips to Algoma between 1918 and 1920.

Frank Carmichael,
Wabajisik: Drowned Land (1929-1930).
Watercolour and gouache over charcoal on wove paper,
51.8 X 69.8 cm.

Frank Carmichael (1890-1945) was the youngest member of the original Group of Seven. Carmichael was always on the fringe of the Group, probably due to the difference in age and possibly because he worked full time as a commercial artist. Most members of the Group seemed to have the attitude that teaching art was an honourable vocation, but they attached a stigma to working in the commercial field. Perhaps Carmichael's greatest contribution to the Group was in reviving the neglected art of watercolour painting.

Paintings by Tom Thomson and The Group of Seven
Foundations: Society, Challenge and Change, Second Edition
Thompson Educational Publishing, Inc., 1999

provided the Group with a narrative, a way for the public to understand what was going on even when it did not understand the artistic issues involved. According to this narrative, members of the Group were young rebels fighting to establish a modern, "Canadian" outlook in the face of overwhelming opposition from an ignorant press and a backward-looking Old Guard. In 1926, with the appearance of Fred Housser's book, *A Canadian Art Movement: The Story of the Group of Seven*, this interpretation of events was enshrined as history. Housser, a financial journalist, was an ardent supporter of the Group. His book described their break with European traditions, their struggle to develop a new style through "direct contact with Nature herself," their disputes with the critics and "the entire press of the country," and their ultimate emergence as the first important art movement to arise in Canada. The Group triumphed, wrote Housser, because it was unafraid to express the native landscape in entirely new ways. No artists before the Group were mature enough to take Canada as its own subject, he claimed, on its own terms. By changing all that, wrote Housser, the Group represented the coming of age of Canada as a culture.

Housser's book was a work of propaganda, not scholarship. Much of what he said about the G7 was simply not true. As he himself admitted, the critical reception of their work actually was pretty favourable, Hector Charlesworth and a few others notwithstanding. The Group were not the pariahs of the art world they made themselves out to be. Nor were they the first to attempt to paint in a distinctively "Canadian" style. Artists before them had chosen similar subject matter, although presented in the manner of the civilized landscapes of Europe. Nor were members of the Group quite as innocent of European training and ideas as Housser claimed. Jackson, Harris, Lismer, Varley and Carmichael all studied abroad. Tom Thomson was the only one who was truly self-taught, and he was not strictly speaking a member of the Group. Regardless, Housser's book went a long way to reconciling the public to the new movement. Its publication roughly marks the transformation of the Group from delinquent sons to patriarchs of the family. "No longer can the Group enjoy the vilification that is the reward of the precocious few," observed playwright Merrill Denison in 1928, "because the many have now joined them and the calliope has become merely an overcrowded bandwagon."

The Group's success was due to other factors besides good public relations. Most importantly, of course, they were tremendously talented artists who produced some of the most beautiful and evocative paintings in the history of Canadian art. But the public usually requires something more than talent. It embraced the Group because the artists so successfully attached themselves to a nationalistic agenda. The Group claimed to be creating a new national consciousness. This was MacDonald's "big idea": the creation of a national purpose through an appreciation of the rugged Canadian landscape. "We believe wholeheartedly in the land," they declared. In this respect the Group perfectly matched the spirit of the times, in Canada at least. During the Twenties Canadians were seeking new ways of imagining themselves as a mature, independent nation. They were receptive, therefore, to a movement of artists which claimed to find in the local landscape a distinctive national identity, and claimed to have found a uniquely Canadian style for expressing it.

The Group's down-to-earth approach to painting also endeared them to a broad public. G7 members were not tweakers of bourgeois noses. They were painters who went into the wilderness to track down their paintings, much like hunters after prey. They were "modern coureurs-de-bois," not effete intellectuals starving in their garrets. They spoke of art as an energetic, manly activity; they identified painting with adventuring and exploring. (The reality was somewhat different. Jackson, for example, described J.E.H. MacDonald as "a quiet, unadventurous person, who could not swim, or paddle, or swing an axe, or find his way in the bush.") They presented their work in simple, accessible language. One of their pre-war exhibitions made no apology for offering "pictures which were suitable for home use, such as one could live with and enjoy." Art was like "any other national Canadian industry," MacDonald wrote: "when our people decide that Art had better be grown at home than imported from Holland, they'll find that they'll get a better article at a lower price." Spoken like a member of the Canadian Manufacturers' Association. These were all attitudes which appealed to Canadians who wanted to feel proud of their youth and vitality and common sense, not shamefaced at their lack of sophistication.

The Group was looking for a domestic audience where one had not existed before. Charles Hill reveals that in 1924 only 2 percent of the paintings purchased in Canada were by Canadian artists. There was virtually no demand for their work, so the G7 had to create one. They did so by going down market. In an early version of the Art Bank, they made their paintings available for rent; they toured them around to small towns; they talked about their work in accessible language and presented themselves in non-threatening ways.

As Hill points out, the Group's relatively tame subject matter also endeared it to the Canadian public. No one had to avert their eyes. There were no nudes descending staircases, no Mona Lisas with moustaches. Admirers could be modern, without being "modern," *au courant* without being immoral and nihilistic like those scandalous Europeans. This was modern art that was clean and bracing and stood for something. "There has not been the slightest attempt at degeneracy," declared Eric Brown, sounding disappointingly conventional for the director of an important art gallery.

Robert Fulford has said that the G7 was Canada's version of Modernism. It is probably more accurate to say that, for better or for worse, the Group was what Canada got *instead* of Modernism. Unlike members of the Group, Modernist painters in other countries did not propagandize for nationalism. Quite the reverse, they despised nationalism as a root cause of the recent war. Nor did Modernists appeal to the comfortable classes. Quite the reverse, they were in revolt against the "botched civilization" of their elders. Merrill Denison could write in 1928 that the G7 was "as Canadian as the North West Mounted

Police or an amateur hockey team." It is impossible to imagine the European avant-garde being compared to a police force.

Hill's survey of cultural life in Canada in the Twenties reveals that there was very little Modernism going on here. His point just as readily applies to the literary world where writers like Morley Callaghan, John Glassco, and even Robert Service (whose northern ballads make a kind of literary parallel to the work of the Group), had to go to Paris to find it. The experimental "isms" of Europe—Cubism, Surrealism, Futurism, Expressionism, Dadaism—gained no adherents in Canada. It is only in comparison to other Canadian artists that the G7 appeared modern. In comparison to European art, the Group was decidedly rearguard.

The Group succeeded in creating an audience for art in Canada, and for Canadian art. Wittingly or not, it also helped to create a very narrow vision of what constituted art. Under the Group's influence paintings came to be judged according to how Canadian they were, which tended to mean how many rocks, trees and totem poles they contained. The G7 became the country's official School because it was conservative, threatened no one, made almost no one uncomfortable, and appealed to a brand of nature worship masquerading as patriotism. With "modernists" like these, there was no need to be modern.

Eventually a new generation of artists and critics grew embarrassed by the G7, as Modernism somewhat belatedly began to find a following in this country. In the 1930s and 1940s, for example, **abstraction** took hold. In this new context, the Group's commitment to landscape seemed old-fashioned. And to a degree this view of the Group persists even in the epoch of Post-modernism in which we currently find ourselves.

The retrospective exhibition which the National Gallery has mounted would like to rescue the Group from such condescension, but evidently some of our cultural gatekeepers continue to feel uneasy in the presence of the west wind and the jackpine. When the show opened at the Art Gallery of Ontario in January, curators there felt obliged to mount a parallel show beside it. Titled The Oh! Canada Project, it aimed to provide an alternative "interactive" space for gallery visitors to express their own feelings about Canada. When critic John Bentley Mays objected to this show on the grounds that it was a politically correct trivialization of the Group's work, he sparked a lively exchange of letters to the editor of the *Globe and Mail*. One side of the debate endorsed Mays's view; the other argued that he was a stuffy white guy who failed to recognize how relevant the AGO was marketing itself to new constituencies of gallery-goers.

If anything, the new show reveals that we have not found a way of being comfortable with our National School of Painters, whose work, whether Modernist or any other-ist, remains unique in the world of art. After all these years, some of us still feel the need to apologize for them. They continue to be an itch we cannot help scratching. Meanwhile, if you get a chance, do what I did. Go see the pictures. All the rest is complication.

KEY TERMS

- National Gallery
- Patrons of the arts
- Modernism
- The Group of Seven
- Canadian landscape painting
- Algonquin School of painting
- National identity
- Abstractionism in painting

REVIEW

1. When did the Group of Seven form? How was it a movement, rather than an organization?

2. What factors contributed to the success of the Group of Seven?

3. Why did members of the Group insist that their work had been negatively received by critics? How did their "narrative" of struggle affect their image? Their popularity?

Guernica

STEPHEN SPENDER

For Spender, the explosion that is Picasso's "Guernica" defied interpretation by the methods of formal art criticism. Instead, he shares the rich impression called forth in him by this painting, leaving the question of its merit for a later day.

PREVIEW

Stephen Spender's 1938 critique of Pablo Picasso's "Guernica" is a chronicling of one man's emotions and opinions upon seeing this well-known painting. Spender's piece serves as a combination of formal art criticism and analysis, and personal reflection. It reads as an intelligent and well-considered reaction to Picasso's famous work. Spender was an English poet and literary critic.

André Gide writes in *Verve* that *Guernica* fails because it is *eccentric*, it breaks away from its centre, or has no centre. Other critics complain that it is neither expressionist nor abstract, but falls between two stools; that it is terrifying without producing any sensation of pity; and so on. All these criticisms are attempts to answer the question whether or not this picture is a great **masterpiece**. Otherwise, they could not be criticisms at all, but just descriptions, which so far from being *against* it, might well be an account of its merits.

Guernica affects one as an explosion, partly no doubt because it is a picture of an explosion. If one attempts to criticize it, one attempts to relate it to the past. So long as a work of art has this explosive quality of newness it is impossible to relate it to the past. People who say that it is *eccentric*, or that it falls between two stools, or that it is too horrible, and so on, are only making the gasping noises they might make if they were blown off their feet by a high-explosive bomb. All I can try to do is to report as faithfully as possible the effect that this very large and very dynamic picture makes on me.

In the first place, it is certainly not **realistic** in the sense that Goya's etchings of another tragedy in Spain are realistic. *Guernica* is in no sense reportage; it is not a picture of some horror which Picasso has seen and been through himself. It is the picture of a horror reported in the newspapers, of which he has read accounts and perhaps seen photographs.

This kind of second-hand experience, from the newspapers, the news-reel, the wireless, is one of the dominating realities of our time.

The many people who are not in direct contact with the disasters falling on civilization live in a waking nightmare of second-hand experiences which in a way are more terrible than real experiences because the person overtaken by a disaster has at least a more limited vision than the camera's wide, cold, recording eye, and at least has no opportunity to imagine horrors worse than what he is seeing and experiencing. The flickering black,

Pablo Picasso's *Guernica* was painted to commemorate the 1937 air raid bombing of Guernica, Spain.

KEY TERMS

- Artistic masterpiece
- Realism
- Collage (as an art form)
- Expressionism
- Abstractionism

white and grey lights of Picasso's picture suggest a moving picture stretched across an elongated screen; the flatness of the shapes again suggests the photographic image, even the reported paper words. The centre of this picture is like a painting of a collage in which strips of newspaper have been pasted across the canvas.

The actual figures on the canvas, the balloon-like floating head of a screaming woman; the figure throwing arms up in despair, the woman running forwards, and leaving behind one reluctant, painful, enormous, clumsy leg, the terror of a horse with open mouth and skin drawn back over the teeth; the hand clutching a lamp and the electric lamp glowing so that it shows the wires, as though at any moment the precious light may go out; the groaning bull, the woman clutching her child, a complex of clustered fingers like over-ripe fruit; all this builds up a picture of horror, but to me there is grandeur in the severed arm of a hero lying in the foreground, clutching the noble, broken, ineffective sword with which he has tried to ward off the horrors of mechanical destruction; and there is pity in the leaves of the little plant growing just above this hand.

Picasso uses every device of **expressionism**, **abstractionism** and effects learnt from collage, to build up the horror of *Guernica*. Diagonal lines of light and shade in the background, suggest searchlights and confusion, and the violent contrasts of the faces revealed in a very white light suggest the despair of light and darkness in air raids; despair of the darkness because it is too complete and you are lost; despair of the light because it is too complete and you are revealed to the enemy raiders.

The impression made on me by this picture is one that I might equally get from a great masterpiece, or some very vivid experience. That, of course, does not mean that it is a masterpiece. I shall be content to wait some years before knowing that. But it is certainly worth seeing. And if you don't like, or resist, or are overwhelmed by explosions, there are the sixty-seven studies for Guernica, some of them quite unlike anything in the picture itself, which are certainly amongst the most beautiful and profound drawings Picasso has ever made.

REVIEW

1. What reason does Spender give for not formally criticizing the painting "Guernica"? What question is art criticism attempting to answer?

2. Why does Spender describe "Guernica" as an "explosion"? What qualities does it possess that support this claim?

3. Spender states that he is willing to "wait some years" before deciding if "Guernica" is a masterpiece. How will the passage of time enable him to more accurately assess the painting?

Survival, Then and Now

Cultural Obsessions

MARGARET ATWOOD

Canada's premier woman of letters takes a razor-sharp (and humorous) look at the state of Canadian literature and finds it may well start to thrive again.... but, paradoxically, perhaps only in Quebec!

PREVIEW

As Canada's international writing superstar, Margaret Atwood has won more than 50 major awards, from the Governor General's Award for her first book of poetry, "The Circle Game," in 1966, to the Giller Prize for her latest novel, "Alias Grace," in 1996. Surprisingly, only the Swedish Humour Association, which honoured her with its International Humorous Writer Award for "The Robber Bride" in 1995, has explicitly recognized one of her most attractive qualities. In this essay, the 59-year-old author turns her finely honed wit on a topic she effectively defined nearly three decades ago: Canadian literature.

In 1972, I wrote and published a book called *Survival: A Thematic Guide to Canadian Literature,* which ignited a ferocious debate and became, as they say, a runaway best-seller. This was a shock to everyone, including me. Canadian writing, interesting? Among the bulk of readers at that time it was largely unknown and among the cognoscenti it was frequently treated as a dreary joke, an oxymoron, a big yawn, or the hole in a non-existent doughnut.

At the beginning of the '60s, the usual sales of poetry books numbered in the hundreds, and a novel was doing well if it hit a thousand copies. But over that decade, things changed rapidly. After the wartime '40s and the beige '50s, Canada was showing a renewed interest in its own cultural doings. **The Canada Council** began supporting writers in earnest in 1965. In Quebec, the **Quiet Revolution** had generated an outburst of literary activity; in the ROC (the Rest of Canada as we call it now but did not then), many poets had emerged through coffee houses and public readings, more novelists and short-story writers were becoming known, and Expo 67, the Montreal world's fair, had created a fresh national self-confidence. Audiences had been building steadily, and by 1972 there was a critical mass of readers who wanted to hear more; and thus, through a combination of good luck, good timing and good reviews, *Survival* became an "overnight publishing sensation," and I myself became an instant sacred monster. "Now you're a target," Farley Mowat said to me, "and they will shoot at you."

How prescient he was. Who could have suspected that this modest cultural artifact would have got so thoroughly up the noses of my elders and betters? If the book had sold the 3,000 copies initially projected, nobody would have bothered their heads much about it, but in the first year alone it sold 10 times that number, and suddenly CanLit was everybody's business. The few dedicated academic souls who had cultivated this neglected pumpkin patch over the meagre years were affronted because a mere chit of a girl had appropriated a pumpkin they regarded as theirs, and the rest were affronted because I had obnoxiously pointed out that there was in fact a pumpkin to appropriate. Even now, after 27 years, some Jack or Jackess emerges with seasonal regularity to take one more crack at *moi*, the supposed Giant, in a never-ending game of Let Us Now Blame Famous Women. You get to feel like the mechanical at the fun-fair shooting gallery, though no one has won the oversized panda yet, because I still seem to be quacking.

Over the years, I've been accused of just about everything, bourgeois superstition to communist rabble-rousing to not being Marshall McLuhan. (I would have liked to have been Marshall McLuhan–it seemed a ton o' fun–but he had the job pretty much cornered.) Yet when I was writing this book–or rather when I was putting it together, for it was more an act of synthesis than of authorship–I attached no particular importance to it. I was, after all, a poet and novelist, wasn't I? I did not consider myself a real critic–just a kind of bake-sale muffin lady, doing a little cottage-industry fundraising in a worthy cause.

The worthy cause was The House of Anansi Press, a small literary publisher formed in 1967 by writers Dennis Lee and David Godfrey as a response to the dearth of publishing opportunities for new writing at that time. Anansi was diverse in scope–Austin Clarke, Harold Sonny Ladoo, Roch Carrier and Jacques Ferron were some of its authors–and had already made quite a few waves by 1971, when Dennis, an old college friend, buttonhooked me onto its board. So there we were one grey November day, a tiny, intrepid, overworked, underpaid band, glumly contemplating the balance sheet, which showed an alarming amount of red ink. Publishing Rule No. 1 is that it's hard to keep small literary publishers solvent unless you have the equivalent of knitting books to support them.

To pay the bills, Anansi had begun a line of user-friendly self-help guides, which had done moderately well: *Law Law Law,* by Clayton Ruby and Paul Copeland, which set forth how to disinherit your relatives, avoid being bled dry by your estranged spouse, and so forth; and *VD,* one of the first venereal disease books, which explicated unwanted goo and warts and such, though AIDS was still a decade into the future.

Thus was born *Survival.* As I'd travelled the country's by-ways, giving poetry readings and toting cardboard boxes of my own books to sell afterwards because often enough there was no bookstore, the absence of views on the subject was spectacular. The two questions I was asked most frequently by audience members were, "Is there any Canadian literature?" and, "Supposing there is, isn't it just a second-rate copy of real literature, which comes from England and the United States?" In Australia they called this attitude the Cultural Cringe; in Canada it was the Colonial Mentality. In both–and in many smaller countries around the world, as it turned out–it was part of a tendency to believe that the Great Good Place was, culturally speaking, elsewhere.

The beginning of Canadian cultural nationalism was not "Am I really that oppressed?" but "Am I really that boring?"

Margaret Atwood

Through no fault of my own, I happened to be doing a one-year teaching stint at York University. Canadian literature formed part of the course load, so I'd had to come up with some easily grasped approaches to it—easily grasped by me as well as by my students, because I was, by training, a Victorianist, and had never formally studied Canadian literature. (Not surprising: it wasn't taught.) I discovered that previous thinkers on the subject, although pithy enough, had been few in number: there was not exactly a wealth of existing lore.

Back to the Anansi meeting. "Hey, I know," I cried, in my Mickey Rooneyish way. "Let's do a *VD* of Canadian literature!" What I meant, I explained, was a sort of handbook for the average reader—for all those people I'd met on my tours who'd wanted to know more, but didn't know where to start. This book would not be for academics. It would have no footnotes, and would not employ the phrase "on the other hand," or at least not much. It would also contain lists of other books that people could actually go into a bookstore and buy. This was a fairly revolutionary concept, because the CanLit of the past was mostly out of print, and that of the present was kept well hidden at the back of the store, in among the Beautiful Canadiana fall foliage calendars.

We now take it for granted that **Canadian literature** exists as a category, but this proposition was not always self-evident. To have any excuse for being, the kind of book I had in mind would have to prove several points. First, that, yes, there was a Canadian literature—such a thing did indeed exist. (This turned out to be a radical proposition at the time, and was disputed by many when the book appeared.) Second, that this body of work was not just a second-rate version of English or American, or, in the case of francophone books, of French literature, but that it had different pre-occupations which were specific to its own history and geopolitics. This too was a radical proposition, although common sense ought to have indicated that it was just common sense: if you were a rocky, watery northern country, cool in climate, large in geographical expanse, small but diverse in population, and with a huge aggressive neighbour to the south, why wouldn't you have concerns that varied from those of the huge aggressive neighbour? Or indeed from those of the crowded, history-packed, tight little island, recently but no longer an imperial power, that had once ruled the waves? Well, you'd think they'd be different, wouldn't you? To justify the teaching of Canadian literature as such, you'd still have to start from the same axioms: i) it exists, and ii) it's distinct.

Back to the Anansi meeting. The desperate will try anything, so the board agreed that this idea should be given a whirl. Over the next four or five months, I wrote away at it, and as I finished each section Dennis Lee edited it, and under Dennis's blue pencil the book grew from the proposed hundred-page handbook to a length of 246 pages. It also took on a more coherent shape and direction. The book's subtitle—A *Thematic Guide to Canadian Literature*—meant that we were aiming, not at an all-inclusive cross-indexed survey such as was provided in 1997 by the 1,199-page *The*

Oxford Companion to Canadian Literature, nor at a series of studies of this author or that, nor at a collection of new critical close readings or *explications du texte.* We were doing the sort of thing that art historian Nikolaus Pevsner had done in *The Englishness of English Art,* or that the American literary critics Perry Miller and Leslie Fiedler were doing in their examinations of American literature: the identification of a series of characteristics and **leitmotifs**, and a comparison of the varying treatments of them in different national and cultural environments.

For example: money as a sign of divine grace or providence is present in the American tradition from the Puritans through Benjamin Franklin through *Moby-Dick* through Henry James through *The Great Gatsby.* The theme is treated now seriously, now cynically, now tragically, now ironically, just as a leitmotif in a symphony may be played in different keys and in different tempos. It varies as time unrolls and circumstances change, of course: the 18th century is not the 20th. Yet the leitmotif persists as a dominating concern—a persistent cultural obsession, if you like.

The persistent **cultural obsession** of Canadian literature, said *Survival,* was, well, survival. In actual life, and in both the anglophone and the francophone sectors, this concern is often enough a factor of the weather, as when the ice storm cuts off the electrical power. *La survivance* has long been an overt theme in Quebec political life, currently manifesting itself as anxiety about the survival of French. In the ROC, it's more like a nervous tic: what'cher gonner do when free trade trashes your ability to control your water supply, or when the Mounties sell themselves to Disney, or when your government says that the magazines from the huge aggressive neighbour to the south are the same as yours really, or when there's a chance that after the next Quebec referendum, that part of the country will no longer be that part of the country? And so on and so forth.

Survival, therefore, began with this dominant note. It then postulated a number of other motifs in Canadian literature—motifs that either did not exist at all in one of the literatures chosen for comparison (for instance, there are almost no "Indians" in English novels), or which did exist, but were not handled in the same way. The Canadian "immigrant story," from fleeing Loyalists, to Scots kicked off their land, to starving Irish, to Latvians emigrating after the Second World War, to the economic refugees of the '70s and '80s, tends to be very different from the one told by Americans: none of their stories is likely to say that the immigrants were really trying to get into Canada but ended up in the United States *faute de mieux.* Canada has rarely been the promised land. About the closest we've come is the title of Wayne Johnston's 1998 novel, *The Colony of Unrequited Dreams.*

The tradition identified in *Survival* was not a bundle of uplifting Pollyanna cheer: quite the reverse. CanLit, at least up until 1970, was on balance a somewhat dour concoction. Some critics who couldn't read very well—a widespread occupational hazard, it seems—thought I was somehow advocating this state of affairs. *Au contraire*: if the book has attitude, it's more like you are here, you really do exist and this is where, so pull up your socks and

It is wonderful to feel the grandness of Canada in the raw, not because she is Canada but because she's something sublime that you were born into, some great rugged power that you are a part of.

Emily Carr, painter

quit whining. As Alice Munro says, "Do what you want and live with the consequences." Or as *Survival* itself says in its last chapter, "Having bleak ground under your feet is better than having no ground at all ... a tradition doesn't necessarily exist to bury you: it can also be used as material for new departures."

Many things have happened in the 27 years since *Survival* was published. In politics, the Quebec cliffhanger and loss of national control and increased U.S. domination brought about by free trade have become, not the tentative warning notes they were in *Survival*, but everyday realities. Canada's well-known failure to embrace a single "identity" of the yodelling or Beefeater variety has come to seem less like a failure than a deliberate and rather brave refusal. In literary criticism, Regionalism, Feminism, Deconstructionism, Political Correctness, Appropriation of Voice, and Identity Politics have all swept across the scene, leaving their traces. The former Canadian-identity question, "Where is here?" has been replaced by "Who are we?" "Discourse" and "text" are the new words for "debate" and "book." "Problematize" has became a verb, "Postmodern"–once a cutting-edge adjective–is used to describe kicky little handbags, and obfuscation, in some academic quarters, has become a mode of being.

Survival, the book, seemed quainter and more out-of-date as these various years went by, and–incidentally–as its wishes were granted and its predictions realized. Yet its central concerns remain with us, and must still be confronted. Are we really that different from anybody else? If so, how? And is that how something worth preserving? In 1972, *Survival* concluded with two questions: *Have we survived? If so, what happens after Survival?* We're still asking the same questions.

People often ask me what I would change about *Survival* if I were writing it today. The obvious answer is that I wouldn't write it today, because I wouldn't need to. The thing I set out to prove has been proven beyond a doubt: few would seriously argue, anymore, that there is no Canadian literature. The other answer is that I wouldn't be able to write it, not only because of my own hardening brain, but because the quantity, range and diversity of books now published would defeat any such effort. Mordecai Richler's well-known jest, "world famous in Canada," ceased to be such a laugh–many Canadian writers are now world-famous, period. The erstwhile molehill of CanLit has grown to a mountain. The year-old, fully bilingual Institute for Canadian Studies at the University of Ottawa lists some 279 Canadian studies centres located in other countries, including 20 in France, 65 in the United States, 16 in Germany and 22 in India. Canadian writers regularly achieve foreign publication, win major prizes, sign movie deals. In fact, so voguish is Canadian writing–or writing in English, at least–that it's become almost embarrassing.

All the more curious that Lucien Bouchard, visiting Paris in March, would quip that he had never seen Canadian culture walking along the street, "but apparently it exists in Ottawa." Of course you don't see much walking along the street if what you're looking at is not the bookstore window, but your own reflection in it. Though even M. Bouchard's reflection is "Canadian culture," considering his status as that archetypical folkloric bogey, the vengeful Scissors Man, used from time immemorial to frighten the fractious: *If you don't sit down and shut up, M. Bouchard will climb in through your window at night and SEPARATE you!*

In Canadian culture, however, there's always a negative side At present we have cuts to grants, threats to magazines, publishers in peril through withdrawal of funding, writers struggling with the effects upon their royalties of book-chain deep discounting, and so forth—not to mention the homogenizing effect of the global economy. *Have we survived?*

But this is Canada, land of contrasts. Indeed it is Canada, land of rugs: no sooner has a rug been placed beneath the nation's artistic feet than it is pulled out, but no sooner has it been pulled out in one place than it is inserted in another. Now, in an astonishing but gratifying development, Quebec has announced that the first $15,000 of **income from copyrights**—from songs to books to computer software—will be tax exempt. (By no great coincidence, $15,000 is the average income from writing in this country.) Will there be unforeseen consequences? Will Quebec become the Ireland of Canada, haven for writers, and the Prague of Europe, the latest chic destination? Will every young, mean and lean creator from all over the country stampede to Montreal, where the rent is cheap and the edible food ditto, so that they can actually have a hope of earning a living from their work? Why stay in Toronto, where the prices are high, the smog is toxic, your vote is worth only a tenth of a vote in North Bay, the public health system is going to rat excrement, and you get sneered at by your own provincial government and the *National Post* for being not-rich? Indeed, why stay in Ontario, where culture and the arts are funded at the rate of $39 a head, as opposed to $79 a head in Quebec?

Experience has shown that where **bohemia** goes, real estate development is sure to follow. First the artists, then the cafés, then the designers, then the lawyers. M. Bouchard must know this: he's been called many things, but rarely stupid. Could it be that this crafty tax move will revitalize downtown Montreal, which for some years has been bleeding at every pore? And revitalize it by means of—*choc, horreur!*—anglophone Canadian writers—incongruous tax exiles from the ROC?

All M. Bouchard has to do is extend the same kind of tax largesse to the publishing industry, and Montreal may once again become the vital centre of anglophone Canadian literary activity, as it was in the '40s and '50s. The street along which Bouchard can see Canadian culture walking may soon be his own. In that case, the 21st century answer to the second-last question posed in *Survival* may be—at least as regards writers—both bizarre and deeply ironic:

Have we survived?

Yes. But only in Quebec.

KEY TERMS

- The Canada Council
- The Quiet Revolution
- Canadian literature
- Cultural obsession
- Leitmotif
- Literary criticism
- Income from copyrights
- Bohemia

REVIEW

1. Explain the dominant theme of Canadian literature as seen by Margaret Atwood in her early book, "Survival."

2. Why wouldn't Margaret Atwood be able to write a book like "Survival" today? What has changed in the interim?

3. Why does Margaret Atwood think that there may be a revival of anglophone Canadian literary activity in francophone Quebec (and why would she see this as both bizarre and deeply ironic)?

ROUGHING IT IN THE BUSH

STEPHEN LEACOCK

For the real men among us, a trip to the bush to hunt moose means doing without and contending with swarms of black flies. However, this is not true for everyone. For those willing to delude themselves, "roughing it" means living it up in high style.

PREVIEW

In this humorous essay, Stephen Leacock reflects on the masculine pretense of relishing the chance to shrug off the veneer of civilization and "rough it." Though described by the author as such, the conditions that await this moose hunter are in no way "rough." Rather, dining and dancing and servants will help soften the ritual hardships. Leacock (1869-1944) was a Canadian economist but he is best remembered for many volumes of humorous essays and stories, including "Literary Lapses" (1910), "Sunshine Sketches of a Little Town" (1912) and "Arcadian Adventures with the Idle Rich" (1914).

The season is now opening when all those who have a manly streak in them like to get out into the bush and "rough it" for a week or two of hunting and fishing. For myself, I never feel that the autumn has been well spent unless I can get out after the moose. And when I go I like to go right into the bush and "rough it"—get clear away from civilization, out in the open, and take fatigue or hardship just as it comes.

So this year I am making all my plans to get away for a couple of weeks of moose hunting along with my brother George and my friend Tom Gass. We generally go together because we are all of us men who like the rough stuff and are tough enough to stand the hardship of living in the open. The place we go to is right in the heart of the primitive Canadian forest, among big timber, broken with lakes as still as glass, just the very ground for moose.

We have a kind of lodge up there. It's just a rough place that we put up, the three of us, the year before last, built out of tamarack logs faced with a broad axe. The flies, while we were building it, were something awful. Two of the men that we sent in there to build it were so badly bitten that we had to bring them out a hundred miles to a hospital. None of us saw the place while we were building it,—we were all busy at the time,—but the teamsters who took in our stuff said it was the worst season for the black flies that they ever remembered.

Still we hung to it, in spite of the flies, and stuck at it till we got it built. It is, as I say, only a plain place but good enough to rough it in. We have one big room with a stone fireplace, and bedrooms round the sides, with a wide verandah, properly screened, all along the front. The verandah has a row of upright tamaracks for its posts and doesn't look altogether bad. In the back part we have quarters where our man sleeps. We had an ice-house knocked up while they were building and water laid on in pipes from a stream. So that on the whole the place has a kind of rough comfort about it,—good enough anyway for fellows hunting moose all day.

The place, nowadays, is not hard to get at. The government has just built a colonization highway, quite all right for motors, that happens to go within a hundred yards of our lodge.

We can get the railway for a hundred miles, and then the highway for forty, and the last hundred yards we can walk. But this season we are going to cut out the railway and go the whole way from the city in George's car with our kit with us. George has one of those great big cars with a roof and thick glass sides. Personally none of the three of us would have preferred to ride in a luxurious dammed thing like that. Tom says that as far as he is concerned he'd much sooner go into the bush over a rough trail in a buckboard, and for my own part a team of oxen would be more the kind of thing that I'd wish.

However the car is there, so we might as well use the thing especially as the provincial government has built the fool highway right into the wilderness. By taking the big car also we can not only carry all the hunting outfit that we need but we can also, if we like, shove in a couple of small trunks with a few clothes. This may be necessary as it seems that somebody has gone and slapped a great big frame hotel right there in the wilderness, not half a mile from the place we go to. The hotel we find a regular nuisance. It gave us the advantage of electric light for our lodge (a thing none of us care about), but it means more fuss about clothes. Clothes, of course, don't really matter when a fellow is roughing it in the bush, but Tom says that we might find it necessary to go over to the hotel in the evenings to borrow coal oil or a side of bacon or any rough stuff that we need; and they do such a lot of dressing up at these fool hotels now that if we do go over for bacon or anything in the evening we might just as well slip on our evening clothes, as we could chuck them off the minute we get back. George thinks it might not be a bad idea,–just as a way of saving all our energy for getting after the moose,–to dine each evening at the hotel itself. He knew some men who did that last year and they told him that the time saved for moose hunting in that way is extraordinary. George's idea is that we could come in each night with our moose,–such and such a number as the case might be—either bringing them with us or burying them where they die,–change our things, slide over to the hotel and get dinner and then beat it back into the bush by moonlight and fetch in the moose. It seems they have a regular two dollar table d'hôte dinner at the hotel,–just rough stuff of course but after all, as we all admit, we don't propose to go out into the wilds to pamper ourselves with high feeding: a plain hotel meal in a home-like style at two dollars a plate is better than cooking up a lot of rich stuff over a camp fire.

If we *do* dine at the hotel we could take our choice each evening between going back into the bush by moonlight to fetch in the dead moose from the different caches where we had hidden them, or sticking round the hotel itself for a while. It seems that there is dancing there. Nowadays such a lot of women and girls get the open air craze for the life in the bush that these big wilderness hotels are crowded with them. There is something about living in the open that attracts modern women and they like to get right away from everybody and everything; and of course hotels of this type in the open are nowadays always well closed in with screens so that there are no flies or anything of that sort.

So it seems that there is dancing at the hotel every evening,–nothing on a large scale or pretentious,–just an ordinary hardwood floor, they may wax it a little for all I know–and some sort of plain, rough Italian orchestra that they fetch up from the city. Not that any of us care for dancing. It's a thing that personally we wouldn't bother with. But it happens that there are a couple of young girls that Tom knows that are going to be staying at the hotel and of course naturally he wants to give them a good time. They are only eighteen and twenty (sisters) and that's really younger than we care for, but with young girls like that,–practically kids,–any man wants to give them a good time. So Tom says, and I think quite rightly, that as the kids are going to be there we may as well put in an appearance at the hotel and see that they are having a good time. Their mother is going to be with them too, and of course we want to give her a good time as well; in fact I think I will lend her my moose rifle and let her go out and shoot a moose. One thing we are all agreed upon in the arrangement of our hunting trip, is in not taking along anything to drink. Drinking spoils a trip of that sort. We all remember how in the old days we'd go out into a camp in the bush (I mean before there used to be any highway or any hotel) and carry in rye whiskey in demijohns (two dollars a gallon it was) and sit around the camp fire drinking it in the evenings.

But there's nothing in it. We all agree that the law being what it is, it is better to stick to it. It makes a fellow feel better. So we shall carry nothing in. I don't say that one might not have a flask or something in one's pocket in the car; but only as a precaution against accident or cold. And when we get to our lodge we all feel that we are a dammed sight better without it. If we *should* need anything,–though it isn't likely,–there are still three cases of old Scotch whiskey, kicking around the lodge somewhere; I think they are kicking round in a little cement cellar with a locked door that we had made so as to use it for butter or anything of that sort. Anyway there are three, possibly four, or maybe, five, cases of Scotch there and if we should for any reason want it, there it is. But we are hardly likely to touch it,–unless we hit a cold snap, or a wet spell;–then we might; or if we strike hot dry weather. Tom says he thinks there are a couple of cases of champagne still in the cellar; some stuff that one of us must have shot in there just before prohibition came in. But we'll hardly use it. When a man is out moose hunting from dawn to dusk he hasn't much use for champagne, not till he gets home anyway. The only thing that Tom says the champagne might come in useful for would be if we cared to ask the two kids over to some sort of dinner; it would be just a rough kind of camp dinner (we could hardly ask their mother to it) but we think we could manage it. The man we keep there used to be a butler in England, or something of the sort, and he could manage some kind of rough meal where the champagne might fit in.

J.E.H. MacDonald, *The Elements* (1916). Oil on board; 71.1 x 91.8 cm.

J.E.H. MacDonald was a founding member of the Group of Seven, a group of Canadian painters formed in 1920 (see page 188). Courtesy of The Art Gallery of Ontario, Toronto. Gift of Dr. Lorne Pierce, 1958, in memory of Edith Chown Pierce (1890-1954).

REVIEW

1. The author apparently scorns the conveniences offered by civilization's encroachment into the bush. How does he justify his plans to make use of them?

2. What is the author's position regarding the luxuries he will encounter on his trip? How is this conveyed?

3. Reflect on the belief that men who have a "manly streak" have an innate urge to go into the bush and hunt. What are the origins of this belief? Is it still valid?

There's only one trouble about our plans for our fall camp that bothers us just a little. The moose are getting damn scarce about that place. There used, so they say, to be any quantity of them. There's an old settler up there that our man buys all our cream from who says that he remembers when the moose were so thick that they would come up and drink whiskey out of his dipper. But somehow they seem to have quit the place. Last year we sent our man out again and again looking for them and he never saw any. Three years ago a boy that works at the hotel said he saw a moose in the cow pasture back of the hotel and there were the tracks of a moose seen last year at the place not ten miles from the hotel where it had come to drink. But apart from these two exceptions the moose hunting has been poor.

Still, what does it matter? What we want is the *life*, the rough life just as I have described it. If any moose comes to our lodge we'll shoot him, or tell the butler to. But if not,—well, we've got along without for ten years, I don't suppose we shall worry.

An Unquiet Awakening

MORDECAI RICHLER

The pleasurable ease of reading a well-written novel may lull us into forgetting its power to transform our perceptions, to bring us to moments of truth. For young Mordecai Richler, the world was decisively changed by the fictional preparation of potato latkes.

PREVIEW

As a young intellectual, Mordecai Richler believed that the make-believe of fiction was unworthy of his attention. When he reads the novel "All Quiet on the Western Front," left for him by the lending library during a bout of illness, his misperceptions, not only of fiction but of his war-time German enemy, are shattered. Mordecai Richler is a Canadian satirist and an author of many essays and novels, including "The Apprenticeship of Duddy Kravitz" (1959), "St. Urbain's Horseman" (1971) and "Soloman Gursky Was Here" (1990). His most recent work of fiction is "Barney's Version," winner of the 1997 Giller Prize.

Reading was not one of my boyhood passions. Girls, or rather the absence of girls, drove me to it. When I was 13 years old, short for my age, more than somewhat pimply, I was terrified of girls. They made me feel sadly inadequate.

Retreating into high seriousness, I acquired a pipe, which I chewed on ostentatiously, and made it my business to be seen everywhere, even at school basketball games, absorbed by books of daunting significance. The two women who ran the lending library, possibly amused by my pretensions, tried to interest me in fiction.

"I want fact. I can't be bothered with stories," I protested, waving my pipe at them affronted, "I just haven't got the time for such nonsense."

Novels, I knew, were mere romantic make-believe, not as bad as poetry, to be fair, but bad enough.

I fell ill with a childhood disease, I no longer remember which, but obviously I meant it as a rebuke to those girls in tight sweaters who continued to ignore me. Never mind, they would mourn at my funeral, burying me with my pipe. Too late, they would say, "Boy, was he ever an intellectual."

The women from the lending library, concerned, dropped off books for me at our house. The real stuff. Fact-filled. Providing me with the inside dope on Theodore Herzl's childhood and *Brazil Yesterday, Today, and Tomorrow.*

One day they brought me a novel: *All Quiet on the Western Front* by Erich Maria Remarque. The painting on the jacket that was taped to the book showed a soldier wearing what was unmistakably a German Army helmet. What was this, I wondered, some sort of bad joke?

Nineteen forty-four that was, and I devoutly wished every German left on the face of the earth an excruciating death. The Allied invasion of France had not yet begun, but I cheered every Russian counterattack, each German city bombed, and—with the help of a map tacked to my bedroom wall—followed the progress of the Canadian troops fighting their way up the Italian boot. Boys from our street had already been among the fallen. Izzy Draper's uncle. Harvey Kegelmass' older brother. The boy who was supposed to marry Gita Holtzman.

All Quiet on the Western Front lay unopened on my bed for two days. Finally, I was driven to picking it up out of boredom. I never expected that a mere novel, a stranger's tale, could actually be dangerous, creating such turbulence in my life, obliging me to question so many received ideas. About Germans. About my own monumental ignorance of the world. About what novels were.

At the age of 13 in 1944, happily as yet untainted by English 104, I couldn't tell you whether Remarque's novel was

a. a slice of life

b. symbolic

c. psychological

d. seminal.

I couldn't even say if it was well or badly written. In fact, as I recall, it didn't seem to be "written" at all. Instead, it just flowed. Now, of course, I understand that writing that doesn't advertise itself is art of a very high order. It doesn't come easily. But at the time I wasn't capable of making such distinctions. I also had no notion of how *All Quiet on the Western Front* rated critically as a war novel. I hadn't read Stendhal or Tolstoy or Crane or Hemingway. I hadn't even heard of them. I didn't know that Thomas Mann, whoever he was, had praised the novel highly. Neither did I know that in 1929 the judges at some outfit called the Book-of-the-Month Club had made it their May selection.

But what I did know is that, hating Germans with a passion, I had read only 20, maybe 30, pages before the author had seduced me into identifying with my enemy, 19-year-old Paul Baumer, thrust into the bloody trenches of the First World War with his schoolmates: Muller, Kemmerich and the reluctant Joseph Behm, one of the first to fall. As if that weren't sufficiently unsettling in itself, the author, having won my love for Paul, my enormous concern for his survival, then betrayed me in the last dreadful paragraphs of his book:

"He fell in October 1918, on a day that was so quiet and still on the whole front, that the army report confined itself to the single sentence: All Quiet on the Western Front.

"He had fallen forward and lay on the earth as though sleeping. Turning him over one saw that he could not have suffered long; his face had an expression of calm, as though almost glad the end had come."

The movies, I knew from experience, never risked letting you down like that. No matter how bloody the battle, how long the odds, Errol Flynn, Robert Taylor, even Humphrey Bogart could be counted on to survive and come home to Ann Sheridan, Lana Turner or—if they were sensitive types—Loretta Young. Only character actors, usually Brooklyn Dodger fans, say George Tobias or William Bendix, were expendable.

Obviously, having waded into the pool of serious fiction by accident, I was not sure I liked or trusted the water. It was too deep. Anything could happen.

There was something else, a minor incident in *All Quiet on the Western Front* that would not have troubled an adult reader but, I'm embarrassed to say, certainly distressed that 13-year-old boy colliding with his first serious novel:

Sent out to guard a village that has been abandoned because it is being shelled too heavily, Katczinsky, the incomparable scrounger, surfaces with suckling pigs and potatoes and carrots for his comrades, a group of eight altogether:

"The suckling pigs are slaughtered, Kat sees to them. We want to make potato cakes to go with the roast. But we cannot find a grater for the potatoes. However, that difficulty is soon over. With a nail we punch a lot of holes in a pot lid and there we have a grater. Three fellows put on thick gloves to protect their fingers against the grater, two others peel the potatoes, and business gets going."

The business, I realized, alarmed—not affronted—was the making of potato latkes, a favourite of mine as well as Paul Baumer's, a dish I had always taken to be Jewish, certainly not a German concoction.

What did I know? Nothing. Or, looked at another way, my real education, my life-long addiction to fiction, began with the trifling discovery that the potato latke was not of Jewish origin, but something borrowed from the German and now a taste that Jew and German shared in spite of everything.

I felt easier about my affection for the German soldier Paul Baumer once I was told by the women from the lending library that when Hitler came to power in 1933 he had burned all of Erich Maria Remarque's books and in 1938 he took away his German citizenship. Obviously Hitler had grasped that novels could be dangerous, something I learned when I was only 13 years old. He burned them; I began to devour them. I started to read at the breakfast table and on streetcars, often missing my stop, and in bed with benefit of a flashlight. It got me into trouble.

I grasped, for the first time, that I didn't live in the centre of the world but had been born into a working-class family in an unimportant country far from the cities of light: London, Paris, New York. Of course this wasn't my fault, it was my inconsiderate parents who were to blame. But there was, I now realized, a larger world out there beyond St. Urbain Street in Montreal.

Preparing myself for the Rive Gauche, I bought a blue beret, but I didn't wear it outside, or even in the house if anybody else was at home. I looked at but lacked the courage to buy a cigarette holder.

As my parents bickered at the supper table, trapped in concerns now far too mundane for the likes of me—what to do if Dworkin raised the rent again, how to manage my brother's college fees—I sat with but actually apart from them in the kitchen, enthralled, reading for the first time, "All happy families are alike but an unhappy family is unhappy after its own fashion." (The opening sentence of *Anna Karenina* by Leo Tolstoy.)

Erich Maria Remarque, born in Westphalia in 1897, went off to war, directly from school, at the age of 18. He was wounded five times. He lost all his friends. After the war he worked briefly as a schoolteacher, a stonecutter, a test driver for a tire company and an editor of *Sportbild* magazine. His first novel, *Im Westen Nichts Neues*, was turned down by several publishers before it was brought out by the Ullstein Press in Berlin in 1928. *All Quiet on the Western Front* sold 1.2 million copies in Germany and was translated in 29 languages, selling some four million copies throughout the world. The novel has been filmed three times; the first time, memorably by Lewis Milestone in 1930. The Milestone version, with Lew Ayres playing Paul Baumer, won Academy Awards for best picture and best direction.

Since *All Quiet on the Western Front* once meant so much to me, I picked it up again with a certain anxiety. After all this time, I find it difficult to be objective about the novel. Its pages still evoke for me a back bedroom with a cracked ceiling and a sizzling radiator on St. Urbain Street: mice scrabbling in the walls, and a window looking out on the sheets frozen stiff on the laundry line.

Over the years the novel has lost something in shock value. The original jacket copy of the 1929 Little, Brown & Company edition of *All Quiet on the Western Front* warns the reader that it is "at times crude" and "will shock the supersensitive by its outspokenness." Contemporary readers, far from being shocked, will be amused by the novel's discretion, the absence of explicit sex scenes, the unbelievably polite dialogue of the men in the trenches.

The novel also has its poignant moments, both in the trenches and when Paul Baumer goes home on leave, an old man of 19, only to find insufferably pompous schoolmasters still recruiting the young with mindless prattle about the fatherland and the glory of battle. Strong characters are deftly sketched. Himmelstoss, the postman who becomes a crazed drillmaster. Tjaden, the peasant soldier. Kantorek, the schoolmaster.

On the front line the enemy is never the Frogs or the Limeys, but the insanity of the war itself. It is the war, in fact, and not even Paul Baumer, that is the novel's true protagonist. In a brief introduction to the novel Remarque wrote: "This book is to be neither an accusation nor a confession, and least of all an adventure, for death is not an adventure to those who stand face to face with it. It will try simply to tell of a generation of men who, even though they may have escaped its shells, were destroyed by the war."

Since the First World War we have become altogether too familiar with larger horrors. The Holocaust, Hiroshima, the threat of a nuclear winter. Death by numbers, cities obliterated by decree. At peace, as it were, we live the daily dread of the missiles in their silos, ours pointed at them, theirs pointed at us. None of this, however, diminishes the power of *All Quiet on the Western Front*, a novel that will endure because of its humanity, its honour and its refusal to lapse into sentimentality or strike a false note.

REVIEW

1. How did reading Remarque's novel "All Quiet on the Western Front" change Richler's opinion of novels?

2. What power does fiction have to alter our perception of the world? Name a work of fiction that has affected you personally.

3. The young Richler believed that real books were fact-filled. Does this prejudice against fiction still exist in our time? If so, where and how is it manifested?

The Game

KEN DRYDEN

Celebrities have it all, don't they? Money, success, admiration; there are plenty of perks to popular heroedom. The whole picture, however, includes struggles with commercial manipulation and feeling, overall, like a fraud.

PREVIEW

In this thoughtful excerpt, Canadian hockey superstar Ken Dryden explores the phenomenon that is the celebrity game. Perceived as harmless, the players of this game do indeed pay a cost. For our modern heroes, it is the burden of hiding every human flaw. For us admirers, it is our feelings of unworthiness in the face of such imaged perfection.

Once I used to wait in line like everyone else. Then one day a bank teller motioned me out of the line, and I haven't been back in one since. I feel no small guilt each time; nonetheless I continue to accept such favours. For the tellers and me, it has become normal and routine. They treat me the way they think people like me expect to be treated. And I accept.

It is the kind of special treatment professional athletes have grown accustomed to, and enjoy. It began with hockey, with teenage names and faces in local papers, with hockey jackets that only the best players on the best teams wore, with parents who competed not so quietly on the side; and it will end with hockey. In between, the longer and better we play the more all-encompassing the treatment becomes. People give, easily and naturally. And we accept. Slippers, sweaters, plant holders, mitts, baby blankets, baby clothes sent in the mail. Paintings, carvings, etchings, sculptures in clay, metal, papier-mâché. Shirts, slacks, coats, suits, ties, underwear; cars, carpets, sofas, chairs, refrigerators, beds, washers, dryers, stoves, TVs, stereos, at cost or no cost at all. After all, a special person deserves a special price. A hundred letters a week, more than 3,000 a year—"You're the best," all but a few of them say. On the street, in restaurants and theatres, we're pointed at, talked about like the weather. "There he is, the famous hockey player," your own kids announce to their friends. In other homes, your picture is on a boy's bedroom wall. Magazines, newspapers, radio, TV; hockey cards, posters, T-shirts, and curios, anywhere, everywhere, name, face, thousands of times.

And we love it. We say we don't, but we do. We hate the nuisance and inconvenience, the bother of untimely, unending autographs, handshakes, and smiles, living out an image of ourselves that isn't quite real, abused if we fail to, feeling encircled and trapped, never able to get away. But we also feel special—head-turning, chin-dropping, forget-your-name special. What others buy Rolls-Royces and votes and hockey teams for, what others take off their clothes for, what others kill for, we have. All we have to do is play.

If exposure is the vehicle of celebrity, attention is what separates one celebrity from another. Guy Lafleur and Yvon Lambert are both celebrities, yet on the same ice, the same screen, Lafleur is noticed, Lambert is not. Lambert, methodical and unspectacular, has nothing readily distinctive about him. His image is passed over, his name unheard. Lafleur is distinctive. The way he skates, the sound of the crowd he carries with him, the goals he scores.

And so, too, others, for other reasons. Mario Tremblay, for his fiery, untamed spirit; Bob Gainey, for his relentless, almost palpable will; Tiger Williams, Eddie Shack, Ron Duguay, each colourful and exciting; and Dave Schultz, once king of the mountain. As sports coverage proliferates beyond games, as it becomes entertainment and moves to prime time, as we look for the story behind the story, off-ice performance becomes important. And so personas are born, and sometimes made, and cameras and microphones are there as it happens. The crazies, the clowns, the "sports intellectuals," the anti-jock rebels (Jim Bouton, Bill "Spaceman" Lee), the playboys (Joe Namath, Derek Sanderson), each a distinctive personality, each a bigger celebrity because of what he does away from the game.

TV has given us a new minimum off-ice standard. The modern player must be articulate (or engagingly inarticulate, especially southern style). It's not enough to score a goal and have it picked apart by the all-seeing eyes of replay cameras. A player must be able to put it in his own eloquent words. How did you do it? How did you feel? Live, on-camera words that cannot be edited for the morning paper.

Celebrity is a full, integrated life, earned on-ice, performed, sustained, strengthened, re-earned off-ice. As Roger Angell once put it, we want our athletes to be "good at life." Role models for children, people we want to believe earned what they have, every bit as good at things off the ice as on. If they're inarticulate, harsh and pejorative, they're suddenly just jocks. Merely lucky, less likable, less good at life, less celebrated; finally, they even seem less good *on* the ice.

At its extreme, the process creates the category of professional celebrity, people "famous for being famous," so accomplished at being celebrities that their original source of deity is forgotten. At the least, it encourages all celebrities to learn the *skills* of the public person. How to look good, how to sound modest and intelligent, funny and self-deprecatory, anything you want. It's a celebrity's short-cut to the real thing, but it works. Walter Cronkite *looks* trustworthy, Ronald Reagan *seems* like a nice guy, Denis Potvin *sounds* intelligent; or is he only articulate? Good enough at something to be a public person, or simply a good public person? You'll never get close enough long enough to know.

All around us are people anxious to help us look better. Not just flacks and PR types but a whole industry of journalists, commentators, biographers, award-givers. Ghost-writers who put well-paid words under our names, then disappear; charity organizers, volunteers who give time and effort so that "honorary presidents," and "honorary directors" may look even better. Children in hospitals, old folks in old folks' homes—we autograph their casts, shake their hands, make them props to our generosity and compassion. And never far away, photographers and cameramen record the event. It is the bandwagon momentum of celebrityhood.

In the end, for us, is an image. After thousands of confused messages, we cut through what is complex and render it simple. One image, concrete and disembodied. What agents call "Ken Dryden."

Recently, I asked an executive at an advertising agency to pretend he was trying to persuade a client to use me as a commercial spokesman for his company. We'd met two or three times, several years before, so he knew me mostly as others do. He wrote the following memo to his client:

> Historically I know you have had some concerns about using an athlete ... either because of potential problems developing out of their careers and public life, or due to simply their lack of availability. I think Ken is quite different from the rest. He is known as a thoughtful, articulate and concerned individual. I think it would go without saying he would not participate in any endorsation unless he was fully committed to and satisfied with the product. (His Ralph Nader exposures would assure that.) He is serious, respected and appears to be very much his own man. I don't think we could ever consider using him in humorous or light approaches (like Eddie Shack) unless it would be by juxtaposition with another ... actor or player. He has good media presence.... His physical presence is also commanding. He is quite tall and impressive.... Other encouraging things would be his intelligence and educational background. He would be more in tune with our target audience with his credentials as a college graduate (Cornell) and a fledgling professional person (law). Also, during production, I think this intelligence and coolness would help in case of commercial production as well as helping to keep costs under control due to mental errors....

So that's my image. Is it accurate? It doesn't matter. It's what people think, it presupposes how they'll react to me. And for the ad man and his client, how people will react is what matters.

If I don't like my image, I can do something about it. I can do things that are "good for my image." I can stop doing things that are "bad for my image." As actors remind us casually and often, I can do things to change my image. Is it too serious? If I run around the dressing room throwing water at the right moment, someone is bound to notice. A journalist with a deadline to meet and space to fill, a new angle, news "Dryden misunderstood."

Want to be known as an antique collector? Collect an antique. A theatre-goer? Go. Once is enough. Tell a journalist, sound enthusiastic, and, above all, play well. Then stand back and watch what happens. Clipped and filed, the news spreads like a chain letter, to other journalists who don't have time to check it out. Presto, it's part of your standard bio. And your image.

If you substitute the word "reputation" for "image" as you might have done a few years ago, you'd have something quite different. A reputation is nothing so trifling or cynical. Like an old barge, it takes time to get going. It's slow and relentless, difficult to manoeuvre, even harder to stop. An image is nothing so solemn. It is merely a commercial asset, a package of all the rights and good-will associated with "Ken Dryden"–something I can sell to whomever I want.

But it's a sticky matter. For the image I'm selling is *your* image of me. The good-will, though it relates to me, is your good-will. Whatever commercial value there is in my name, my image, it's you who puts it there. You like me or trust me, and any prospective buyer of my image, anxious to put my name alongside his product, knows that and counts on it to make you buy his product. And you might, even though it may not be in your best interest. So by selling my name, I have perhaps taken your trust and turned it against you.

I did a commercial once, six years ago. I'd decided I never would, but this one was different enough to start a web of rationalizations until I forgot the point and accepted. A fast-food chain was looking for a winter promotion; Hockey Canada, the advisory and promotional body, wanted a fundraiser and a way to deliver the message to kids and their parents that minor hockey can be approached and played differently. The idea was a mini-book done by Hockey Canada, then sold through the restaurant chain. I was to be a collaborator on the book, and its public spokesman. But after doing the TV and radio ads (for the book, but with a corporate jingle at the end), and seeing the point-of-purchase cardboard likenesses of me in the restaurant, I realized my mistake.

Since then, I have turned down endorsements for, among other things, a candy bar ("The way I see it, a full body shot of you in the net, mask up, talking, then we draw in tight on your catching glove, you open it, the bar's inside…"), a credit card company ("You may not know me without my mask, but…"), and a roll-on deodorant that would also be promoted by several other people whose names begin with the sound "dry."

It's a game—an ad game, an image game, a celebrity game—that no one really loses. Everyone needs someone to talk about—why not about us? Everyone needs heroes and villains. We earn a little money, get some exposure. The commercials are going to be done anyway. Besides, it doesn't last long. A few years and images change, celebrity cools, it's over. It all evens out.

But it doesn't. We all lose, at least a little. We lose because you think I'm better than I am. Brighter than I am, kinder, more compassionate, capable of more things, as good at life as I am at the game. I'm not. Off the ice I struggle as you do, but off the ice you never see me, even when you think you do. I appear good at other things because I'm good at being a goalie; because I'm a celebrity; because there's always someone around to say I'm good. Because in the cozy glow of success, of good news, you want me to be good. It's my angle, and so long as I play well the angle won't change. I appear bright and articulate because I'm an athlete, and many athletes are not bright and articulate. "Like a dog's walking on his hind legs," as Dr. Johnson once put it, "it is not done well; but you are surprised to find it done at all."

But you don't believe that, just as I don't believe it about celebrities I don't know. They're taller, more talented, more compassionate. They glitter into cameras and microphones, give each other awards for talent and compassion, "great human beings" every one. Wet-eyed I applaud, and believe. And all of us lose. You, because you feel less worthy than you are. Me, because once, when I was twenty-three years old and trying to learn about myself, I wanted to believe I was, or soon would be, everything others said I was. Instead, having learned much and grown older, I feel co-conspirator to a fraud.

> In the world of the celebrity, the hierarchy of publicity has replaced the hierarchy of descent and even of great wealth.
>
> C. Wright Mills, sociologist

Professional athletes do exciting, sometimes courageous, sometimes ennobling things, as heroes do, but no more than you do. Blown up on a TV screen or a page, hyped by distance and imagination, we seem more heroic, but we're not. Our achievement seems grander, but it isn't. Our cause, our commitment, is no different from yours. We are no more than examples, metaphors, because we enter every home; we're models for the young because their world is small and we do what they do.

A few years ago, Joe McGinniss, author of *The Selling of the President, 1968*, wrote a book called *Heroes*. It sketches McGinniss's own tormented trail from being the youngest, to the highly acclaimed, to the former–all before he was thirty. At the same time, he ostensibly searches for the vanished American hero. He talks to George McGovern and Teddy Kennedy, General William Westmoreland, John Glenn, Eugene McCarthy, author William Styron, playwright Arthur Miller, some of them heroes of his, all of them heroes to many.

But it's like chasing a rainbow. He finds that, as he gets closer, his heroes disappear. In homes and bars, on campaign trails, they're distinctly, disappointingly normal. Not wonderfully, triumphantly, down to-earth normal, but up-close, drinking-too-much, sweating, stinking, unheroically normal. And for heroes, normal isn't enough. We are allowed one image; everything must fit.

The Greeks gave their gods human imperfections. In the modern hero, however, every flaw is a fatal flaw. It has only to be found, and it will be. Moving from celebrity to hero is like moving from a city to a small town. In a city, the camera's eye, though always present, is distant. In a small town, there isn't that distance. There's no place to hide.

"Whom the gods would destroy," Wilfrid Sheed wrote in *Transatlantic Blues*, "they first oversell." Superficially created, superficially destroyed–for the hero, for the celebrity, it all evens out. Except a heavy price is paid along the way. We all lose again. You, because, saddened and hurt by heroes who turn out not to be heroes at all, you become cynical and stop believing. Me, because I'm in a box. What is my responsibility? Is it, as I'm often told, to be the hero that children think I am? Or is it to live what is real, to be something else?

Recently, a friend asked me to speak to his college seminar. Near the end of two hours, we began to talk about many of these questions. A girl raised her hand. She said that a year or two earlier, on the Academy Awards, she had seen Charlton Heston receive an award for his "humanitarian" work. Heston had made the point, the girl said, that thousands of volunteers had done far more than he, that they deserved the award.

I asked the class what that story told them about Charlton Heston. That he's even modest, they decided. A few of the students laughed; then, one by one, several others joined in.

REVIEW

1. How is a celebrity's image created? How can it be changed?

2. Celebrities are often pressured to endorse products. What issues are involved for the celebrity in responding to these requests?

3. Dryden points that the gods of the Greeks were given human imperfections. Why do you think that we, in contrast, demand that our modern-day heroes excel in every area of life?

THE SKATING PARTY

MERNA SUMMERS

Are we humans capable of loving when and whom we choose? Can reason overpower true love? The haunting story of one man's choices, and their irreparable consequences, is told in this powerful short work.

PREVIEW

This short story by Canadian author Merna Summers focuses on the universal theme of choice, and the crucial situations in which all of us find ourselves at some point. People must often make choices instantaneously and under considerable stress. Summer's story illustrates that it can be difficult to ascertain the reasons for other people's actions in these situations.

Our house looked down on the lake. From the east windows you could see it: a long sickle of blue, its banks hung with willow. Beyond was a wooded ridge, which, like all such ridges in our part of the country, ran from northeast to south west.

In another part of the world, both lake and ridge would have had names. Here, only people had names. I was Maida; my father was Will, my mother was Winnie. Take us all together and we were the Singletons. The Will Singletons, that is, as opposed to the Dan Singletons, who were my grandparents and dead, or Nathan Singleton, who was my uncle and lived in the city.

In the books I read, lakes and hills had names, and so did ponds and houses. Their names made them more real to me, of greater importance, than the hills and lakes and sloughs that I saw every day. I was eleven years old before I learned that the hill on which our house was built had once had a name. It was called Stone Man Hill. My parents had never thought to tell me that.

It was my uncle, Nathan Singleton, who told me. Uncle Nathan was a bachelor. He had been a teacher before he came to Willow Bunch, but he had wanted to be a farmer. He had farmed for a few years when he was a young man, on a quarter that was now part of our farm. His quarter was just south of what had been my grandfather's home place, and was now ours. But then he had moved to the city and become a teacher again.

In some ways it seemed as if he had never really left Willow Bunch. He spent all his holidays at our place taking walks with me, talking to my mother, helping my father with such chores as he hadn't lost the knack of performing. Our home was his home. I found it hard to imagine him as I knew he must be in his classroom: wearing a suit, chalk dust on his sleeve, putting seat work on the blackboard. He didn't even talk like a teacher.

Uncle Nathan was older than my father, quite a lot older but he didn't seem so to me. In some ways he seemed younger, for he told me things and my father did not. Not that my father was either silent or unloving. He talked as much as anybody, and he was fond of some people—me included—and showed it. What he did not give away was information.

Some children are sensitive: an eye and an ear and a taking-in of subtleties. I wasn't like that. I wanted to be told. I wanted to know how things really were and how people really acted. Sometimes it seemed to me that collecting the facts was uphill work. I persisted because it was important for me to have them. I wanted to know who to praise and who to blame. Until I was in my mid-teens, that didn't seem to me to be too much to ask.

Perhaps my father had a reluctance to look at things too closely himself. He wanted to like people, and he may have found it easier to do if he kept them a little out of focus. Besides that he believed that life was something that children should be protected from knowing about for as long as possible.

I got most of my information from my mother. She believed that knowledge was protection: that children had a right to know and parents had an obligation to teach. She didn't know all there was to know, but what she did know she intended to pass on to me.

I knew this because I heard her say so one night after I had gone to bed. Uncle Nathan, who was at the farm for the weekend, saw things my mother's way. "What you don't know can hurt you," he said. "Especially what you don't know about yourself."

So my mother and my uncle talked to me, both as a sort of inoculation against life and because I now believe, both of them liked to talk anyway. I was also willing to listen. My father listened too. He might feel that my mother told me too much, but his conviction wasn't strong enough to stop her.

It was Uncle Nathan, talking for pleasure, not policy, who gave me the pleasure of knowing that I lived in a place with a name. Stone Man Hill was so named, he said, because long ago there had existed on the slopes below our house the shape of a man, outlined in fieldstones.

"He was big," Uncle Nathan said. "Maybe fifteen yards, head to foot."

It was a summer afternoon. I was eleven. My father, in from the fields for coffee was sitting at the kitchen table. His eyelashes were sooty with field dust. My mother was perched on a kitchen stool by the cupboard, picking over berries.

"He must have been quite a sight," my father said.

I walked to the east window of the kitchen and looked out, trying to imagine our hillside field of brome as unbroken prairie sod, trying to picture what a stone man would look like stretched out among the buffalo beans and gopher holes, his face to the sky.

"You get me a writing pad and I'll show you what he looked like," Uncle Nathan said.

I got the pad and Uncle Nathan sat down at the table opposite my father. I sat beside him, watching as he began to trace a series of dots. His hand worked quickly, as if the dots were already visible, but only to his eyes. The outline of a man took shape.

"Who made the stone man?" I asked.

"Indians," Uncle Nathan said. He held the picture up, as if considering additions. "But I don't know when and I don't know why."

"He could have been there a hundred years," my father said. "Maybe more. There was no way of telling"

"I used to wonder why the Indians chose this hill," Uncle Nathan said. "I still do."

He got up and walked to the window looking out at the hill and the lake and the ridge. "It may be that it was some sort of holy place to them," he said.

My mother left the cupboard and came across to the table. She picked up Uncle Nathan's drawing. Looking at it, the corners of her mouth twitched upwards.

"You're sure you haven't forgotten anything?" she asked. "Your mother used to say that the stone man was very complete."

Uncle Nathan returned her smile. "The pencil's right here, Winnie," he said. "You're welcome to it."

My father spoke quickly. "It was too bad the folks didn't have a camera," he said. "It would have been nice to have a picture of the stone man."

My mother went back to her berries.

"I've always been sorry I was too young to remember him," my father said. "Before he turned into a rock pile, that is."

I hadn't yet got around to wondering about the stone man's disappearance. Now I did. He should still have been on his hillside for me to look at. My father had been a baby when his people came to Willow Bunch, and he couldn't remember the stone man. My uncle had been a young man and could. But the difference in their ages and experience hadn't kept them from sharing a feeling of excitement at the thought of a stone man on our hillside. Why had my grandfather been insensible to this appeal? Hadn't he liked the stone man?

"Liking wouldn't enter into it," my father said. "Your grandfather had a family to feed. He knew where his duty lay."

"There was 30 acres broke when Pa bought this place," Uncle Nathan said. "He thought he needed more. And this hill was the only land he could break without brushing it first."

Somebody else had owned our place before my grandfather hadn't they? I asked. He hadn't turned the stone man into a rock pile.

"He was a bachelor," my father said.

"The way your grandfather saw it," Uncle Nathan said, "it was a case of wheat or stones. And he chose wheat."

"Which would you have chosen?" I asked Uncle Nathan. "Which did you want?"

"I wanted both," Uncle Nathan said.

"The choice wasn't yours to make." My mother spoke as if she were defending him.

"That's what I thought then," Uncle Nathan said. "I thought when Pa told me to get those rocks picked, that that was what I had to do. I think now I should have spoken up. I know for years I felt guilty whenever I remembered that I had done just what was expected of me."

He looked up, a half-smile on his face. "I know it sounds crazy," he said, "but I felt as if the stone man had more claim on me than my own father did."

"We all of us think some crazy things sometimes," my father said.

From my point of view, Uncle Nathan had only one peculiarity. He had never married. And though I sometimes asked him why, I never found any satisfaction in his answers.

"Maybe it wasn't every girl who took my eye," he told me once. "I'd pity the girl who had to count on me to take care of her," he said another time.

Then my mother told me about the skating party. It had been a dark night in November, and my mother, five years old, had come to our lake with her parents, and spent the night pushing a kitchen chair in front of her across the ice, trying to learn to skate. The party was being held in honour of Uncle Nathan and a girl called Eunice Lathem. The were to be married soon, and their friends planned after the skating, to go up to the house and present a gift to them. The gift and the fact that the party was in her honour were to be a surprise to Eunice. Nathan, for some reason, had been told about it.

There had been cold that year but no snow, so you could skate all over the lake. My mother remembered them skimming by, the golden lads and girls who made up the world when she was small, and Nathan and Eunice the most romantic of all. Nathan was handsome and Eunice was beautiful and they were very much in love, she said.

She remembered the skaters by moonlight, slim black shapes mysterious against the silver fields. There were a lot of clouds in the sky that night and when the moon went behind one of them friends, neighbours, and parents' friends became alike: all equally unknown, unidentifiable.

My grandfather and Uncle Nathan had built a big wood fire at the near end of the lake. My mother said that it was a grand experience to skate off into the darkness and the perils and dangers of the night, and then turn and come back toward the light, following the fire's reflection on the ice.

Late on, when some people were already making their way up the hill to the house, Eunice Lathem went skating off into the darkness with her sister. They didn't skate up the middle of the lake as most of the skaters had been doing. Instead they went off toward the east bank. There is a place there where a spring rises and the water is deep but they didn't know that. The ice was thinner there. They broke through.

Near the fire, people heard their cries for help. A group of men skated out to rescue them. When the men got close to the place where the girls were in the water, the ice began to crack under their feet.

All the men lay down then and formed a chain, each holding the ankles of the man in front of him. Uncle Nathan was at the front. He inched forward, feeling the ice tremble beneath his body until he came to the point where he could reach either of two pairs of hands clinging to the fractured edge.

It was dark. He couldn't see the girls' faces. All he could do was grasp the nearest pair of wrists and pull. The men behind him pulled on his feet. Together they dragged one girl back to safety. But as they were doing it, the ice broke away beneath them and the second girl went under. The moon came out and they saw it was Eunice Lathem's sister they had saved. They went back to the hole, but Eunice had vanished. There wasn't any way they could even get her body.

"It was an awful thing to have happen on our place," my father said.

"Your Uncle Nathan risked his life," my mother said. Her voice was earnest, for she too believed in identifying heroes and villains.

"There was no way on earth he could save both girls," she said. "The ice was already breaking, and the extra weight of the first one was bound to be too much for it."

Why hadn't he saved Eunice first?

"I told you," my mother said. "He couldn't see their faces."

It troubled me that he hadn't had some way of knowing. I would have expected love to be able to call out to love. If it couldn't do that, what was it good for? And why had the moon been behind a cloud anyway?

"Your grandmother used to say that the Lord moves in a mysterious way," my father said.

"What does that mean?" I asked.

"It means that nobody knows," my mother said.

I'd seen Eunice Lathem's name on a grave in the yard of St. Chad's, where we attended services every second Sunday. If I'd thought of her at all, it was as a person who had always been dead. Now she seemed real to me, almost like a relative. She was a girl who had loved and been loved. I began to make up stories about her. But I no longer skated on the lake alone. Eunice Lathem's sister, whose name was Delia Sykes, moved away from Willow Bunch right after the accident. She didn't wait until her husband sold out; she went straight to Edmonton and waited for him there. Even when they buried Eunice in the spring, she didn't come back.

Years later, someone from Willow Bunch had seen her in Edmonton. She didn't mention Eunice or the accident or even Willow Bunch.

"It must have been a short conversation," my mother said practically.

Is it surprising that I continued to wonder why Uncle Nathan didn't marry? Some people remember their childhoods as a time when they thought of anybody over the age of 25 as being so decrepit as to be beyond all thought of romance or adventure. I remember feeling that way about women, but I never thought of men that way, whatever their ages. It seemed to me that Uncle Nathan could still pick out a girl and marry her if he set his mind to it.

"No," he said when I asked him. "Not 'still' and not 'pick out a girl.' A person doesn't have that much say in the matter. You can't love where you choose."

And then, making joke of it, "See that you remember that when your time comes," he said.

One day my mother showed me a picture of Eunice Lathem and her sister. Two girls and a pony stood looking at the camera. Both girls were pretty. The one who wasn't Eunice was laughing; she looked like a girl who loved to laugh. Eunice was pretty too but there was a stillness about her, almost a sternness. If she hadn't been Eunice Lathem, I would have said she was sulking.

I felt cheated. Was the laughing one also prettier?

"She may have been," my mother said. "I remember Eunice Lathem as being beautiful. But since Delia Sykes was married I don't suppose I gave her looks a thought one way or the other."

As I grew older I spent less time wondering about the girl who'd been Eunice Lathem. I'd never wondered about her sister, and perhaps never would have if I hadn't happened to be with Uncle Nathan the day he heard that Delia Sykes had died.

It was the spring I was fifteen. My parents were away for the weekend, attending a silver wedding in Rochfort Bridge. Uncle Nathan and I were alone on the farm and so, if he wanted to talk about Delia Sykes, he hadn't much choice about who to talk to.

It was a morning for bad news. The frost was coming out of the ground, setting the very ditches and wheel-ruts to weeping. Out in the barn, a ewe was mourning her lost lamb. We had put her in a pen by herself and we were saving the dead lamb, so we could use its skin to dress another lamb in case one of the ewes died in lambing or had no milk.

Uncle Nathan and I left the barn and walked out to the road to pick up the mail. The news of Delia's death was in the local paper. "Old-timers will be saddened to learn of the death in Duncan, B.C. of Mrs. Delia Sykes, a former resident of this district," the paper said.

Uncle Nathan shook his head slowly, as if he found the news hard to believe. "So Delia's gone," he said. "She was a grand girl, Delia Sykes. No matter what anybody said she was a grand girl."

There was a picture of Mrs. Sykes with the death notice. I saw a middle-aged woman who had gone from the hairdresser's to the photographer's. Her cheeks were as firm and round as two peach halves, and she had snappy eyes. She was wearing a white dress. She looked as if she might have belonged to the Eastern Star or the Rebekahs.

Uncle Nathan looked at the picture too. "Delia always was a beauty," he said.

He sat in silence for a while and then bit by bit, he began to tell me the story of how he had met Delia Sykes and before her, her husband.

"Only I didn't realize that he was her husband," Uncle Nathan said. "I thought when I met her that she was single, that was the joke of it."

It was late July and late afternoon. Uncle Nathan was teaching school, to make enough money to live on until his farm got going. But he was hoping to get out of it.

"The land was new then and we thought there was no limit to how rich we were all going to be some day. Besides that," he added, "what I wanted to do was farm. School-teaching seemed to me to be no proper job for a man."

There were two things Uncle Nathan wanted. One was to stop teaching. The other was to find a wife.

There were more men than girls around then, he told me, so the man who wanted a good selection had to be prepared to cover a lot of territory.

"Harold Knight and I took in dances and ball games as far away as Hasty Hills," he said.

They'd already seen a fair sampling, but there were still girls they hadn't seen.

"I had a pretty fair idea of what I was looking for," Uncle Nathan said. "I imagine it was the same sort of thing every young fellow thinks he's looking for, but I thought I had standards. I wasn't willing to settle for just anyone."

It was with the idea of looking over another couple of girls that he went to see Harold Knight that late July afternoon. A family with two daughters was rumoured to have moved in somewhere near Morningside School. He'd come to suggest to Harold that they take in the church service at the school the next Sunday.

The Knights, Uncle Nathan said, had hay and seed wheat to sell to people with the money to buy it. When Uncle Nathan walked into their yard that day, he saw that Mr. Knight was talking to a buyer. It was a man he'd never seen before, but he guessed by the cut of the man's rig that he must be well fixed.

"Nathan," Mr. Knight said, "meet Dobson Sykes."

Mr. Sykes was a straight-standing man with greying hair. He put out his hand and Uncle Nathan shook it.

"His driving horses," Uncle Nathan said "were as showy a team as I'd ever seen–big bays with coats the colour of red willow."

"You'd go a long way before you'd find a better-matched team than that," Mr. Knight said.

"Oh, they match well enough." Dobson Sykes spoke as if that was a matter of little importance to him, as if no effort was made in the acquiring of such a team. "I'd trade them in a minute if something better came along," he said carelessly. "I have a job to keep Spark, here, up to his collar."

"I had a fair amount of respect then for men who'd done well in life," Uncle Nathan told me. "This man was about my father's age, old enough to have made it on his own. When a man like that came my way, I studied him. I thought if I was going to be a farmer instead of a teacher, I'd have to start figuring out how people went about getting things in life."

"I wasn't really surprised when Mr. Knight said that Sykes had a crew of men–men he was paying–putting up a set of buildings for him on a place he'd bought near Bannock Hill. He looked like a man with that kind of money."

"We're not building anything fancy," Dobson Sykes said. "If I'd wanted to stay farming on a big scale, I wouldn't have moved from Manitoba."

After a while Uncle Nathan left the two older men talking and walked out toward the meadow, where Harold was fetching a load of hay for Mr. Sykes.

It was on the trail between buildings and meadow that he met Delia Sykes.

He didn't see her at first because she wasn't sitting up front with Harold. She must have been lying back in the hay, Uncle Nathan said, just watching the clouds drift by overhead. She sat up.

Uncle Nathan saw at once that she was not very old; he had girls almost as old as she was in his classroom. But there was nothing of the schoolgirl about

Delia. She was young but womanly. Everything about her curved, from the line of her cheek to the way she carried her arms.

Uncle Nathan saw all this in the instant that she appeared looking down over the edge of the load. He saw too that she had a kind of class he'd never seen around Willow Bunch. She looked like a girl perfectly suited to riding around the country behind a team of perfectly matched bays.

She reached behind her into the hay and came up with a crown of french-braided dandelions. She set it on top of her hair and smiled.

He knew right then, Uncle Nathan said, that his voice wouldn't be among those swelling the hymns at Morningside School next Sunday. And he felt as if he understood for the first time how men must feel when they are called to the ministry. Choosing and decision and standards have nothing to do with it. You're called or you're not called, and when you're called you know it.

The girl smiled and opened her arms as if to take in the clouds in the sky and the bees buzzing in the air and the red-topped grasses stirring in the wind. Then she spoke.

"You've got no worries on a load of hay," she said. Those were the first words Uncle Nathan heard Delia Sykes say. "You've got no worries on a load of hay."

There was a patch of milkweed blooming near the path where Uncle Nathan was standing. In late July, small pink blossoms appear and the milk, rich and white, is ready to run as soon as you break the stalk. Uncle Nathan picked a branch, climbed the load of hay, and presented it to the girl.

"It's not roses," he said "but the sap is supposed to cure warts."

She laughed. "My name is Delia Sykes," she said.

"I thought she was Dobson's daughter," Uncle Nathan said, "and it crossed my mind to wonder if he'd have traded her off if she hadn't moved along smart in her harness."

"There didn't seem to be much fear of that. You could see right away she had spirit. If she had too much, it was nothing that marriage to a good man wouldn't cure, I thought."

Uncle Nathan gave a rueful smile. "Of course when we got back to the yard I found out that she wasn't Dobson's daughter but his wife. Later I wonder why she hadn't introduced herself as Mrs. Sykes. And she'd called me Nathan too, and girls didn't do that then.

"The truth is," Uncle Nathan said, "I had kind of fallen for her."

Did she feel the same way about him?

If she did, Uncle Nathan wasn't willing to say so. "Delia was only nineteen," he said. "I don't think she knew what she wanted."

He was silent for a while. Then he went on with his story. "Once I knew she was married," he said "I knew right away what I had to do. I remember I gave myself a good talking to. I said, 'If you can fall in love in twenty minutes, you can fall out of love just as fast.'"

"And could you?"

"Some people could, I guess," Uncle Nathan said. "It seemed to take me a bit longer than that."

The story stopped then because we had to go out to the barn to check the sheep. While we'd been in the house, another ewe had dropped her lamb. We heard it bleat as we came in the barn, and the ewe whose lamb had died heard it too. It was at the far end of the barn, out of sight, but at the sound of it, milk began to run from her udder. She couldn't help herself.

We checked the rest of the sheep and then we went back into the house. I made us a pot of tea.

"I was afraid to go to see Dobson and Delia after they got moved in," Uncle Nathan said. "I think I was afraid somebody would read my mind."

He went, he said, because Delia soon made her house a gathering place for all the young people of the district, and he didn't see how he could be the only one to stay away. Delia didn't make things any easier for him.

"She used to keep saying she'd only been married three months … as if that made it any less final. And when she spoke of anything they had–whether it was a buggy or a kitchen safe or the pet dog–she would say 'my buggy' or 'my kitchen safe' or 'my dog.' 'We' and 'us' were words she didn't use at all."

I poured our tea then, trying to imagine the house that Delia Sykes had lived in.

"It was something of a showplace for its time," Uncle Nathan told me. Everything in it was the best of its kind, he said, from the Home Comfort stove in the kitchen to the pump organ in the parlour. What puzzled Uncle Nathan was Delia's attitude to her things. She'd picked them out herself in Winnipeg and ordered them sent, but when they got here, she seemed to feel they weren't important.

"The more things you've got, the more things you've got to take care of," she said. She didn't even unpack most of her trunks.

Dobson was worried. He thought that moving away from her family had unsettled her. "Delia wasn't like this in Manitoba," he said.

"I kept wondering," Uncle Nathan said, "where we would go from here. It never occurred to me that there could be another girl for me. And then Eunice came along."

It was on an October afternoon, Uncle Nathan said, that he met Eunice Lathem.

The sun was low in the southwest when he drove into the Sykes yard, and Dobson, as usual, was out around the buildings showing the younger men his grinding mill, his blacksmith shop, his threshing machine.

Uncle Nathan remembered that the trees were leafless except for the plumes of new growth at the top. He tied up his horse and, as he headed for the house, saw that the afternoon sun was turning the west-facing walls all gold and blue. It looked like a day for endings, not beginnings. But he went into the house, and there stood Eunice Lathem.

Eunice was a year or two older than Delia but she looked just like her. Uncle Nathan noticed that she was quieter.

Supper was already on the table when Uncle Nathan got there. The news of Eunice's arrival had attracted such a company of bachelors that there weren't enough plates or chairs for everybody to eat at once.

"I don't know about anybody else, but I'm starving," Delia announced, taking her place at the head of the table. Eunice, though she was the guest of honour, insisted on waiting until the second sitting.

As the first eaters prepared to deal with their pie, Eunice began to ladle water out of a stonewear crock into a dishpan. Uncle Nathan went to help her. He said something funny and she laughed.

Delia's voice startled them both. "I invited Eunice out here to find a husband," she said with a high-pitched laugh. "I said to myself, 'With all the bachelors we've got around, if she can't find a husband here there's no hope for her.'"

Delia spoke as if she was making a joke and there was a nervous round of laughter. Blood rose in Eunice's face.

"If I'd known that was why you were asking me," Eunice said, "I would never have come."

And indeed, Uncle Nathan said, Eunice wasn't the sort of girl to need anyone's help in finding a husband. She was, if anything, prettier than Delia. Not as showy, perhaps, perhaps not as rounded. But if you went over them point by point comparing noses, chins, teeth and all the rest of it, Eunice's might well have come out on top.

Later, when the others had gone, Delia apologized. "I shouldn't have said that," she said. "It sounded awful." She didn't even claim to have been making joke.

"I want you two to be friends," she said.

In the weeks that followed, Uncle Nathan saw that Delia was pushing her sister his way. He didn't know why, but he didn't find the idea unpleasant.

"I suppose I liked Eunice at first because she looked so much like Delia," he said, "but as I got to know her better it seemed to me that she might be easier to get along with in the long run. I wouldn't be the first man to marry the sister of the girl who first took his fancy, nor the last one either.

"It seemed to me that a man could love one girl as easily as another if he put his mind to it. I reasoned it out. How much did the person matter anyway? That was what I asked myself. It seemed to me that when all was said and done, it would be the life that two people made together that would count, not who the people were.

"I remember thinking that getting married would be like learning to dance. Some people are born knowing how; they have a natural beat. Other people have to make an effort to learn. But all of them, finally, are moving along to the music one way or the other.

"Anyway," Uncle Nathan said "I spoke to Eunice and she agreed, and we decided to be married at Christmas.

"It was September, I think, when we got engaged," Uncle Nathan said. "I remember thinking about telling Dobson and Delia. I could imagine the four of us–Dobson and Delia, Eunice and me–living side by side, spending our Sundays together, raising children who would be cousins and might even look like each other.

"I came over early on the Sunday and we told them. Delia didn't have very much to say then. But in the afternoon when quite a crowd had gathered and Eunice and I were waiting for the rest of them to get there before we made our announcement, a strange thing happened.

"The day before, Dobson had brought home a new saddle pony and Delia had wanted to ride it. Dobson didn't know how well broke it was, or if it could be trusted, and he refused. I guess that refusal rankled. Delia didn't like to be told she couldn't do a thing or have a thing she had set her heart on.

"Anyway, on Sunday afternoon Eunice was sitting at the pump organ playing for us, and she looked beautiful. We were all sitting around looking at her.

"And then somebody happened to glance out of the window," Uncle Nathan said. "And there was Delia on the pony and the pair of them putting on a regular rodeo.

"She didn't break her neck which was a wonder. By the time she finally got off the pony, we were all out in the yard, and somebody had the idea of taking a picture of Delia and Eunice and the pony."

After that, Uncle Nathan said, Delia seemed to want to get the wedding over with as soon as possible. She hemmed sheets and ordered linen and initialled pillow-cases. When November finally came and the neighbours decided on a skating party for Eunice and Uncle Nathan, it was Delia who sewed white rabbit fur around the sleeves and bottom of Eunice's coat, so that it would look like a skating dress.

The night of the party was dark. There was a moon, but the sky was cloudy. They walked down the hill together, all those young people laughing and talking.

"One minute you could see their faces and the next they would all disappear," Uncle Nathan said. "I touched a match to a bonfire we had laid in the afternoon, and we all sat down to screw on our skates.

"I skated first with Eunice. She wanted to stay near the fire so we could see where we were going. I skated with several other girls, putting off, for some reason, the time when I would skate with Delia. But then she came gliding up to me and held out her hands and I took them and we headed out together into the darkness.

"As soon as we turned our backs on the fire it was as if something came over us. We wanted to skate out farther and farther. It seemed to me that we could keep on like this all our lives, just skating outward farther and farther, and the lake would keep getting longer and longer so that we would never come to the end of it."

Uncle Nathan sighed. "I didn't know then that in three days Delia would have left Willow Bunch for good, and in six months I would have followed her," he said.

Why had he given up farming?

"Farming's no life for a man alone," he said. "And I couldn't imagine ever wanting to marry again."

He resumed his story. "Once the moon came out and I could see Delia's face, determined in the moonlight.

"'Do you want to turn back?' I asked her.

"'I'm game as long as you are,' she said.

"Another time, 'I don't ever want to turn back,' she said.

"I gave in before Delia did," Uncle Nathan said. "'If we don't turn around pretty soon,' I told her 'we're going to be skating straight up Pa's stubble fields.'

"We turned around then, and there was the light from the fire and our feet already set on its path. And I found I wanted to be back there with all the people around me. Eunice deserved better, and I knew it."

As they came toward the fire, Eunice skated out to meet them. "I might as well have been someplace else for all the attention she paid me," Uncle Nathan said. Her words were all for Delia.

"If this is what you got me out here for," Eunice said, "you can just forget about it. I'm not going to be your window blind."

"I don't know what you're talking about," Delia said.

She looked unhappy. "She knew as well as I did," Uncle Nathan said "that whatever we were doing out there it was more than just skating."

"We were only skating," Delia said. And then her temper rose. "You always were jealous of me," she said.

"Who would you say was jealous now?" Eunice asked.

"We were far enough away from the fire for the girls not to be heard," Uncle Nathan said. "At least I hoped we were.

"What was worrying me was the thought of Eunice having to meet all the people up at the house, and finding out she was the guest of honour, and having to try to rise to the occasion.

"That was why I suggested that the two of them go for a skate. I thought it would give them a chance to cool down. Besides," he added, "I couldn't think of anything else to do."

The girls let themselves be persuaded. They skated off together and Uncle Nathan watched them go. First he could see their two silhouettes, slim and graceful against the silver lake. Then all he could see was the white fur on Eunice's coat. And then they were swallowed up by the darkness.

"It was several minutes before we heard them calling for help," Uncle Nathan said.

Uncle Nathan and I sat silent for some time then: he remembering, I pondering. "If only you could have seen how beautiful she was," he said at last, and I didn't know whether it was Eunice he was speaking of, or Delia.

"I wonder if I would have felt any better about it if I'd got Eunice instead of Delia," he said. I realized that he'd been trying to make the judgement for 30 years.

"You didn't have any choice," I reminded him. "It was dark. You couldn't see their faces."

"No," Uncle Nathan said. "I couldn't see their faces." The sound of old winters was in his voice, a sound of infinite sadness.

"But I could see their hands on the edge of the ice," he said. "The one pair of arms had white fur around them.

"And I reached for the other pair."

REVIEW

1. What characteristic does the act of "naming" bestow on objects, according to the narrator?

2. Uncle Nathan decides to marry Eunice, stating that "a man could love one girl as easily as another." How does his belief change regarding choice in the matter of love? Does this justify his actions at the skating party?

3. How does this story speak to our human tendency to abdicate our power to choose, and our unwillingness to accept responsibility for our choices?

IMAGES OF RELATIONSHIP

CONCEPTIONS OF MORALITY AND SELF

CAROL GILLIGAN

A man named Heinz considers whether or not to steal a drug that he cannot afford to buy in order to save his wife's life. Two 11-year-olds, a boy and a girl, both intelligent and perceptive about life, respond differently to this hypothetical "moral dilemma." Right and wrong is not a simple matter—it seems that girls and boys see such dilemmas differently.

In 1914, with his essay "On Narcissism," Freud swallows his distaste at the thought of "abandoning observation for barren theoretical controversy" and extends his map of the psychological domain. Tracing the development of the capacity to love, which he equates with maturity and psychic health, he locates its origins in the contrast between love for the mother and love for the self. But in thus dividing the world of love into narcissism and "object" relationships, he finds that while men's development becomes clear, women's becomes increasingly opaque. The problem arises because the contrast between mother and self yields two different images of relationships. Relying on the imagery of men's lives in charting the course of human growth, Freud is unable to trace in women the development of relationships, morality, or a clear sense of self. This difficulty in fitting the logic of his theory to women's experience leads him in the end to set women apart, marking their relationships, like their sexual life, as "a 'dark continent' for psychology"....

Thus the problem of interpretation that shadows the understanding of women's development arises from the differences observed in their experience of relationships. To Freud, though living surrounded by women and otherwise seeing so much and so well, women's relationships seemed increasingly mysterious, difficult to discern, and hard to describe. While this mystery indicates how theory can blind observation, it also suggests that development in women is masked by a particular conception of human relationships. Since the imagery of relationships shapes the narrative of human development, the inclusion of women, by changing that imagery, implies a change in the entire account.

The shift in imagery that creates the problem in interpreting women's development is elucidated by the **moral judgements** of two eleven-year-old children, a boy and a girl, who see, in the same dilemma, two very different moral problems. While current theory brightly illuminates the line and the

PREVIEW

In this excerpt from her book "In a Different Voice" (1982) Harvard psychologist Carol Gilligan explores the way in which the psychological development of women has been trivialized and in many cases ignored by research in the field. She takes particular exception to the work of Lawrence Kohlberg, whose paradigm of child moral development defined the area of child psychology until Gilligan's criticism.

logic of the boy's thought, it casts scant light on that of the girl. The choice of a girl whose moral judgements elude existing categories of developmental assessment is meant to highlight the issue of interpretation rather than to exemplify sex differences per se. Adding a new line of interpretation, based on the imagery of the girl's thought, makes it possible not only to see development where previously development was not discerned but also to consider differences in the understanding of relationships without scaling these differences from better to worse.

The two children were in the same sixth-grade class at school and were participants in the rights and responsibilities study, designed to explore different **conceptions of morality and self**. The sample selected for this study was chosen to focus the variables of gender and age while maximizing developmental potential by holding constant, at a high level, the factors of intelligence, education, and social class that have been associated with moral development at least as measured by existing scales.

The two children in question, Amy and Jake, were both bright and articulate and, at least in their eleven-year-old aspirations, resisted easy categories of sex-role stereotyping, since Amy aspired to become a scientist while Jake preferred English to math. Yet their moral judgements seem initially to confirm familiar notions about differences between the sexes, suggesting that the edge girls have on moral development during the early school years gives way at puberty with the ascendance of formal logical thought in boys.

The dilemma that these eleven-year-olds were asked to resolve was one in the series devised by Kohlberg to measure moral development in adolescence by presenting a conflict between moral norms and exploring the logic of its resolution. In this particular dilemma, a man named Heinz considers whether or not to steal a drug which he cannot afford to buy in order to save the life of his wife. In the standard format of Kohlberg's interviewing procedure, the description of the dilemma itself–Heinz's predicament, the wife's disease, the druggist's refusal to lower his price–is followed by the question, "Should Heinz steal the drug?" The reasons for and against stealing are then explored through a series of questions that vary and extend the parameters of the dilemma in a way designed to reveal the underlying **structure of moral thought**.

Jake, at eleven, is clear from the outset that Heinz should steal the drug. Constructing the dilemma, as Kohlberg did, as a conflict between the values of property and life, he discerns the logical priority of life and uses that logic to justify his choice:

> For one thing, a human life is worth more than money, and if the druggist only makes $1,000, he is still going to live, but if Heinz doesn't steal the drug, his wife is going to die. (*Why is life worth more than money?*) Because the druggist can get a thousand dollars later from rich people with cancer, but Heinz can't get his wife again. (*Why not?*) Because people are all different and so you couldn't get Heinz's wife again.

Asked whether Heinz should steal the drug if he does not love his wife, Jake replies that he should, saying that not only is there "a difference between hating and killing," but also, if Heinz were caught, "the judge would probably think it was the right thing to do." Asked about the fact that, in stealing, Heinz would be breaking the law, he says that "the laws have mistakes, and you can't go writing up a law for everything that you can imagine."

Thus, while taking the law into account and recognizing its function in maintaining social order (the judge, Jake says, "should give Heinz the lightest possible sentence"), he also sees the law as man-made and therefore subject to error and change. Yet his judgement that Heinz should steal the drug, like his view of the law as having mistakes, rests on the assumption of agreement, a societal consensus around moral values that allows one to know and expect others to recognize what is "the right thing to do."

Fascinated by the power of logic, this eleven-year-old boy locates truth in math, which, he says, is "the only thing that is totally logical." Considering the moral dilemma to be "sort of like a math problem with humans," he sets it up as an equation and proceeds to work out the solution. Since his solution is rationally derived, he assumes that anyone following reason would arrive at the same conclusion and thus that a judge would also consider stealing to be the right thing for Heinz to do. Yet he is also aware of the limits of logic. Asked whether there is a right answer to moral problems, Jake replies that "there can only be right and wrong in judgement," since the parameters of action are variable and complex. Illustrating how actions undertaken with the best of intentions can eventuate in the most disastrous of consequences, he says, "like if you give an old lady your seat on the trolley, if you are in a trolley crash and that seat goes through the window, it might be that reason that the old lady dies."

Theories of **developmental psychology** illuminate well the position of this child, standing at the juncture of childhood and adolescence, at what Piaget describes as the pinnacle of childhood intelligence, and beginning through thought to discover a wider universe of possibility. The moment of preadolescence is caught by the conjunction of formal operational thought with a description of self still anchored in the factual parameters of his childhood world–his age, his town, his father's occupation, the substance of his likes, dislikes, and beliefs. Yet as his self-description radiates the self-confidence of a child who has arrived, in Erikson's terms, at a favourable balance of industry over inferiority–competent, sure of himself, and knowing well the rules of the game–so his emergent capacity for formal thought, his ability to think about thinking and to reason things out in a logical way, frees him from dependence on authority and allows him to find solutions to problems by himself.

This emergent autonomy follows the trajectory that **Kohlberg's six stages** of moral development trace, a three-level progression from an egocentric understanding of fairness based on individual need (stages one and two), to a conception of fairness anchored in the shared conventions of societal agreement (stages three and four), and finally to a principled understanding of fairness that rests on the free-standing logic of equality and reciprocity (stages five and six). While this boy's judgements at eleven are scored as conventional on Kohlberg's scale, a mixture of stages three and four, his ability to bring deductive logic to bear on the solution of moral dilemmas, to differentiate morality from law, and to see how laws can be considered to have mistakes points toward the principled conception of justice that Kohlberg equates with moral maturity.

In contrast, Amy's response to the dilemma conveys a very different impression, an image of development stunted by a failure of logic, an inability to think for herself. Asked if Heinz should steal the drug, she replies in a way that seems evasive and unsure:

> Well, I don't think so. I think there might be other ways besides stealing it, like if he could borrow the money or make a loan or something, but he really shouldn't steal the drug–but his wife shouldn't die either.

Asked why he should not steal the drug, she considers neither property nor law but rather the effect that theft could have on the relationship between Heinz and his wife:

> If he stole the drug, he might save his wife then, but if he did, he might have to go to jail, and then his wife might get sicker again, and he couldn't get more of the drug, and it might not be good. So, they should really just talk it out and find some other way to make the money.

Seeing in the dilemma not a math problem with humans but a narrative of relationships that extends over time, Amy envisions the wife's continuing need for her husband and the husband's continuing concern for his wife and seeks to respond to the druggist's need in a way that would sustain rather than sever connection. Just as she ties the wife's survival to the preservation of relationships, so she considers the value of the wife's life in a context of relationships, saying that it would be wrong to let her die because, "if she died, it hurts a lot of people and it hurts her." Since Amy's moral judgement is grounded in the belief that, "if somebody has something that would keep somebody alive, then it's not right not to give it to them," she considers the problem in the dilemma to arise not from the druggist's assertion of rights but from his failure of response.

As the interviewer proceeds with the series of questions that follow from Kohlberg's construction of the dilemma, Amy's answers remain essentially unchanged, the various probes serving neither to elucidate nor to modify her initial response. Whether or not Heinz loves his wife, he still shouldn't steal or let her die; if it were a stranger dying instead, Amy says that "if the stranger didn't have anybody near or anyone she knew," then Heinz should try to save her life, but he should not steal the drug. But as the interviewer conveys through the repetition of questions that the answers she gave were not heard or nor right, Amy's confidence begins to diminish, and her replies become more constrained and unsure. Asked again why Heinz should not steal the drug, she simply repeats, "Because it's not right." Asked again to explain why, she states again that theft would not be a good solution, adding lamely, "if he took it, he might not know how to give it to his wife, and so his wife might still die." Failing to see the dilemma as a self-contained problem in moral logic, she does not discern the internal structure of its resolution; as she constructs the problem differently herself, Kohlberg's conception completely evades her.

Instead, seeing a world comprised of relationships rather than of people standing alone, a world that coheres through human connection rather than through systems of rules, she finds the puzzle in the dilemma to lie in the failure of the druggist to respond to the wife. Saying that "it is not right for someone to die when their life could be saved," she assumes that if the druggist were to see the consequences of his refusal to lower his price, he would realize that, "he should just give it to the wife and then have the husband pay back the money later." Thus she considers the solution to the dilemma to lie in making the wife's condition more salient to the druggist or, that failing, in appealing to others who are in a position to help.

Just as Jake is confident the judge would agree that stealing is the right thing for Heinz to do, so Amy is confident that, "if Heinz and the druggist had talked it out long enough, they could reach something besides stealing." As he considers the law to "have mistakes," so she sees this drama as a mistake, believing that "the world should just share things more and then people wouldn't have to steal." Both children thus recognize the need for agreement but see it as mediated in different ways–he impersonally through systems of logic and law, she personally through communication in relationship. Just as he relies on the conventions of logic to deduce the solution to this dilemma, assuming these conventions to be shared, so she relies on a process of communication, assuming connection and believing that her voice will be heard. Yet while his assumptions about agreement are confirmed by the convergence in logic between his answers and the questions posed, her assumptions are belied by the failure of communication, the interviewer's inability to understand her response.

Although the frustration of the interview with Amy is apparent in the repetition of questions and its ultimate circularity, the problem of interpretation is focused by the assessment of her response. When considered in the light of Kohlberg's definition of the stages and sequence of moral development, her moral judgements appear to be a full stage lower in maturity than those of the boy. Scored as a mixture of stages two and three, her responses seem to reveal a feeling of powerlessness in the world, an inability to think systematically about the concepts of morality or law, a reluctance to challenge authority or to examine the logic of received moral truths, a failure even to conceive of acting directly to save a life or to consider that such action, if taken, could possibly have an effect. As her reliance on relationships seems to reveal a continuing dependence and vulnerability, so her belief in communication as the mode through which to resolve moral dilemmas appears naive and cognitively immature.

Yet Amy's description of herself conveys a markedly different impression. Once again, the hallmarks of the preadolescent child depict a child secure in her sense of herself, confident in the substance of her beliefs, and sure of her ability to do something of value in the world. Describing herself

REVIEW

1. Why do psychologists use the "Heinz" dilemma to test ethical judgements in children? What is it about this case that makes it an ideal test?

2. What is the fundamental difference, according to Gilligan's research, in the way in which girls and boys attempt to resolve dilemmas such as the one involving Heinz and his wife?

3. Which psychological approach makes more sense today, Kohlberg's or Gilligan's?

at eleven as "growing and changing," she says that she "sees some things differently now, just because I know myself really well now, and I know a lot more about the world." Yet the world she knows is a different world from that refracted by Kohlberg's construction of Heinz's dilemma. Her world is a world of relationships and psychological truths where an awareness of the connection between people gives rise to a recognition of responsibility for one another, a perception of the need for response. Seen in this light, her understanding of morality as arising from the recognition of relationship, her belief in communication as the mode of conflict resolution, and her conviction that the solution to the dilemma will follow from its compelling representation seem far from naive or cognitively immature. Instead, Amy's judgements contain the insights central to an **ethic of care**, just as Jake's judgements reflect the logic of the justice approach. Her incipient awareness of the "method of truth," the central tenet of nonviolent conflict resolution, and her belief in the restorative activity of care, lead her to see the actors in the dilemma arrayed not as opponents in a contest of rights but as members of a **network of relationships** on whose continuation they all depend. Consequently her solution to the dilemma lies in activating the network by communication, securing the inclusion of the wife by strengthening rather than severing connections....

In this way, these two eleven-year-old children, both highly intelligent and perceptive about life, though in different ways, display different modes of moral understanding, different ways of thinking about conflict and choice. In resolving Heinz's dilemma, Jake relies on theft to avoid confrontation and turns to the law to mediate the dispute. Transposing a hierarchy of power into a hierarchy of values, he defuses a potentially explosive conflict between people by casting it as an impersonal conflict of claims. In this way, he abstracts the moral problem from the interpersonal situation, finding in the logic of fairness an objective way to decide who will win the dispute. But this hierarchical ordering, with its imagery of winning and losing and the potential for violence which it contains, gives way in Amy's construction of the dilemma to a network of connection, a web of relationships that is sustained by a process of communication. With this shift, the moral problem changes from one of unfair domination, the imposition of property over life, to one of unnecessary exclusion, the failure of the druggist to respond to the wife....

WHETHER God Exists

Five Proofs

SAINT THOMAS AQUINAS

To objections that God does not exist and that there is no need to suppose God's existence, Aquinas responds with five logical proofs of the reality of a First Mover, a First Efficient Cause, to which we give the name of God.

OBJECTION 1. It seems that God does not exist; because if one of two contraries be infinite, the other would be altogether destroyed. But the word "God" means that He is infinite goodness. If, therefore, God existed, there would be no evil discoverable; but there is evil in the world. Therefore God does not exist.

Obj. 2. Further, it is superfluous to suppose that, what can be accounted for by a few principles has been produced by many. But it seems that everything that appears in the world can be accounted for by other principles, supposing God did not exist. For all natural things can be reduced to one principle, which is nature; and all things that happen intentionally can be reduced to one principle, which is human reason, or will. Therefore there is no need to suppose God's existence.

On the contrary, It is said in the person of God: *I am Who am* (Exod. iii. 14).

I answer that, The existence of God can be proved in five ways.

The first and more manifest way is the **argument from motion**. It is certain and evident to our senses that some things are in motion. Whatever is in motion is moved by another, for nothing can be in motion except it have a potentiality for that towards which it is being moved; whereas a thing moves inasmuch as it is in act. By "motion" we mean nothing else than the reduction of something from a state of potentiality into a state of actuality. Nothing, however, can be reduced from a state of potentiality into a state of actuality unless by something already in a state of actuality. Thus, that which is actually hot as fire, makes wood, which is potentially hot, to be actually hot, and thereby moves and changes it. It is not possible that the same thing should be at once in a state of actuality and potentiality from the same point of view, but only from different points of view. What is actually hot cannot simultaneously be only potentially hot; still, it is simultaneously potentially cold. It is therefore impossible that from the same point of view and in the same way anything should be both moved and mover, or that it

PREVIEW

Saint Thomas Aquinas (1225-1274) was the architect of the most comprehensive theological structure of the Roman Catholic Church, the "Summa Theologica." It has long been recognized as the "official" statement of orthodox Christian beliefs by many theologians. Aquinas borrowed many of his arguments from Aristotle, as can be seen in his "five ways" of demonstrating God's existence.

should move itself. Therefore, whatever is in motion must be put in motion by another. If that by which it is put in motion be itself put in motion, then this also must needs be put in motion by another, and that by another again. This cannot go on to infinity, because then there would be no first mover, and, consequently, no other mover—seeing that subsequent movers only move inasmuch as they are put in motion by the first mover; as the staff only moves because it is put in motion by the hand. Therefore it is necessary to arrive at a First Mover, put in motion by no other; and this everyone understands to be God.

The second way is from the formality of **efficient causation**. In the world of sense we find there is an order of efficient causation. There is no case known (neither is it, indeed, possible) in which a thing is found to be the efficient cause of itself; for so it would be prior to itself, which is impossible. In efficient causes it is not possible to go on to infinity, because in all efficient causes following in order the first is the cause of the intermediate cause, and the intermediate is the cause of the ultimate cause, whether the intermediate cause be several, or one only. To take away the cause is to take away the effect. Therefore, if there be no first cause among efficient causes, there will be no ultimate cause, nor any intermediate. If in efficient causes it is possible to go on to infinity, there will be no first efficient cause, neither will there be an ultimate effect, nor any intermediate efficient causes; all of which is plainly false. Therefore it is necessary to put forward a First Efficient Cause, to which everyone gives the name of God.

The third way is taken from **possibility and necessity**, and runs thus: We find in nature things that could either exist or not exist, since they are found to be generated, and then to corrupt; and, consequently, they can exist, and then not exist. It is impossible for these always to exist, for that which can one day cease to exist must at some time have not existed. Therefore, if everything could cease to exist, then at one time there could have been nothing in existence. If this were true, even now there would be nothing in existence, because that which does not exist only begins to exist by something already existing. Therefore, if at one time nothing was in existence, it would have been impossible for anything to have begun to exist; and thus even now nothing would be in existence—which is absurd. Therefore, not all beings are merely possible, but there must exist something the existence of which is necessary. Every necessary thing either has its necessity caused by another, or not. It is impossible to go on to infinity in necessary things which have their necessity caused by another, as has been already proved in regard to efficient causes. Therefore we cannot but postulate the existence of some being having of itself its own necessity, and not receiving it from another, but rather causing in others their necessity. This all men speak of as God.

The fourth way is taken from the **gradation** to be found in things. Among beings there are some more and some less good, true, noble, and the like. But , "more" and "less" are predicated of different things, according as they resemble in their different ways something which is in the degree of

A medieval manuscript by St. Thomas Aquinas; the forerunner of his great *Summa Theologica*.

"most," as a thing is said to be hotter according as it more nearly resembles that which is hottest; so that there is something which is truest, something best, something noblest, and, consequently, something which is uttermost being; for the truer things are, the more truly they exist. What is most complete in any genus is the cause of all in that genus; as fire, which is the most complete form of heat, is the cause whereby all things are made hot. Therefore there must also be something which is to all beings the cause of their being, goodness, and every other perfection; and this we call God.

The fifth way is taken from the **governance of the world**; for we see that things which lack intelligence, such as natural bodies, act for some purpose, which fact is evident from their acting always, or nearly always, in the same way, so as to obtain the best result. Hence it is plain that not fortuitously, but designedly, do they achieve their purpose. Whatever lacks intelligence cannot fulfil some purpose, unless it be directed by some being endowed with intelligence and knowledge; as the arrow is shot to its mark by the archer. Therefore some intelligent being exists by whom all natural things are ordained towards a definite purpose; and this being we call God.

Reply Obj. 1. As Augustine says: *Since God is wholly good, He would not allow any evil to exist in His works, unless His omnipotence and goodness were such as to bring good even out of evil.* This is part of the infinite goodness of God, that He should allow evil to exist, and out of it produce good.

Reply Obj. 2. Since nature works out its determinate end under the direction of a higher agent, whatever is done by nature must needs be traced back to God, as to its first cause. So also whatever is done designedly must also be traced back to some higher cause other than human reason or will, for these can suffer change and are defective; whereas things capable of motion and of defect must be traced back to an immovable and self-necessary first principle.

KEY TERMS

- Thomas Aquinas's "Five Proofs"
- Proof 1. Argument from motion
- Proof 2. Efficient causation
- Proof 3. Possibility and necessity
- Proof 4. Gradation
- Proof 5. Governance of the world

REVIEW

1. According to the second objection, what principles explain natural things and things that happen intentionally?

2. What are the five logical arguments offered by Aquinas to prove the existence of God?

3. How does Aquinas justify the existence of evil in light of a "wholly good" First Mover?

On the Existence of God

BERTRAND RUSSELL

Christian beliefs and Christ's character and teachings are far from sanctified for this philosopher, as he urges us to shun the fear and dependence generated by "words uttered long ago by ignorant men," and make the best of the world as it is.

PREVIEW

Bertrand Russell (1872-1970) was one of the great philosophers of this century. He wrote an enormous number of philosophical books and articles, from "Principia Mathematica" (with Alfred North Whitehead) to some notorious polemics in favor of "free love" and atheism. He was too controversial for most universities, and a famous court case prevented him from teaching at City College of New York. He did, however, win the Nobel Prize for Literature in 1950. At the age of eighty-nine, he was jailed for protesting against nuclear arms. The selection here was delivered as a public lecture.

To come to this question of the existence of God: it is a large and serious question, and if I were to attempt to deal with it in any adequate manner I should have to keep you here until Kingdom Come, so that you will have to excuse me if I deal with it in a somewhat summary fashion. You know, of course, that the Catholic Church has laid it down as a **dogma** that the existence of God can be proved by the unaided reason. That is a somewhat curious dogma, but it is one of their dogmas. They had to introduce it because at one time the freethinkers adopted the habit of saying that there were such and such arguments which mere reason might urge against the existence of God, but of course they knew as a matter of faith that God did exist. The arguments and the reasons were set out at great length, and the Catholic Church felt that they must stop it. Therefore they laid it down that the existence of God can be proved by the unaided reason and they had to set up what they considered were arguments to prove it. There are, of course, a number of them, but I shall take only a few.

THE FIRST-CAUSE ARGUMENT

Perhaps the simplest and easiest to understand is the **argument of the First Cause**. (It is maintained that everything we see in this world has a cause, and as you go back in the chain of causes further and further you must come to a First Cause, and to that First Cause you give the name of God.) That argument, I suppose, does not carry very much weight nowadays, because, in the first place, cause is not quite what it used to be. The philosophers and the men of science have got going on cause, and it has not anything like the vitality it used to have; but, apart from that, you can see that the argument that there must be a First Cause is one that cannot have any validity. I may say that when I was a young man and was debating these questions very seriously in my mind, I for a long time accepted the argument of the First Cause, until one day, at the age of eighteen, I read John Stuart Mill's Autobiography, and I there found this sentence: "My father taught me that the question 'Who made me?' cannot be answered, since it immediately suggests the further question 'Who made God?'" That very simple sentence showed me, as I still think, the fallacy in the argument of the First Cause. If everything must have a cause, then God must have a cause. If there can be anything without a cause, it may just as well be the world as God, so that there cannot be any validity in that argument. It is exactly of the same nature as the Hindu's view, that the world rested upon an elephant and the elephant rested upon a tortoise; and when they said, "How about the tortoise?" the Indian said, "Suppose we change the subject." The argument is really no better than that. There is no reason why the world could not have come into being without a cause; nor, on the other hand, is there any reason why it should not have always existed. There is no reason to suppose that the world had a beginning at all. The idea that things must have a beginning is really due to the poverty of our imagination. Therefore, perhaps, I need not waste any more time upon the argument about the First Cause....

THE ARGUMENT FROM DESIGN

The next step in this process brings us to the **argument from design**. You all know the argument from design: everything in the world is made just so that we can manage to live in the world, and if the world was ever so little different, we could not manage to live in it. That is the argument from design. It sometimes takes a rather curious form; for instance, it is argued that rabbits have white tails in order to be easy to shoot. I do not know how rabbits would view that application. It is an easy argument to parody. You all know Voltaire's remark, that obviously the nose was designed to be such as to fit spectacles. That sort of parody has turned out to be not nearly so wide of the mark as it might have seemed in the eighteenth century, because since the time of Darwin we understand much better why living creatures are adapted to their environment. It is not that their environment was made to be suitable to them but that they grew to be suitable to it, and that is the basis of adaptation. There is no evidence of design about it.

When you come to look into this argument from design, it is a most astonishing thing that people can believe that this world, with all the things that are in it, with all its defects, should be the best that omnipotence and omniscience have been able to produce in millions of years. I really cannot believe it. Do you think that, if you were granted omnipotence and omniscience and millions of years in which to perfect your world, you could produce nothing better than the Ku Klux Klan or the Fascists? Moreover, if you accept the ordinary laws of science, you have to suppose that human life and life in general on this planet will die out in due course: it is a stage in the decay of the solar system; at a certain stage of decay you get the sort of conditions of temperature and so forth which are suitable to protoplasm, and there is life for a short time in the life of the whole solar system. You see in the moon the sort of thing to which the earth is tending–something dead, cold, and lifeless.

I am told that that sort of view is depressing, and people will sometimes tell you that if they believed that, they would not be able to go on living. Do not believe it; it is all nonsense. Nobody really worries much about what is going to happen millions of years hence. Even if they think they are worrying much about that, they are really deceiving themselves. They are worried about something much more mundane, or it may merely be a bad digestion; but nobody is really seriously rendered unhappy by the thought of something that is going to happen to this world millions and millions of years hence. There-fore, although it is of course a gloomy view to suppose that life will die out–at least I suppose we may say so, although sometimes when I contemplate the things that people do with their lives I think it is almost a consolation–it is not such as to render life miserable. It merely makes you turn your attention to other things.

… Of course I know that the sort of intellectual arguments that I have been talking to you about are not what really moves people. What really moves people to believe in God is not any intellectual argument at all. Most people believe in God because they have been taught from early infancy to do it, and that is the main reason.

Then I think that the next most powerful reason is the wish for safety, a sort of feeling that there is a big brother who will look after you. That plays a very profound part in influencing people's desire for a belief in God.

THE CHARACTER OF CHRIST

I now want to say a few words upon a topic which I often think is not quite sufficiently dealt with by **Rationalists**, and that is the question whether Christ was the best and the wisest of men. It is generally taken for granted that we should all agree that that was so. I do not myself. I think that there are a good many points upon which I agree with Christ a great deal more than the pro-fessing Christians do. I do not know that I could go with Him all the way, but I could go with Him much further than most professing Christians can. You will remember that He said, "Resist not evil: but whosoever shall smite thee on thy right cheek, turn to him the other also." That is not a new precept or a new principle. It was used by Lao-tse and Buddha some 500 or 600 years before Christ, but it is not a principle which as a matter of fact Christians accept. I have no doubt that the present Prime Minister [Stanley Baldwin], for instance, is a most sincere Christian, but I should not advise any of you to go and smite him on one cheek. I think you might find that he thought this text was intended in a figurative sense.

Then there is another point which I consider excellent. You will remember that Christ said, "Judge not lest ye be judged." That principle I do not think you would find was popular in the law courts of Christian countries. I have known in my time quite a number of judges who were very earnest Christians, and none of them felt that they were acting contrary to Christian principles in what they did. Then Christ says, "Give to him that asketh of thee, and from him that would borrow of thee turn not thou away." That is a very good principle. Your Chairman has reminded you that we are not here to talk politics, but I cannot help observing that the last general election was fought on the question of how desirable it was to turn away from him that would borrow of thee, so that one must assume that the Liberals and Conservatives of this country are composed of people who do not agree with the teaching of Christ, because they certainly did very emphatically turn away on that occasion.

Then there is one other **maxim** of Christ which I think has a great deal in it, but I do not find that it is very popular among some of our Christian friends. He says, "If thou wilt be perfect, go and sell that which thou hast, and give to the poor." That is a very excellent maxim, but, as I say, it is not much practiced. All these, I think, are good maxims, although they are a little difficult to live up to. I do not profess to live up to them myself; but then, after all, it is not quite the same thing as for a Christian.

• Defects in Christ's Teaching

Having granted the excellence of these maxims, I come to certain points in which I do not believe that one can grant either the superlative wisdom or the superlative goodness of Christ as depicted in the Gospels; and here I may say that one is not concerned with the historical question. Historically it is quite doubtful whether Christ ever existed at all, and if He did we do not know anything about Him, so that I am not concerned with the historical question, which is a very difficult one. I am concerned with Christ as He appears in the Gospels, taking the Gospel narrative as it stands, and there one does find some things that do not seem to be very wise. For one thing, He certainly thought that His second coming would occur in clouds of glory before the death of all the people who were living at that time. There are a great many texts that prove that. He says, for instance, "Ye shall not have gone over the cities of Israel till the Son of Man be come." Then He says, "There are some standing here which shall not taste death till the Son of Man comes into His kingdom"; and there are a lot of places where it is quite clear that He believed that His second coming would happen during the lifetime of many then living. That was the belief of His earlier followers, and it was the basis of a good deal of His moral teaching. When He said, "Take no thought for the morrow," and things of that sort, it was very largely because He thought that the second coming was going to be very soon, and that all ordinary mundane affairs did not count. I have, as a matter of fact, known some Christians who did believe that the second coming was imminent. I knew a parson who frightened his congregation terribly by telling them that the second coming was very imminent indeed, but they were much consoled when they found that he was planting trees in his garden. The early Christians did really believe it, and they did abstain from such things as planting trees in their gardens, because they did accept from Christ the belief that the second coming was imminent. In that respect, clearly He was not so wise as some other people have been, and He was certainly not superlatively wise.

> *Dost thou think because thou art virtuous there shall be no more cakes and ale?*
>
> *William Shakespeare*

Bertrand Russell, a Nobel laureate and philosopher, championed unilateral nuclear disarmament.

• The Moral Problem

Then you come to **moral questions**. There is one very serious defect to my mind in Christ's moral character, and that is that He believed in hell. I do not myself feel that any person who is really profoundly humane can believe in everlasting punishment. Christ certainly as depicted in the Gospels did believe in everlasting punishment, and one does find repeatedly a vindictive fury against those people who would not listen to His preaching–an attitude which is not uncommon with preachers, but which does somewhat detract from superlative excellence. You do not, for instance find that attitude in Socrates. You find him quite bland and urbane toward the people who would not listen to him; and it is, to my mind, far more worthy of a sage to take that line than to take the line of indignation. You probably all remember the sort of things that Socrates was saying when he was dying, and the sort of things that he generally did say to people who did not agree with him.

You will find that in the Gospels Christ said, "Ye serpents, ye generation of vipers, how can ye escape the damnation of hell." That was said to people who did not like His preaching. It is not really to my mind quite the best tone, and there are a great many of these things about hell. There is, of course, the familiar text about the sin against the Holy Ghost: "Whosoever speaketh against the Holy Ghost it shall not be forgiven him neither in this World nor in the world to come." That text has caused an unspeakable amount of misery in the world, for all sorts of people have imagined that they have committed the sin against the Holy Ghost, and thought that it would not be forgiven them either in this world or in the world to come. I really do not think that a person with a proper degree of kindliness in his nature would have put fears and terrors of that sort into the world.

Then Christ says, "The Son of Man shall send forth His angels, and they shall gather out of His kingdom all things that offend, and them which do iniquity, and shall cast them into a furnace of fire; there shall be wailing and gnashing of teeth"; and He goes on about the wailing and gnashing of teeth. It comes in one verse after another, and it is quite manifest to the reader that there is a certain pleasure in contemplating wailing and gnashing of teeth, or else it would not occur so often. Then you all, of course, remember about the sheep and the goats; how at the second coming He is going to divide the sheep from the goats, and He is going to say to the goats, "Depart from me, ye cursed, into everlasting fire." He continues, "And these shall go away into everlasting fire." Then He says again, "If thy hand offend thee, cut it off; it is better for thee to enter into life maimed, than having two hands to go into hell, into the fire that never shall be quenched; where the worm dieth not and the fire is not quenched." He repeats that again and again also. I must say that I think all this doctrine, that hell-fire is a punishment for sin, is a doctrine of cruelty. It is a doctrine that put cruelty into the world and gave the world generations of cruel torture; and the Christ of the Gospels, if you could take Him as His chroniclers represent Him, would certainly have to be considered partly responsible for that....

THE EMOTIONAL FACTOR

As I said before, I do not think that the real reason why people accept religion has anything to do with argumentation. They accept religion on **emotional grounds**. One is often told that it is a very wrong thing to attack religion, because religion makes men virtuous. So I am told; I have not noticed it. You know, of course, the parody of that argument in Samuel Butler's book, *Erewhon Revisited*. You will remember that in *Erewhon* there is a certain Higgs who arrives in a remote country, and after spending some time there he escapes from that country in a balloon. Twenty years later he comes back to that country and finds a new religion in which he is worshipped under the name of the "Sun Child," and it is said that he ascended into heaven. He finds that the Feast of the Ascension is about to be celebrated, and he hears Professors Hanky and Panky say to each other that they never set eyes on the man Higgs, and they hope they never will; but they are the high priests of the religion of the Sun Child. He is very indignant, and he comes up to them, and he says, "I am going to expose all this humbug and tell the people of Erewhon that it was only I, the man Higgs, and I went up in a balloon." He was told, "You must not do that, because all the morals of this country are bound round this myth, and if they once know that you did not ascend into heaven they will all become wicked"; and so he is persuaded of that and he goes quietly away.

That is the idea–that we should all be wicked if we did not hold to the Christian religion. It seems to me that the people who have held to it have been for the most part extremely wicked. You find this curious fact, that the more intense has been the religion of any period and the more profound has been the dogmatic belief, the greater has been the cruelty and the worse has been the state of affairs. In the so-called ages of faith, when men really did believe the Christian religion in all its completeness, there was the **Inquisition**, with its tortures; there were millions of unfortunate women burned as witches; and there was every kind of cruelty practiced upon all sorts of people in the name of religion.

You find as you look around the world that every single bit of progress in humane feeling, every improvement in the criminal law, every step toward the diminution of war, every step toward better treatment of the coloured races, or every mitigation of slavery, every moral progress that there has been in the world, has been consistently opposed by the organized churches of the world. I say quite deliberately that the Christian religion, as organized in its churches, has been and still is the principal enemy of moral progress in the world....

There are a great many ways in which, at the present moment, the church, by its insistence upon what it chooses to call morality, inflicts upon all sorts of people undeserved and unnecessary suffering. And of course, as we know, it is in its major part an opponent still of progress and of improvement in all the ways that diminish suffering in the world, because it has chosen to label as morality a certain narrow set of rules of conduct which have nothing to do with human happiness; and when you say that this or that ought to be done

> *What terrible questions we are learning to ask! The former men believed in magic, by which temples, cities, and men were swallowed up, and all trace of them gone. We are coming on the secret of a magic which sweeps out of men's minds all vestige of theism and beliefs which they and their fathers held and were framed upon.*
>
> Ralph Waldo Emerson

REVIEW

1. What reasons does Russell give for most people's faith in God? On what grounds does he feel that people accept religion?

2. According to Russell, how has the Christian religion, both historically and currently, contributed to the wickedness in the world?

3. Russell states that the conception of God is "quite unworthy of free men." On what would he have us rely, rather than on religion?

because it would make for human happiness, they think that has nothing to do with the matter at all. "What has human happiness to do with morals? The object of morals is not to make people happy...."

Religion is based, I think, primarily and mainly upon fear. It is partly the terror of the unknown and partly, as I have said, the wish to feel that you have a kind of elder brother who will stand by you in all your troubles and disputes. Fear is the basis of the whole thing–fear of the mysterious, fear of defeat, fear of death. Fear is the parent of cruelty, and therefore it is no wonder if cruelty and religion have gone hand in hand. It is because fear is at the basis of those two things. In this world we can now begin a little to understand things, and a little to master them by help of science, which has forced its way step by step against the Christian religion, against the churches, and against the opposition of all the old precepts. Science can help us to get over this craven fear in which mankind has lived for so many generations. Science can teach us, and I think our own hearts can teach us, no longer to look around for imaginary supports, no longer to invent allies in the sky, but rather to look to our own efforts here below to make this world a fit place to live in, instead of the sort of place that the churches in all these centuries have made it.

WHAT WE MUST DO

We want to stand upon our own feet and look fair and square at the world–its good facts, its bad facts, its beauties, and its ugliness; see the world as it is and be not afraid of it. Conquer the world by intelligence and not merely by being slavishly subdued by the terror that comes from it. The whole conception of God is a conception derived from the ancient **Oriental despotisms**. It is a conception quite unworthy of free men. When you hear people in church debasing themselves and saying that they are miserable sinners, and all the rest of it, it seems contemptible and not worthy of self-respecting human beings. We ought to stand up and look the world frankly in the face. We ought to make the best we can of the world, and if it is not so good as we wish, after all it will still be better than what these others have made of it in all these ages. A good world needs knowledge, kindliness, and courage; it does not need a regretful hankering after the past or a fettering of the free intelligence by the words uttered long ago by ignorant men. It needs a fearless outlook and a free intelligence. It needs hope for the future, not looking back all the time toward a past that is dead, which we trust will be far surpassed by the future that our intelligence can create.

THE DIMENSIONS OF A COMPLETE LIFE

I HAVE A DREAM

MARTIN LUTHER KING, JR.

A complete life is one in which all dimensions are in harmony. In this passionate appeal, in words intended for his fellow clergymen, King speaks to us all of the need to embrace a life equally balanced by love of self, love of humanity and love of God.

PREVIEW

Martin Luther King, Jr. (1929-1968) wrote this letter to eight fellow clergymen from his jail cell in Birmingham, Alabama, where he had been detained after being arrested at a nonviolent protest in that city. In it he asks for the assistance of other religious leaders in the civil rights struggle, and answers criticism they had levelled against him for his involvement. This version was edited by King for publication in his book "Why We Can't Wait."

Many, many centuries ago, out on a lonely, obscure island called Patmos, a man by the name of John caught a vision of the new Jerusalem descending out of heaven from God. One of the greatest glories of this new city of God that John saw was its completeness. It was not partial and one-sided, but it was complete in all three of its dimensions. And so, in describing the city in the twenty-first chapter of the book of Revelation, John says this: "The length and the breadth and the height of it are equal." In other words, this new city of God, this city of ideal humanity, is not an unbalanced entity but it is complete on all sides.

Now John is saying something quite significant here. For so many of us the book of Revelation is a very difficult book, puzzling to decode. We look upon it as something of a great enigma wrapped in mystery. And certainly if we accept the book of Revelation as a record of actual historical occurrences it is a difficult book, shrouded with impenetrable mysteries. But if we will look beneath the peculiar jargon of its author and the prevailing apocalyptic symbolism, we will find in this book many eternal truths which continue to challenge us. One such truth is that of this text. What John is really saying is this: that life as it should be and life at its best is the life that is complete on all sides.

There are three dimensions of any complete life to which we can fitly give the words of this text: length, breadth, and height. The length of life as we shall think of it here is not its duration or its longevity, but it is the push of a life forward to achieve its personal ends and ambitions. It is the inward concern for one's own welfare. The breadth of life is the outward concern for the welfare of others. The height of life is the upward reach for God.

These are the three dimensions of life, and without the three being correlated, working harmoniously together, life is incomplete. Life is something of a great triangle. At one angle stands the individual person, at the other angle stand other persons, and at the top stands the Supreme, Infinite Person, God. These three must meet in every individual life if that life is to be complete.

Now let us notice first the length of life. I have said that this is the dimension of life in which the individual is concerned with developing his inner powers. It is that dimension of life in which the individual pursues personal ends and ambitions. This is perhaps the selfish dimension of life, and there is such a thing as moral and rational self-interest. If one is not concerned about himself he cannot be totally concerned about other selves.

Some years ago a learned rabbi, the late Joshua Liebman, wrote a book entitled *Peace of Mind*. He has a chapter in the book entitled "Love Thyself Properly." In this chapter he says in substance that it is impossible to love other selves adequately unless you love your own self properly. Many people have been plunged into the abyss of emotional fatalism because they did not love themselves properly. So every individual has a responsibility to be concerned about himself enough to discover what he is made for. After he discovers his calling he should set out to do it with all of the strength and power in his being. He should do it as if God Almighty called him at this particular moment in history to do it. He should seek to do his job so well that the living, the dead, or the unborn could not do it better. No matter how small one thinks his life's work is in terms of the norms of the world and the so-called big jobs, he must realize that it has cosmic significance if he is serving humanity and doing the will of God.

To carry this to one extreme, if it falls your lot to be a streetsweeper, sweep streets as Raphael painted pictures, sweep streets as Michelangelo carved marble, sweep streets as Beethoven composed music, sweep streets as Shakespeare wrote poetry. Sweep streets so well that all the hosts of heaven and earth will have to pause and say, "Here lived a great street-sweeper who swept his job well." In the words of Douglas Mallock:

> If you can't be a highway, just be a trail;
> If you can't be the sun, be a star,
> For it isn't by size that you win or you fail—
> Be the best of whatever you are.

When you do this, you have mastered the first dimension of life—the length of life.

But don't stop here; it is dangerous to stop here. There are some people who never get beyond this first dimension. They are brilliant people; often they do an excellent job in developing their inner powers; but they live as if nobody else lived in the world but themselves. There is nothing more tragic than to find an individual bogged down in the length of life, devoid of the breadth.

The breadth of life is that dimension of life in which we are concerned about others. An individual has not started living until he can rise above the narrow confines of his individualistic concerns to the broader concerns of all humanity.

You remember one day a man came to Jesus and he raised some significant questions. Finally he got around to the question, "Who is my neighbour?" This could easily have been a very abstract question left in mid-air. But Jesus immediately pulled that question out of mid-air and placed it on a dangerous curve

Martin Luther King Jr. and Malcolm X were leaders of the civil rights movement in the U.S.

between Jerusalem and Jericho. He talked about a certain man who fell among thieves. Three men passed; two of them on the other side. And finally another man came and helped the injured man on the ground. He is known to us as the good Samaritan. Jesus says in substance that this is a great man. He was great because he could project the "I" into the "thou."

So often we say that the priest and the Levite were in a big hurry to get to some ecclesiastical meeting and so they did not have time. They were concerned about that. I would rather think of it another way. I can well imagine that they were quite afraid. You see, the Jericho road is a dangerous road, and the same thing that happened to the man who was robbed and beaten could have happened to them. So I imagine the first question that the priest and the Levite asked was this: "If I stop to help this man, what will happen to me?" Then the good Samaritan came by, and by the very nature of his concern reversed the question: "If I do not stop to help this man, what will happen to him?" And so this man was great because he had the mental equipment for a dangerous altruism. He was great because he could surround the length of his life with the breadth of life. He was great not only because he had ascended to certain heights of economic security, but because he could condescend to the depths of human need.

All this has a great deal of bearing in our situation in the world today. So often racial groups are concerned about the length of life, their economic privileged position, their social status. So often nations of the world are concerned about the length of life, perpetuating their nationalistic concerns, and their economic ends. May it not be that the problem in the world today is that individuals as well as nations have been overly concerned with the length of life, devoid of the breadth? But there is still something to remind us that we are interdependent, that we are all involved in a single process, that we are all somehow caught in an inescapable network of mutuality. Therefore whatever affects one directly affects all indirectly.

As long as there is poverty in the world I can never be rich, even if I have a billion dollars. As long as diseases are rampant and millions of people in this world cannot expect to live more than twenty-eight or thirty years, I can never be totally healthy even if I just got a good check-up at Mayo Clinic. I can never be what I ought to be until you are what you ought to be. This is the way our world is made. No individual or nation can stand out boasting of being independent. We are interdependent. So John Donne placed it in graphic terms when he affirmed, "No man is an island entire of itself. Every man is a piece of the continent, a part of the main." Then he goes on to say, "Any man's death diminishes me because I am involved in mankind, and therefore never send to know for whom the bell tolls; it tolls for thee." When we discover this, we master the second dimension of life.

Finally, there is a third dimension. Some people never get beyond the first two dimensions of life. They master the first two. They develop their inner powers; they love humanity, but they stop right here. They end up with the feeling that man is the end of all things and that humanity is God. Philosophically or theologically, many of them would call themselves humanists.

Let freedom ring and when this happens, when we allow freedom to ring, when we let it ring from every village and every hamlet, from every state and every city, we will be able to speed up that day when all of God's children, black men and white men, Jews and Gentiles, Protestants and Catholics, will be able to join hands and sing in the words of the old Negro spiritual, "Free at last, free at last. Thank God Almighty, we are free at last."

Martin Luther King, Jr.

They seek to live life without a sky. They find themselves bogged down on the horizontal plane without being integrated on the vertical plane. But if we are to live the complete life we must reach up and discover God. H.G. Wells was right: "The man who is not religious begins at nowhere and ends at nothing." Religion is like a mighty wind that breaks down doors and makes that possible and even easy which seems difficult and impossible.

In our modern world it is easy for us to forget this. We so often find ourselves unconsciously neglecting this third dimension of life. Not that we go up and say, "Good-by, God, we are going to leave you now." But we become so involved in the things of this world that we are unconsciously carried away by the rushing tide of materialism which leaves us treading in the confused waters of secularism....

Something should remind us once more that the great things in this universe are things that we never see. You walk out at night and look up at the beautiful stars as they bedeck the heavens like swinging lanterns of eternity, and you think you can see all. Oh, no. You can never see the law of gravitation that holds them there. You walk around this vast campus and you probably have a great esthetic experience as I have had walking about and looking at the beautiful buildings, and you think you see all. Oh, no. You can never see the mind of the architect who drew the blueprint. You can never see the love and the faith and the hope of the individuals who made it so....

In a real sense everything that we see is a shadow cast by that which we do not see. Plato was right: "The visible is a shadow cast by the invisible." And so God is still around. All of our new knowledge, all of our new developments, cannot diminish his being one iota. These new advances have banished God neither from the microcosmic compass of the atom nor from the vast, unfathomable ranges of interstellar space. The more we learn about this universe, the more mysterious and awesome it becomes. God is still here.

So I say to you, seek God and discover him and make him a power in your life. Without him all of our efforts turn to ashes and our sunrises into darkest nights. Without him, life is a meaningless drama with the decisive scenes missing. But with him we are able to rise from the fatigue of despair to the buoyancy of hope. With him we are able to rise from the midnight of desperation to the daybreak of joy. St. Augustine was right—we were made for God and we will be restless until we find rest in him.

Love yourself, if that means rational, healthy, and moral self-interest. You are commanded to do that. That is the length of life. Love your neighbour as you love yourself. You are commanded to do that. That is the breadth of life. But never forget that there is a first and even greater commandment, "Love the Lord thy God with all thy heart and all thy soul and all thy mind." This is the height of life. And when you do this you live the complete life.

Thank God for John who, centuries ago, caught a vision of the new Jerusalem. God grant that those of us who still walk the road of life will catch this vision and decide to move forward to that city of complete life in which the length and the breadth and the height are equal.

REVIEW

1. What does King mean when he speaks of life's "length, breadth and height?"

2. Why does King assert that "no individual can stand out boasting of being independent?" What is his basis for such an opinion?

3. How does King combine the philosophy of Plato with Christianity? Is this a convincing comparison?

TEXT AND IMAGE CREDITS

Grateful acknowledgement is made for permission to reprint excerpts from copyrighted material. All efforts were made to obtain copyright permission. Any error or omissions will be corrected in future printings.

Introduction

- "Modern Ode to a Modern School" by John Erskine. Original source unknown.
- "The Road Not Taken." From Robert Frost, *Mountain Interval* (New York: Henry Holt, 1916).

Part 1: General Education

- "The New World Order." From Council of Regents, *Vision 2000: Quality and Opportunity—the Final Report of Vision 2000* (Toronto: Ministry of Colleges and Universities, 1990). The material reproduced here was edited for the present work.
- "Education for What?" by Jim Turk. Courtesy of the author.
- "Why College Grads Get the Jobs" by Robert Sheppard, *Maclean's,* Oct. 26, 1998. Reprinted with permission.
- "A Neo-Luddite Reflects on the Internet" by Gertrude Himmelfarb. From *Times Higher Education Supplement,* Nov. 1996.
- "Honing Generic Skills." From Robert H. Lauer, *Social Problems and the Quality of Life,* 5th ed. Copyright © 1992 Wm. C. Brown Communications, Inc. Reprinted by permission of Times Mirror Higher Education Group, Inc., Dubuque, Iowa. All rights reserved.
- "Little Red Riding Hood—Revisited" by Russell Baker. From *The New York Times* (January 13, 1980). Copyright © 1980 by the New York Times company. Reprinted by permission.
- "Rules for Writers." TEP archives. Original source unknown.

Part 2: Science and Technology

- "Science as a Way of Thinking." From Carl Sagan, *Broca's Brain* (New York: Random House, 1979).
- "From the Big Bang to Black Holes." From *A Brief History of Time* by Stephen W. Hawking. Copyright © 1988 by Stephen W. Hawking. Interior illustrations copyright © 1988 by Ron Miller. Used by permission of Bantam Books, a division of Random House, Inc.
- "Unexpected Vistas" by James Trefil. Reprinted with the permission of Scribner, a Division of Simon & Schuster, Inc. from *THE UNEXPECTED VISTA: A PHYSICIST'S VIEW OF NATURE* by James Trefil. Copyright © 1983 by James S. Trefil.
- "The Discovery of Radium." From a lecture given by Marie Curie at Vassar College in the 1920s.
- "How Did Life Begin?" by James Trefil. Excerpts from *THE EDGE OF THE UNKNOWN: 101 Things You Don't Know About Science and No One Else Does Either,* by James Trefil. Copyright © 1996 by James Trefil. Reprinted by permission of Houghton Mifflin Company. All rights reserved.
- "Unscrambling Life" by James Trefil. Excerpts from *THE EDGE OF THE UNKNOWN: 101 Things You Don't Know About Science and No One Else Does Either,* by James Trefil.

Copyright © 1996 by James Trefil. Reprinted by permission of Houghton Mifflin Company. All rights reserved.
- "Consciousness: The Final Frontier" by James Trefil. Excerpts from *THE EDGE OF THE UNKNOWN: 101 Things You Don't Know About Science and No One Else Does Either,* by James Trefil. Copyright © 1996 by James Trefil. Reprinted by permission of Houghton Mifflin Company. All rights reserved.
- "Do NOT Use the F-Word" by Tom Pollard. Courtesy of the author.
- "The Pain of Animals" from *Inventing the Future.* Copyright © 1989 by David Suzuki. Reprinted by permission of Stoddart Publishing Co. Limited, 34 Lesmill Road, Toronto, Ontario, Canada, M3B 2T6.
- "The Obligation to Endure," from *Silent Spring* by Rachel Carson. Copyright © by Rachel L. Carson, renewed 1990 by Roger Christie. Reprinted by permission of Houghton Mifflin Company. All rights reserved.
- "On the Origin of Species." From Charles Darwin, *On the Origin of Species* (London: John Murray, 1859).
- "Why Sex Works" by Nicholas Wade. From *The New York Times* (January 31, 1999, WK4). Copyright © 1999 by the New York Times company. Reprinted by permission.
- "Posture Maketh the Man." From Stephen Jay Gould, *Ever Since Darwin, Reflections in Natural History* (New York: W.W. Norton & Company, Inc., 1973).
- "The Body in the Bog" by Geoffrey Bibby. *Horizon* (Winter, 1968). Vol X No. 1. Reprinted by permission of *American Heritage Magazine,* a division of Forbes, Inc. © Forbes, Inc., 1968.
- "Mind-Boggling Medical Milestones" by Daniel Q. Haney. From *The Globe and Mail* (March 27, 1999, D5). Reprinted with permission of The Associated Press.
- "MP3—Profiting from Technology." Appeared as "Roll-your-own CDs roll on" in *The Economist* (April 10, 1999). © 1999. The Economist Newspaper Group, Inc. Reprinted with permission. Further reproduction prohibited, www.economist.com.
- "Shall I Compare Thee to a Swarm of Insects?" by George Johnson. From *The New York Times* (April 11, 1999, WK1). Copyright © 1999 by the New York Times company. Reprinted by permission.

Part 3: The Social Sciences

- "The Debate Goes On: Nature or Nurture?" by James Trefil. Excerpts from *THE EDGE OF THE UNKNOWN: 101 Things You Don't Know About Science and No One Else Does Either,* by James Trefil. Copyright © 1996 by James Trefil. Reprinted by permission of Houghton Mifflin Company. All rights reserved.
- "Following Orders" by Philip Meyer. Courtesy of the author.
- "Talking Cures" by Brian Burnie. Courtesy of the author.
- "Freud's Falling Market Share" by Krista Foss. From *The Globe and Mail* (February 16, 1999, A1). Reprinted by permission of *The Globe and Mail.*
- "A Nation without Memory?" by Mark Starowicz. From an address to the conference on The Future of Canadian History, Montreal, 1999. Mark Starowicz is Head of CBC's

Index of Key Terms

U
unified theory (of the universe), 55
union certification, 158
union meeting, 158
union organizing, 157
university degree versus college diploma, 23

V
vaccines, discovery of, 96
Vision 2000, 16

W
white-dominated society, 143
women's movement, the, 132
    See also feminist movement
work and children, choice for many women, 133
worker discretion, limitations on, 152
workers' rights, 162
working conditions, 160
workplace harassment, 134

X
X-rays, 95